CW00530901

The Lotus® Guide to
1-2-3® @Functions

THE LOTUS® GUIDE TO

1-2-3® @FUNCTIONS

Mary Campbell

Lotus
Books™

ADDISON-WESLEY PUBLISHING COMPANY, INC.

Reading, Massachusetts   Menlo Park, California   New York
Don Mills, Ontario   Wokingham, England   Amsterdam   Bonn
Sydney   Singapore   Tokyo   Madrid   San Juan

This book is part of the Lotus Learning Series.

Many of the designations used by manufacturers and sellers to distinguish their products are claimed as trademarks. Where those designations appear in this book, and Addison-Wesley was aware of a trademark claim, the designations have been printed in initial caps or all caps.

Lotus, 1-2-3, and Lotus HAL are registered trademarks of Lotus Development Corporation, Inc.

Lotus HAL is distinguished from HAL, which is a trademark of Qantel for its Hotel And Leisure software.

Limitation of Liability
While every reasonable precaution has been taken in the preparation of this book, the author and the publishers assume no responsibility for errors or omissions, or for the uses made of the material contained herein or the decisions based on such use. **No warranties are made, express or implied, with regard to the contents of this work, its merchantability, or fitness for a particular purpose.** Neither the author nor the publishers shall be liable for direct, indirect, special, incidental, or consequential damages arising out of the use or inability to use the contents of this book.

Library of Congress Cataloging-in-Publication Data
Campbell, Mary V.
    The Lotus guide to 1-2-3 @ functions / Mary Campbell.
      p.   cm. — (Lotus learning series)
    Includes index.
    ISBN 0-201-12948-5
    1. Lotus 1-2-3 (Computer program) 2. Business—Data processing.
    I. Title. II. Series.
    HF5548.4.L67C355 1989   005.369'—dc19   88-34655

Under the copyright laws, this book may not be copied, photocopied, reproduced, translated, modified, or reduced to any electronic medium or machine-readable form, in whole or in part, without the prior written consent of Lotus Development Corporation.

Copyright © 1989 by Lotus Development Corporation
               55 Cambridge Parkway
               Cambridge, MA 02142
All rights reserved. Printed in the United States. Published simultaneously in Canada.

Managing Editor: Mark Boyer
Cover Designer: Celia Miller

ISBN 0-201-12948-5
ABCDEFGHIJ-AL-89
First printing, July, 1989

Acknowledgments

This book is the result of the efforts of many people. I would like to extend my special thanks to the following individuals:

Leslie Boerke, who created the many models for the book as we waited for Release 3.

Gabrielle Lawrence, who helped with every phase of the book, including suggestions for practical applications for which the @functions could be used.

Julie Stillman, acquisitions editor, who remained patient and assured me that we would one day soon finish this book.

Debbie McKenna, who helped with many of the details at Addison-Wesley as we worked to turn the manuscript into a final product.

Susan Lane Riley, who copy edited the manuscript.

Beth Burleigh, who handled the production at Addison-Wesley.

Mark Boyer at Lotus, for his idea to do this book to better acquaint 1-2-3 users with the power of @functions.

Scott Tucker at Lotus, for taking the time to review the entire manuscript.

To all the others at Lotus who were such an immense help through the beta process for Releases 2.2 and 3, including Susan Erabino, Chris Noble, Mary Beth Rettger, Danielle Romance, and Alexandra Trevelyan.

Contents

About This Book

The Lotus Guide to 1-2-3 @Functions introduces you to the varied applications for the Lotus @functions. Even if you are an experienced 1-2-3 user, you may not have explored their full capabilities. You can use the @functions to add power and flexibility to your models, to simplify your formulas, and to extend the capabilities of the 1-2-3 macro language. This book will show you how to do all of these things. It will also show you how to use the features of Lotus HAL that offer functionality similar to the @functions.

This book explores every feature of @functions, from the basics of entering @functions to advanced applications. In-depth coverage of each @function in each 1-2-3 release version is provided. Included are the syntax for every @function, a description of the function and each of its arguments, and one or more practical application examples that can be used directly or further adapted for other applications.

Organization of the Book

This book is organized into eleven chapters. Chapter 1 introduces you to the basics of @functions and the rules for their entry. Chapters 2 through 9 each address an @function category, with a separate section that includes examples for each @function. Chapter 10 covers the use of @functions with HAL. Chapter 11 shows you how to use @functions with 1-2-3's macro features.

The Lotus Guide to 1-2-3 @Functions starts with a tutorial approach to the entry of @functions to provide a firm foundation in the steps needed to enter them correctly. Later chapters provide the details for the function entries but do not require you to enter all the keystrokes for model creation to benefit from the application examples. This increases the number of different application ideas that can be presented and provides a concise guide for you to refer to as you create your own models.

Conventions Used in the Book

For consistency, the function keywords used throughout the book are always shown in uppercase letters, although you may use either uppercase or lowercase in your entries. Function arguments are shown in lowercase. When you enter the argument names, you will be substituting the value of the function argument for the argument names in the examples. Menu selections and names of keys are shown with initial capital letters.

1

Getting Acquainted with the @Functions

Lotus 1–2–3 allows you to create models to solve problems in a number of applications areas such as finance, accounting, science, and mathematics. The diverse applications that you can develop with this package make it one of the most popular software packages for microcomputers.

Formulas are an important part of 1–2–3's model-building process. Whether simple or complex, these formulas always require time for recording and testing. However, 1–2–3 provides a group of prerecorded formulas known as @functions, which can save a great deal of time during both formula entry and testing. You can use @functions by themselves or as part of another formula entry.

WHAT THE BUILT-IN FUNCTIONS OFFER

1–2–3's @functions provide formulas that meet your needs in a variety of application areas. For example, some functions let you total or average numbers stored within a range of the worksheet. Other functions perform more specialized tasks such as calculating the sine of an angle or the internal rate of return for an investment.

In addition to their flexibility in meeting your computational needs in a wide range of applications, there are many other advantages to @functions. First, because they have been well tested, they offer proven reliability.

Second, the concise recording used with the @function format is shorter than a formula that you might create yourself. Third, because they are prerecorded, the @functions greatly minimize the errors that often occur during formula entry. Finally, the @functions perform some tasks that you simply could not do on your own such as looking at the contents of a cell, choosing a value from a table of values, and telling you the amount of memory still available. These functions add power and functionality to models beyond what you can create with formulas.

CATEGORIES OF FUNCTIONS

1-2-3 Release 3 provides 103 functions that are organized into the following eight categories: database, date and time, financial, logical, mathematical, special, statistical, and string. Some categories are very closely related in terms of their functionality. For example, the date and time functions are a homogeneous group of functions since all of the functions in this group perform date and time calculations. Other function categories, such as the special functions, provide a diverse array of functions that include a table lookup function and error trapping functions. A brief description of the eight categories of @functions follows. Appendix A provides a complete list of 1-2-3's functions. The releases of 1-2-3 that support each function are listed.

The database functions offer selective statistical computations based on your specifications. If you have a list of employees from many locations, these functions allow you to perform tasks such as totaling the salaries for Dallas employees. Although the database may include employees from many locations, the database functions work with this information selectively.

1-2-3's date and time functions give you a method for recording date and time entries in worksheet cells. They also provide a way of extracting a portion of a date or time entry such as the month or the hour.

The financial functions perform tasks related to finance and accounting. A number of the functions in this category use the time value of money concept, which states that a dollar today is worth more than a dollar in the future. Other functions in this group focus on the various accounting methods used for computing asset depreciation such as the double-declining balance or the sum-of-the-years' digits methods.

1-2-3's logical functions revolve around the truth of a condition test. One application of the logical functions is to determine whether a purchase amount is sufficient to qualify for a discount. You can use these functions to store a true or false value in a cell. Also, you can perform actions depending on the result of a condition test.

The mathematical functions perform simple and complex mathematical computations. The round function is one of the simplest and allows you to compute the value of a number rounded to the nearest whole number or the nearest thousandth. A more complex computation is the arctangent function, which is one of the trigonometric calculations supported by the @functions.

1-2-3's special functions are the most diverse of all the categories. Functions that do not fit neatly in another category are in the special function category. Some functions in this group provide information about individual cells and ranges on the worksheet; other functions in this group assist you with error trapping. These functions can check for errors or data that is currently unavailable for calculations. A new Release 3 function in this category examines system information.

The statistical functions perform very elementary statistical calculations such as sum, average, count, minimum, and maximum. The standard deviation and variance are two slightly more complex but manageable statistical functions.

String functions,which were introduced in Release 2, manipulate a group of characters. 1-2-3 can extract characters from the middle or either end of a character string with these functions. You can also use a string function to change the case used for text entry.

This book groups all functions in a single category in one chapter. In addition, there is also a chapter on the use of HAL for Release 1A, 2, and 2.01 users, which is a separate program that works with 1-2-3 and provides a short-cut approach to functions. The final chapter provides macro examples that utilize functions for special features.

COMPONENTS OF FUNCTIONS

1-2-3's functions are much more structured than ordinary formulas. The rules governing function entries are easy to master and provide consistency as you use the 103 available functions. These rules are syntax rules that cover the construction of a function entry, and you must follow these rules in much the same way that you adhere to syntax rules for English grammar. As you know, if you do not follow syntax rules for English grammar others will not understand what you say or write. Similarly, if you do not follow 1–2–3's syntax rules for @functions, 1–2–3 will not understand what you need and you will be unable to perform the computation. Figure 1.1 shows the various components of the syntax for a typical @function.

Figure 1.1 Syntax for an @function

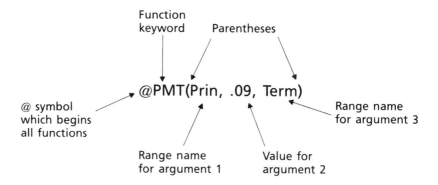

The first component of any @function is the commercial at sign (@), which tells 1–2–3 that you are entering a value in a cell. The @ tells 1–2–3 that the next sequence of characters should represent a function keyword such as SUM or PMT.

The keyword that follows the @ can be in either uppercase or lowercase characters; 1–2–3 always translates your entry into uppercase if you choose lowercase for entry. In this book, all function keywords are shown in uppercase.

Be sure to use the exact spelling of each keyword shown in this book. Although it may seem that using AVERAGE instead of AVG is a request for the average of a group of numbers, 1–2–3 will not perform the calculation unless you use AVG for the function keyword.

Except for the eight functions listed in Table 1.1, a set of parentheses follows the keyword. The parentheses contain the arguments, which tell 1–2–3 the data you want to use in the function's computation. Depending on the function, these arguments might be a single range of worksheet cells reference with a range address, or a series of individual cell references and logical formulas. The next section of this chapter more closely examines the range of options for expressing function arguments.

TABLE 1.1: FUNCTIONS THAT DO NOT REQUIRE ARGUMENTS	
@ERR	@PI
@FALSE	@RAND
@NA	@TODAY
@NOW	@TRUE

Do not add extra spaces anywhere in a function. The keyword follows immediately after the @ symbol, and the parenthesis follows after the keyword. There are no spaces between the function arguments. The closing parenthesis follows immediately after the last argument. There is no space between the argument and parenthesis.

A CLOSER LOOK AT FUNCTION ARGUMENTS

Many types of entries are used to represent function arguments. Regardless of the type of data used, all function arguments are either lists or individual arguments that are position-dependent. The function you select determines the choice of the argument type. A few functions accept lists for arguments; the remaining functions expect the arguments you supply to be in a specific order. The following examples will clarify the differences between the two types of arguments.

Using Functions That Expect an Argument List

Only the statistical functions accept a list for an argument. The argument list for these functions can consist of a range address or a range name that references a range of values as in @SUM(B10..B25) or @SUM(SALES), where SALES is a range name assigned to a range on the worksheet. In releases prior to Release 3, if you use a range name in a function, it must exist at the time you enter the formula or you will not be able to finalize the formula entry. In Release 3, however, you can use undefined range names in a function. Although the cell initially displays an error message, the error condition is resolved once you assign the range name. Figure 1.2 shows the @SUM function referencing a list that consists of a range address.

Figure 1.2 An
@SUM with a
range address for
the list

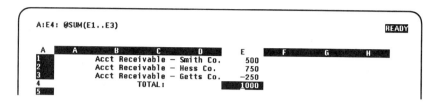

A list can consist of either a series of individual cell addresses separated by commas, or a series of range names separated by commas. @SUM(K2,P5,T7) and @SUM(SALARIES,BENEFITS,TRAVEL) are examples of these two options. In the latter example, the three range names refer to individual cell addresses. The number of individual references supported is dependent on the total length of the formula containing the @function. In Release 2.01 the limit is 240 characters; in Release 3, the limit for a formula is 512 characters.

The third option for an argument expressed as a list is a combination of individual cell addresses and ranges. To compute a total for two ranges of entries and a few individual cell addresses, the formula might look like @SUM(A1..A10,B3,C3..C8).

Using Functions with Position-Dependent Arguments

You must supply the arguments to most functions in a specific order. For example, the @PMT function computes the payment amount for a loan if you supply the loan principal, the interest, and the term of the loan. The sequence of @PMT arguments must be @PMT(principal,interest, term). In this example each argument is provided as a cell address on the current worksheet. Figure 1.3 displays an @PMT function entry.

Figure 1.3 An
@PMT function

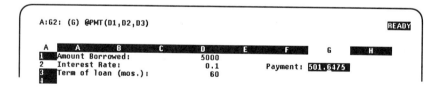

The type of entry that can be used as an argument for this type of function varies by function. Cell addresses, range addresses, range names referring to a single cell or a range, logical formulas, values, strings, arithmetic or string formulas, and three-dimensional ranges are all possibilities.

ENTERING A FUNCTION

You can enter a function in any worksheet cell, but first be sure that 1–2–3 is in READY mode before starting your entry. If 1–2–3 is in another mode, you must cancel the activity or complete it before making a new entry.

Entering the @SUM Function

You can try a few 1–2–3 functions by entering several data values on a clear worksheet. If you have entries on the worksheet, enter /Worksheet Erase Yes to clear memory. Next, type the entries in B2..D15 exactly as shown in Figure 1.4. If you use /Range Format Other Automatic in Release 3 before entering the date, 1–2–3 automatically enters date serial numbers and formats them as dates. In earlier releases, use label entries like '15-Jul-89 for the date entries. Use /Range Format Currency 0 with a range of C5..C16 to format all the entries and one additional cell as currency. You can sum the numbers in column C by following these steps:

Figure 1.4
Entering @SUM

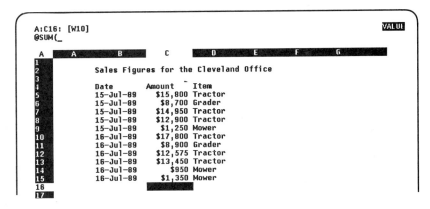

1. Move the cell pointer to C16.
2. Type @SUM(. (The period that ends each sentence should not be typed.) Notice in Figure 1.4 that the mode indicator has changed to value. With Release 3, you can use a shortcut. Type an @, press the Name (F3) key twice, use the Down Arrow key to highlight @SUM(, and press Enter.

3. Move the cell pointer to C5, type a ., and move the cell pointer to C15, or type **C5..C15**.

4. Type a).

5. Press Enter.

The result $108,625 appears in cell C16, as shown in Figure 1.5. The function entry appears as @SUM(C5..C15) in the control panel for this cell. (Note that 1–2–3 records the single period in the range specification as a double period.)

Figure 1.5
Producing a total
with @SUM

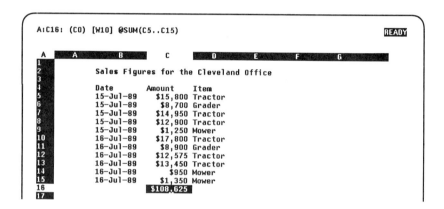

Entering the @PMT Function

The numbers in A1..A3 in Figure 1.6 can be used to test the @PMT function. This function requires three arguments. The first is the principal amount borrowed. (The 100000 entry in A1 will work fine for this.) The second argument is the interest rate for the loan. When calculating an annual payment amount, the interest rate should be expressed in annual terms; when calculating a monthly payment amount, the interest rate should be expressed as a monthly rate, otherwise interest will not be compounded correctly.

Figure 1.6 Using
@PMT with
computations for
two arguments

To use the number in A3 as a monthly interest rate, divide by 12 as in A3/12. The third argument, the term for the loan, should be expressed in years for an annual payment amount and in months for a monthly payment amount. The entry of 20 in A2 could represent a number of years. Multiplying the entry in A2 by 12 yields a number of months. The completed entry would look like @PMT(A1,A3/12,A2*12). The steps required to make this entry are shown below in two ways. The first set of steps uses the pointing method to build the formula. The second set of steps lets you build the formula by typing each of the cell references.

To build the @PMT function using the pointing method of formula entry:

1. Move the cell pointer to B2.
2. Type **@PMT(**. With Release 3, type an @, press F3 (Name) twice, and select @PMT from the list presented.
3. Move the cell pointer to A1 and type a **,**.
4. Move the cell pointer to A3 and type **/12,**.
5. Move the cell pointer to A2 and type ***12)**.
6. Press Enter.

Build the @PMT function by typing the references:

1. Move the cell pointer to B2.
2. Type **@PMT(**. With Release 3, type an @, press F3 (Name) twice, and select @PMT from the list presented.
3. Type **A1**.
4. Type a **,** followed by **A3/12,**.
5. Type **A2*12)**.
6. Press Enter.

The formulas in B1 and B2 provide identical results despite the difference in formula entry. Although the first method requires a little additional time, the visual verification helps to ensure accuracy.

GETTING HELP

1-2-3's help features are especially valuable when you forget the order for a function's arguments. Press the F1 (Help) key from READY mode and 1-2-3 displays the initial help menu shown in Figure 1.7. You can select from the list of topics displayed on the screen by using the arrow keys to move to the desired topic and pressing Enter. The Down Arrow key will move you down the screen in the current column. The Left and Right Arrow keys will allow you to move to topics in different columns. With Release 3 there is a special @function index entry. When the Topic @Function index is highlighted, press Enter. The next help screen you see provides an index listing each individual @function, as shown in Figure 1.8. By using the End key to move to the bottom of the screen and using the arrow keys to highlight the continued option, you can select additional functions or one of the function categories. If you choose to look at a statistical function in more detail in Release 2.01, for example, the next screen will look like Figure 1.9.

Figure 1.7 The initial help screen

```
A:A1:                                                          HELP

1-2-3 Help Index — Highlight a bold topic and press ENTER.

█████████          @Function Index        Mode Indicators
1-2-3 commands     About Ranges           Status Indicators
/Copy                Highlighting         Using Help
/Data                Specifying
/File              Cell References
/Graph             Control Panel
/Move              Error Message Index
/Print             Formulas
/Quit              Function Keys
/Range             Keys, Summary
/System            Macro Command Index
/Worksheet         Macro Introduction


To highlight a bold topic, press a pointer movement key.
To return to a previous Help screen, press BACKSPACE.
To leave Help and return to the worksheet, press ESC.

27-Mar-89 11:53 AM
```

Figure 1.8 The @function index

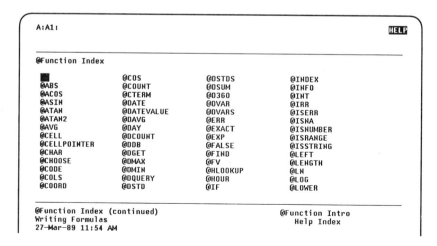

```
A:A1:                                                          HELP

@Function Index

█              @COS          @DSTDS        @INDEX
@ABS           @COUNT        @DSUM         @INFO
@ACOS          @CTERM        @D360         @INT
@ASIN          @DATE         @DVAR         @IRR
@ATAN          @DATEVALUE    @DVARS        @ISERR
@ATAN2         @DAVG         @ERR          @ISNA
@AVG           @DAY          @EXACT        @ISNUMBER
@CELL          @DCOUNT       @EXP          @ISRANGE
@CELLPOINTER   @DDB          @FALSE        @ISSTRING
@CHAR          @DGET         @FIND         @LEFT
@CHOOSE        @DMAX         @FV           @LENGTH
@CODE          @DMIN         @HLOOKUP      @LN
@COLS          @DQUERY       @HOUR         @LOG
@COORD         @DSTD         @IF           @LOWER

@Function Index (continued)                @Function Intro
Writing Formulas                           Help Index
27-Mar-89 11:54 AM
```

Figure 1.9 Help
requested for the
@SUM function

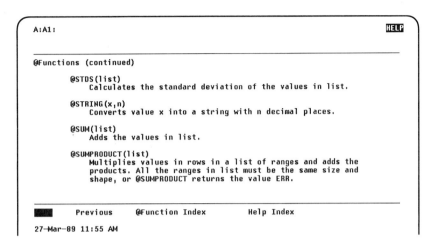

```
A:A1:                                                              HELP
_____

@Functions (continued)
        @STDS(list)
            Calculates the standard deviation of the values in list.

        @STRING(x,n)
            Converts value x into a string with n decimal places.

        @SUM(list)
            Adds the values in list.

        @SUMPRODUCT(list)
            Multiplies values in rows in a list of ranges and adds the
            products. All the ranges in list must be the same size and
            shape, or @SUMPRODUCT returns the value ERR.

    _____
    ▮▮▮▮      Previous      @Function Index        Help Index

27-Mar-89 11:55 AM
```

If you have already started to enter the function, 1–2–3 saves you a little
time. When you press the F1 (Help) key, 1–2–3 displays the @function
index. You can make additional selections for more specific information.

CORRECTING ERRORS

Everyone who makes entries in 1–2–3 worksheets occasionally makes
mistakes. 1–2–3 lets you correct errors in function entries in the same
way that you correct errors in other entries. Correction techniques are
reviewed below and are summarized in Table 1.2.

TABLE 1.2: STEPS FOR ERROR CORRECTION

Status of Entry	Action
Not finalized	Press Esc to eliminate the entry
	Press Backspace to eliminate one character at a time
	Press F2 (Edit) followed by the appropriate cursor movement
Finalized	Retype the entry
	Press F2 (Edit) followed by the appropriate cursor movement

The exact method used for error correction depends upon whether you have finalized the entry of the function in the worksheet cell. You can always finalize cell entries by pressing Enter, and you can sometimes finalize entries by pressing the arrow keys. If you have typed a formula, the arrow keys will always finalize an entry for you. However, when you have used the pointing method to select the last reference in the formula, 1-2-3 interprets a press of the arrow key as an indication that you want to change the reference that Point mode is electing and requires you to finalize with Enter. If 1-2-3 rejects your entry due to a syntax problem or other mistake, your entry will still be finalized. 1-2-3 will be in Edit mode to allow for your correction.

Correcting a Mistake Before Finalizing

You have several options for making a correction if you have not finalized your entry. If you notice your mistake immediately after typing a character, use the Backspace key to delete the previous character. Continue pressing the Backspace key until all errors have been eliminated. For example, if you intended to type **Budget – 1989** in a worksheet cell and accidentally typed **Budget – 1990**, the correction is easy. Press the backspace key twice, type **89** and press Enter.

If correcting the error with the Backspace key would delete many correct entries, press the Edit (F2) key. Once in Edit mode, you can use the Left and Right Arrow keys to move within the entry. This allows you to make changes without deleting correct entries. If you need to insert a character, move one position past where the new character should appear and type the character. If you are going to make more significant changes to the entries, use the Insert key and type in the new characters. Press Enter to finalize your changes.

A few examples will clarify these more extensive corrections. If you type **Bdget 1990**, the missing character is closer to the beginning of the entry. Using the backspace key would delete almost the entire entry. Pressing F2, then pressing the Home key, moves you to the beginning of the entry. The mode indicator should read EDIT. Pressing the Right Arrow key twice moves the small cursor in the edit line at the top of your screen to the d. Type a u and press Enter. Characters are always inserted in the space before the cursor as long as you are in Edit mode and the default of Insert is still on. When Insert is not on, OVR will appear in the bottom line of your screen, and entries from the keyboard will replace characters on the screen.

If you accidentally type **Budget 1989** when you intend to type **Sales 1989**, switch Insert to Overstrike to facilitate the correction once you enter Edit mode. First, press F2 (Edit) to enter Edit mode. Next, press Home followed by the Right Arrow key to move to the B. Press the Insert key to set the Overstrike mode on (the OVR indicator will display at the bottom of the screen). Type **Sales** and the characters entered replace existing characters. Press the Delete key once to delete the t from the original entry and press Enter to finalize.

Correcting a Mistake After Finalizing

To correct a mistake after finalizing an entry, you can either retype the entry or edit it. To edit a finalized entry, use the same procedure that you used when editing an entry that was not finalized. First, press the Edit (F2) key; the mode indicator will change to Edit, and you can use the Left and Right Arrow keys to move within the entry. You can also use the Home key to move to the first position in the entry, and the End key to move to the last position. Avoid using the Backspace key since it will delete a character each time you strike the key.

You can also type characters to be inserted to the left of the cursor. If you press the Insert key to toggle the overstrike feature, the characters you type will replace characters in the existing entry. Once you complete the changes, press Enter.

RELEASE DIFFERENCES

There have been five releases of 1-2-3 since its introduction with Release 1.0. Each new release contains new functions. You can utilize the information in this book regardless of the release you work with. Note, however, that you will be unable to use the full set of functions in the current release if you are using an older release. If you use the Lotus translation facility to convert a worksheet created with a higher release to a lower one, 1-2-3 will only translate function entries that are part of the lower release.

Release 1 Through Release 2.2

Release 1A followed shortly after Release 1 but provided the same @function support as 1.0. Release 2.0 offered many new functions over Release 1A, including the entire category of string functions. In addition, time functions were added to the date functions present since Release 1, and thirty-seven new functions supplemented the special, financial, and logical categories.

Shortly after the introduction of Release 2, Release 2.01 was introduced as a maintenance release. Although it contained no new functions, some subtle differences are present. Perhaps the most significant is the way 1-2-3 handles label entries in computations. In Release 2.0, a label entry caused an error when referenced in a formula, such as +A1+A2 if A1 contains ''ABC'' and A2 contains 100. A problem occurs since these cells are referenced as individual cells, not as ranges. @SUM(A1.A2) would return the correct answer since it uses range references. However, Release 2.01 treats these entries as zeros, allowing you to include a blank cell at the beginning of a range you are adding or to generate a series of underline symbols in a cell to separate detail entries from a total. You can reference both of these in a range for @SUM without any impact on the total, yet these extra rows make it easy to expand a range at the top or bottom in order to add additional detail entries. In Release 2.0 and above, a function that expects a string will return an error message if you supply a value.

In 1989, Lotus released version 2.2 with expanded features for users with 8088 machines. Although this release does not provide any new functions, it enhances performance with features like minimal recalculation, macro recording, and settings sheets.

Special Release 3 Considerations

Although Release 3 offers no new function categories, there are sixteen new functions within the existing function categories. Each new function is marked. New functions will not be available to those using an earlier release.

The most significant difference in Release 3 is its ability to use multiple sheets in one worksheet file. Every worksheet can have as many as 256 levels with each sheet level represented by one or two letters. Sheet letters are assigned the same way as column letters, running from A to Z then proceeding to double letter combinations from AA to IV. You can access data in other worksheet levels by entering the letter representing the worksheet level, a colon, and the cell address. This feature can total data across worksheets or reference an interest rate stored in another level of the current worksheet.

Using Arguments from Another Level of the Worksheet

Release 3's ability to support multi-level worksheets allows you to organize your models. Since you can store different types of information on different levels, you might need to reference data from a number of worksheet levels when you enter functions that use several arguments.

The only difference in entering references to cells or ranges in different sheets is that you must specify the sheet letter. To access a principal amount from G2 of sheet A, you would type **A:G2** rather than G2. To refer to an interest rate in F3 of sheet B, type **B:F3**. A reference to a term stored in H1 of sheet C would be **C:H1**. The payment function accessing data from three different sheets might look like @PMT(G2,B:F3/12,C:H1*12), as shown in Figure 1.10.

Figure 1.10 Using @PMT with multiple-sheet references in Release 3

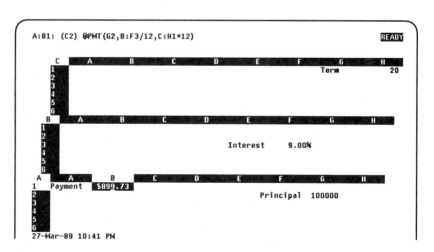

Referencing a List of Values Across Worksheet Levels

Release 3's three-dimensional features let you create ranges that span sheets. Functions that accept range references for arguments will accept a range reference that spans worksheet levels. To determine the average of the entries in cells D2.F10 of the current worksheet, type @AVG(D2.F10). To average the entries in D2.F10 of levels A, B, and C, type @AVG(A:D2.C:F10). The single-level reference averages twenty-seven values. The multi-level reference includes eighty-one entries in the average calculation.

Linking Argument Values from Other Worksheet Files

Release 3 supports links to data stored in other worksheet files. Once the link is established, 1-2-3 obtains the current value for this reference each time you execute the /File Admin Link-Refresh command. This allows you to create a model that accesses up-to-date information in your other models or those created by others in your organization.

To create a link within a function, you need to specify a source file and a cell address, range address, or range name in the other file that you wish to access. You must use the special angle bracket symbols (<< >>) with the filename to tell 1-2-3 that you are creating a link.

To create a payment calculation that references a range named Interest in a file named PRIME, type @PMT(A1, << PRIME >> INTEREST/ 12,A3*12), as shown in Figure 1.11.

Figure 1.11 Using @PMT with an external file reference in Release 3

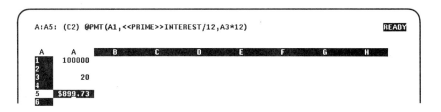

If you use addresses rather than range names, you must provide a complete address including the sheet. 1-2-3 would accept @PMT(A1, << PRIME >> A:F2,A3) because the address referenced is complete. It would not accept @PMT(A1, << PRIME >> F2,A3) since the external reference does not include the sheet.

Using Wildcard Reference Features

Release 3's wildcard reference features allow you to access a specific range name in one of the active files. The difference between this and an explicit reference to an external file is that the filename is not specified. 1-2-3 returns an error message if the range name specified is found in multiple locations or if it does not find the range name in any of the files.

The wildcard feature allows you to develop applications that many users can use. All users may have their own files,and they can use the wildcard feature to access the data in their own file if they conform to the restrictions of this feature.

Figure 1.12 shows a formula with a wildcard reference to a range name Interest. 1-2-3 searches for Interest in an active worksheet file, using the value associated with the name in the function. If 1-2-3 does not find the range name or if it finds multiple occurrences of the range name, the function results in an error message.

Figure 1.12 Using a wildcard reference to a range name in an active sheet in Release 3

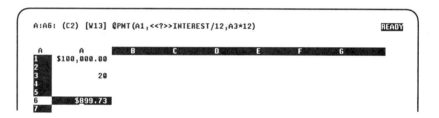

NESTED FUNCTIONS

Although most functions are used alone, you can combine function entries. The use of one function as the argument for another function is referred to as nesting functions. You can determine whether or not a function is acceptable as an argument based upon the type of argument needed and the type of result which the function returns.

Since the @SUM function expects a list of values or references to values as an argument, any function that produces a value could be nested within the sum function. The following are examples of acceptable nested functions within the sum function:

@SUM(A2.B7,@SUM(D3.G7),Z2)
@SUM(@AVG(S2.S25),@AVG(D3..F7))
@SUM(@PMT(D2,D3,D4),TAXES,INSURANCE)

You will notice in all the examples that each nested function is entered exactly as if you were entering it alone. The parentheses and function arguments are provided in the same fashion as stand-alone functions. Although 1-2-3 does not reject the first example, it produces the same result if entered as @SUM(A2.B7,D3.G7,Z2). The latter approach is simpler, clearer, and uses less memory.

The arguments for @PMT are all value entries or references to value entries. As previously explained, functions that return character strings are treated as a zero when used in functions that expect a value. A string function such as @RIGHT returns a string of characters rather than a value. Entering @PMT(@RIGHT(A2,5),A3,A4) would always return 0 since @RIGHT returns a string regardless of the entry in A2. If A2 contains a value entry, an error message is returned since the @RIGHT function expects a string.

Nesting is used frequently with logical condition tests. The ability to use nesting allows for complex condition test. Examples of nested functions are covered with @IF in Chapter 3, Logical Functions.

2

Statistical Functions

1-2-3's statistical functions provide basic statistical measures that anyone can use since they do not require an understanding of advanced statistical concepts.

The statistical functions permit an easy way to compute measurements for a group of data values. These measurements provide some information about the values as a group. Rather than examining each data value, you can use the statistical measures to provide an overview of what the data looks like.

The statistical functions can total a group of values to provide a sum. If a group of values represents expenses for a period, the sum of each individual purchase provides the total purchases for the period. You can also use these functions to compute averages. Thus, if the individual values represent the prices paid for a ton of salt in 1988, you can use the average to project the cost of this chemical for future periods.

Other statistical functions compute a count of the values in a group, the maximum value in the group, and the minimum value in the group. Because the statistical functions provide so many practical applications, you will want to master this group of functions before any other.

A COMMON SYNTAX FOR ALL STATISTICAL FUNCTIONS

Since all statistical functions have the same format, you will know how to use the entire group once you master your first statistical function. The only change is the keyword that begins the function.

All the statistical functions operate on lists. A list is a group of one or more values. Each entry in the list can be a cell address, a value, a range address, or a range name. If a list consists of more than one type of entry, commas separate the entries. Note that cell addresses function as values in formulas. Even when the cell is blank, the cell evaluates as a zero, not as a blank. This means that @COUNT(A1,A2,A3) is always 3 since the individual cell never evaluates as a blank. The same function excludes blank cells from a referenced range, so @COUNT (A1..A3) would equal zero.

Like the arguments for other functions, you enclose lists in parentheses. Some of the values you might record in lists are as follows:

```
(A1.A10)
(B6.D20,Z2,F14)
(B6,SALES,Z72)
(A5,3,10,Z2,5*4,Z10,EXPENSES)
```

In these examples, A1.A10 and B6.D20 are range addresses, Z2 and F14 are individual cell addresses, and the numbers 3 and 10 in the last example are values. The entry 5*4 is a formula but is treated as a value since it evaluates as 20 when the computation is performed. Sales and Expenses are range names that have been applied to a single cell or a range of cells. You can assign range names with the /Range Name Create or /Range Name Labels command.

New Release 3 Options with Statistical Functions

1-2-3 Release 3 expands statistical functions to include working with lists that span sheets and references to external data. Since you can have as many as 256 sheets in one Release 3 worksheet file, the statistical functions can work with arguments from different sheets or ranges that span sheets. Using an external file link, the data in Release 3 functions can reside in an external worksheet file.

The following entries represent list entries that would be acceptable only in Release 3:

- (A:A1..B:C10), where the current file has at least two sheets

- (B:S2..B:S25,A:L10,C1), where C1 is in the current sheet and the file has at least two sheets, A and B

- (<< ACCT.WK3 >>A:B2..H:B25), where ACCT.WK3 is a file on disk with sheet levels A through H

- (<< ? >> SALES), where SALES is a defined range name in an active worksheet

Using Three Dimensional Ranges

If you are currently working with a single sheet Release 3 file and wish to add sheets, you can use the /Worksheet Insert Sheet command. You can add the sheets either before or after the current sheet and can add more than one sheet at a time by specifying the number you wish to add. Once the new sheets are added, you will find that they have the same structure and organization as the original sheet. (In other words, they have columns A through IV and rows 1 through 8192.) You can look at a view showing data from three sheets by entering /Worksheet Window Perspective. This helps you obtain a perspective of the entries you want to make before beginning. You can move from sheet to sheet with Ctrl-PGUP and Ctrl-PGDN. To zoom in for a close-up look at the current sheet, press Alt-F6 (Zoom). Pressing it a second time returns you to the three-window display and entering the /Worksheet Window Clear command eliminates the extra windows permanently.

You can enter data in any cell on any sheet. Figure 2.1 shows quarterly product sales information for three regions on sheets B through D. The @AVG (average) function is used with this data to compute average product sales by product and quarter. A summary sheet is created on sheet A to compute average sales for all regions.

Figure 2.1
Release 3 data for
several regions

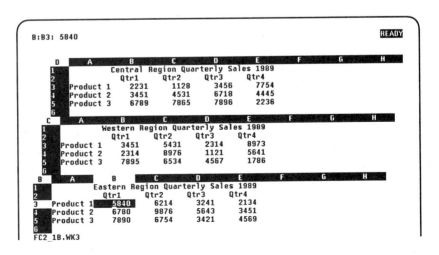

Creating an average for values that span several sheets requires the use of a sheet indicator in front of each cell address. Release 3 assumes that your cell references are for the current sheet if it does not find this sheet indicator in your formulas. The sheet indicator is separated from the cell address by a colon (:) as in A:D1 to represent cell D1 on sheet A.

The first formula on sheet A is in cell B3; it references product 1 sales in quarter 1 for all three regions with the formula @AVG(B:B3..D:B3), a range consisting of a cell on each of the three sheets as shown in Figure 2.2. This formula structure is used for the remaining formulas and can be copied across and down to obtain the average for the remaining quarters and products. The sheet letters do not interfere with the copy process and are automatically adjusted by /Copy when required.

Figure 2.2 Average sales for all three regions

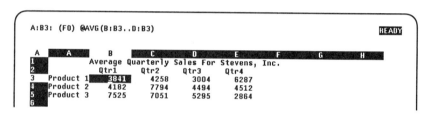

You can obtain the product totals for each year by adding each of the quarter totals on the three region sheets. To total yearly sales for product 1, enter the formula @SUM(B:B3..D:E3) on a summary sheet. The size of the range is dictated by the number of cells included from each sheet and the number of sheets involved. Even though the range is three-dimensional, the basic technique of using diagonally opposite corners to specify a range still works.

Like ranges that are on one sheet, three-dimensional ranges are adjusted if you insert sheets in the middle of the range. For example, inserting a sheet before or after sheet C would automatically include the cells on the new sheet within the range.

Using External File Links

You can reference data stored in worksheet files on disk by using the statistical functions. For instance, you might create a worksheet that contains both detail and consolidation information on one sheet and may need to store the detail files separately due to size constraints or to the fact that they are updated by other people. In this case, the consolidation sheet may show sums or averages obtained with external data references.

Figure 2.3 shows data from one of the external sheets. To total the 1989 tire sales for the Eastern region and display the total on the current sheet, you would type @SUM(<< C:\123\EASTSLS.WK3 >> B3..E3). (The name of the file is enclosed in the double angle bracket symbols << >>.) If the file is a .WK3 file, only the file name must be enclosed within the symbols. The entire file extension is required when the file is a .WKS, .WK1, .WRK, or .WR1 file. If the file is in a directory other than the current directory, the complete path must be specified.

Figure 2.3 Tire sales for the Eastern region

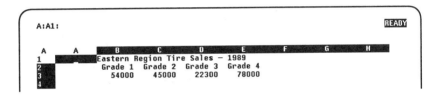

Release 3 is able to access all the cells in the range specified with the external reference and use them to compute the @AVG formula. It can even combine external references from many sheets if each is a separate element within the list, as in

@AVG(<< C:\ACCT\EASTSLS.WK3 >> B3..E3,
<< C:\ACCT\WESTSLS.WK3 >> B3..E3)

The two referenced ranges are averaged within the @function, as shown in Figure 2.4.

Figure 2.4 Average tire sales in two regions

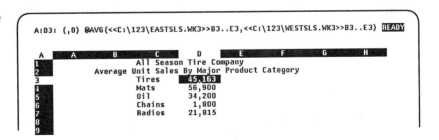

If you are using 1–2–3 on a network, it is possible that some of the files to which you have external links may be updated while you are using a worksheet. Use the /File Admin Link-Refresh command to update all of the links in all of the active files.

External References in Release 2.2

Release 2.2 of 1–2–3 also supports external references. Although the special symbols that indicate the external file reference are the same, file links within Release 2.2 offer only a subset of Release 3's features; they are cell links that bring a value from a cell in an external file to a cell in the current worksheet. In Release 2.2, you cannot use an external link within an @function. Instead, you can bring values into cells and reference these values in a function. The same results as Release 3 can be achieved, although an extra step is required. Assuming that you want to create a total of the sales for the Eastern and Western regions with Release 2.2, the best approach would be to total the sales for both regions on the region worksheets, then use + <<EASTSLS.WK1 >>F3 to bring the Eastern region total into the current worksheet. The entry + <<WESTSLS.WK1 >>F3 will bring the sales for the Western region into the current sheet. Assuming the entries for the two regions are stored in Z2 and Z3 on the current sheet, you can enter +Z2+Z3 or @SUM(Z2,Z3) to compute the same total shown in the earlier Release 3 example.

There are several special circumstances that affect list entries for all of the statistical functions. 1–2–3 ignores blank cells that are part of a range; a blank cell referred to by a cell address or range name has the numeric value of zero, which enters into the computation. 1–2–3 treats strings as zeros and considers a cell containing a label indicator with no other entry to be a string and returns a zero. Therefore, if you count the entries in a column that contains numbers and strings, both the numbers and the strings increment the count.

@SUM

To total the values in A1 and A2, you can type the formula +A1+A2. However, to add all the numbers from cell A1 to A100, you would not want to type +A1+A2+ ... +A100, since that approach is time-consuming and error prone. Instead, you should use the @SUM function to tell 1–2–3 to add a range of numbers that you specify.

The format of the @SUM function is @SUM(list). This function is extremely flexible, and allows you to sum a range of values, individual cell entries, or a combination of ranges and individual cell values.

Example

@SUM is most frequently used for adding a column or row of numbers. Figure 2.5 shows how @SUM is used to quickly total a number of purchases.

Figure 2.5 Using @SUM to add a column of numbers

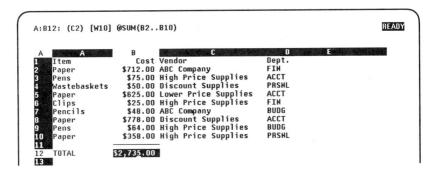

Of course, you could replace the @SUM function used in this model with a formula entry consisting of a series of additions. However, a formula takes longer to enter, is more likely to produce errors, and does not clearly indicate which numbers are being added.

Functions like @SUM that support ranges for an argument easily withstand expansions and contractions in the data. Thus, a new computation will be correct if you add or delete a row from the middle of the range referenced in a list. However, adding or deleting a row at the beginning or the end of a range does not offer the same success. If you insert a row at the beginning or the end of a range, the computation will remain unaffected; if you delete a row at the beginning or the end of a range, the function range shrinks in Release 3 although earlier releases return an error message.

With Release 2.01 and above, you can use a row of dashes at the top and bottom of the range to eliminate this problem. With the dashes included in the range, you can add or delete entries at the top or bottom of the range. Figure 2.6 shows a worksheet with dashes at the top and bottom. The function @SUM(E5..E18) calculates total salaries. The correct answer results since 1–2–3 treats the dashes as zeros in the calculation.

Figure 2.6 Using @SUM to add a column of salaries

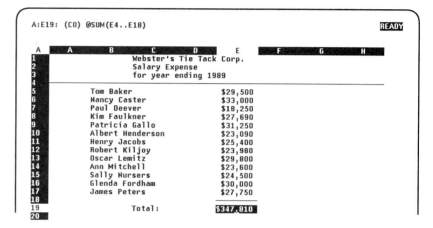

If you move the cell pointer to E6 and enter /Worksheet Insert Row, 1–2–3 prompts you to insert a row. Since you need only add one row, press Enter to have 1–2–3 add a new row at the top. To add the new entry, type **Mary Abbott** in B6 and **$26,385** in E6. The total at the bottom is updated for the new entry as shown in Figure 2.7.

Figure 2.7 Using @SUM to add a column of salaries after adding a new row

```
A:E20: (C0) @SUM(E4..E19)                                    READY

A    A        B         C         D      E       F      G      H
1                      Webster's Tie Tack Corp.
2                      Salary Expense
3                      for year ending 1989
4
5             Mary Abbott              $26,385
6             Tom Baker                $29,500
7             Nancy Caster             $33,000
8             Paul Deever              $18,250
9             Kim Faulkner             $27,690
10            Patricia Gallo           $31,250
11            Albert Henderson         $23,090
12            Henry Jacobs             $25,400
13            Robert Kiljoy            $23,980
14            Oscar Lemitz             $29,800
15            Ann Mitchell             $23,600
16            Sally Nursers            $24,500
17            Glenda Fordham           $30,000
18            James Peters             $27,750
19
20                       Total:        $374,195
```

Other Applications

In addition to adding a column or row of numbers, @SUM also adds groups of numbers that are outside a contiguous range. You can include other computations within the argument list. These additional computations can include the standard arithmetic computations or other functions. For example, to add sales tax to the cost of the items purchased, change the formula for total purchases in cell B12 to @SUM(B2..B10,.07*@SUM(B2..B10)) or simply @SUM(B2.B10)*1.07. This formula computes a seven percent sales tax based on the sum of the purchases. The function adds the computed tax to the sum of the individual purchases. Note that the comma separating the two entries in the list tells 1-2-3 to treat them as separate items.

SPECIAL RELEASE 3 FEATURES

@SUM works the same in Release 3 as in earlier releases of 1-2-3. Release 3's multilevel worksheets and support for file links extend these features even further. Thus, with the new features you can total entries on different levels of the worksheet, or you can access the data stored in other worksheet files on disk to produce a consolidated budget or an expense report from details in many different worksheets.

Create Summaries Across Worksheets

Release 3 lets you add data values stored in many levels of the current worksheet just as you were able to use the average function to work with data in multiple-sheets. You can use this feature to total the sales for sales personnel even if the sales figures for each person are stored on a different level of the worksheet. Figure 2.8 shows the sales entries for John Smith in each of the product sales sheets. Using @SUM across levels produces a total sales computation for John and other sales personnel as shown in Figure 2.9 in the summary sheet. You can enable Group Mode with /Worksheet Global Group Enable, enter a range or global format of comma for the entries, widen column A, and increase the global column width, and have the changes you make to one sheet affect all the sheets.

Figure 2.8 An example of sales worksheets by product

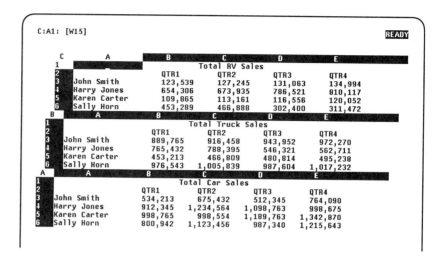

Figure 2.9 Using @SUM to add numbers from different sheets

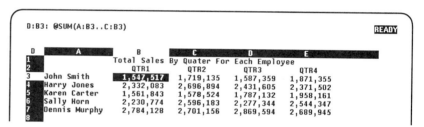

Totaling Data from Other Files

Release 3 also allows you to sum data from different files. Figure 2.10 presents the detail travel expenses, by employee. While this amount of detail is useful in evaluating the fiscal responsibility of each employee, it is too detailed for a summary report of expenses. The summary report in Figure 2.11 requires only the total for each expense type. By utilizing @SUM to reference the detail expense entries, you can obtain a total figure for the summary. Although the general procedure remains the same, you can modify the formula for different detail expense worksheets.

Figure 2.10 An example of travel expense detail

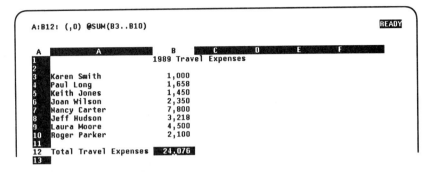

Figure 2.11 Using @SUM to add numbers from different worksheets

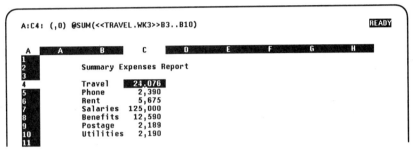

The formula in cell E7 is @SUM(<< TRAVEL.WK3 >> B3..B10). The opening double angle brackets (<<) tell 1–2–3 that an external worksheet file is to be accessed. The name of the file and its extension follow the arrows. The closing double angle brackets (>>) are followed by the range reference, which tells 1–2–3 which cells to reference. This feature lets you produce an aggregate report on expenses by accessing the data in the detail worksheet files. Since the external sheet contains a total, you can achieve the same result with a reference to this total. Keep the @SUM alternative in mind for situations where a total is not on the sheet. Figure 2.12 shows a similar expense consolidation with each of the external reference formulas displayed on the sheet.

Figure 2.12
External file
references in
formulas

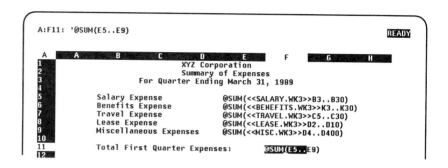

```
A:F11:  '@SUM(E5..E9)                                                    READY

  A      A         B         C         D         E       F      G      H
 1                            XYZ Corporation
 2                           Summary of Expenses
 3                       For Quarter Ending March 31, 1989
 4
 5          Salary Expense              @SUM(<<SALARY.WK3>>B3..B30)
 6          Benefits Expense            @SUM(<<BENEFITS.WK3>>K3..K30)
 7          Travel Expense              @SUM(<<TRAVEL.WK3>>C5..C30)
 8          Lease Expense               @SUM(<<LEASE.WK3>>D2..D10)
 9          Miscellaneous Expenses      @SUM(<<MISC.WK3>>D4..D400)
10
11          Total First Quarter Expenses:       @SUM(E5..E9)
12
```

Wildcard References

Release 3 allows you to reference a named range in an active worksheet file without specifying the name of the worksheet containing the range. This feature offers flexibility, but poses additional restrictions. For this feature to work properly the following must be true:

- Only one of the active files can have a named range that matches the specified entry.

- One of the files must have a range that matches.

1-2-3 returns an error message if either condition is not met.

The wildcard reference to the range name SALES is written as <<?>>SALES. You can use a wildcard reference any place you can use a named range, including as an argument in an @SUM function. For example, to reference the PROFIT1 and PROFIT2 in an @SUM formula, you would type @SUM(<?>PROFIT1,<?>PROFIT2).

@COUNT

Some calculations require that you know the number of cells that contain entries; other calculations require that you know the number of non-blank cells. In an application in which the entries represent overtime hours, the count indicates how many people worked overtime during a particular period. You may need to know that number for reasons that do not involve calculations (such as determining if the worksheet fits on one page). The @COUNT function counts the number of cells in the list with non-blank entries. Since the format of this function is @COUNT(list), you have all the flexibility of lists described earlier in the chapter although you should avoid using individual cell addresses as part of the list.

1-2-3 handles blank entries differently depending on whether they are within a range or provided as an individual cell address. If the list contains a range, @COUNT ignores blank cells. If the list contains individual cell references and names for individual cells, @COUNT counts each cell reference or name as 1 even though it may be blank.

@COUNT is different from any of the other statistical functions since the entries in the list can be labels. @COUNT can count the entries in a row or a column and obtain the same result regardless of whether the entries are labels or values.

Example

You can use @COUNT to count the number of items purchased. If you are operating a large purchasing department, you might judge the performance of your department by the number of purchase orders processed. If you set up a worksheet like Figure 2.13, you can use @COUNT to determine the number of cells in column B that contain purchases. Attempting to compute a count by subtracting the beginning row from the last row will not produce correct results in all cases due to the presence of blank rows. By using @COUNT, you eliminate blank rows in the report. Entering @COUNT(B2..B10) in cell B13, will yield the correct count.

Figure 2.13 Using @COUNT to count the number of items purchased

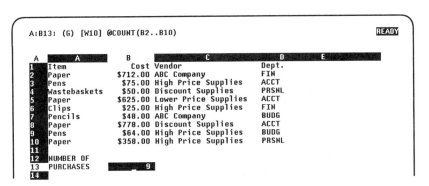

A formula like @COUNT(B2..B10,E1) might not provide the results you expect. Because of the individual cell address, you will get one number higher than the original count even though E1 is blank. 1-2-3 counts single cell references as one rather than zero even though the cell is blank.

Other Applications

@COUNT can provide useful information when you know the number of entries you should have. A comparison of @COUNT and the expected number of entries tells you how many blank cells remain in the range. A list of 500 employees with a @COUNT result of 497 for the range containing social security numbers indicates that three employee records have blanks in the social security number column.

@AVG

The average of a group of numbers is an important statistical computation that provides meaningful information about the range of entries. You can compute the average sales for a sales report, the average purchase price for an invoice, or the average grade for a test.

The average is the sum of each entry divided by the total number of entries. Rather than create a formula that adds the entries and divides the sum by the count of the items that you want to average, @AVG does it for you. @AVG is equivalent to the @SUM function divided by the @COUNT function. The format for this function is @AVG(list). 1–2–3 defines list in the same way as for other statistical functions.

Example

Since @AVG is equal to @SUM/@COUNT, you can test the results by computing the average purchase for the purchases used in the @SUM and @COUNT example. In Figure 2.14, the average purchase is computed as the average of the range B2 to B10. While you could use the @SUM and @COUNT instead, @AVG is quicker and clearer to other users of your worksheet model.

Figure 2.14 Using @AVG to calculate the average price of the items purchased

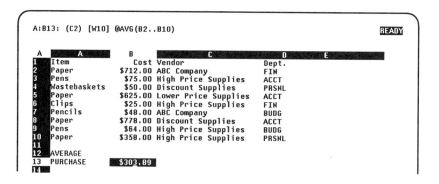

As with the other statistical functions, if you reference a single cell, the count increases by one even if the cell is blank, thereby distorting the average. For example, refer to Figure 2.14. If the formula in cell B13 looked like: @AVG(B2..B10,E1), the result would be 273.50 rather than the correct result of 303.89. The incorrect result is caused by the use of the single cell reference within the list of function arguments. Entering the formula as @AVG(B2..B10,E1..E1) does not eliminate the problem because 1-2-3 converts the entry to E1.

Other Applications

Another example of @AVG is the computation of student semester averages. A teacher can record the students' grades in a worksheet and add the @AVG function to perform the computation. In addition to computing student averages, the teacher can use @AVG to compute the class average for specific assignments. This can help the teacher judge whether the assignment was the appropriate difficulty level.

@MIN

With large worksheets, you often need to know the lowest number in a range of entries. You might be using this number in another formula, displaying the lowest cost in a group of expenses, or, if the numbers in the group are negative, to check that a column is wide enough. The @MIN function determines the lowest number in the group of entries represented by the list used as the function argument. The format of this function is @MIN(list). As with the other statistical functions, @MIN accepts any combination of ranges, cell addresses, values, or range names. If there is a string in your list, remember that 1-2-3 treats the entry as a zero.

Example

Finding the lowest number in a range is necessary for determining the lowest purchase amount. In Figure 2.15, @MIN calculates the lowest value of the different items purchased. In addition to determining the lowest purchase amount, you can use @MIN to verify the accuracy of entries. Thus, if the result of @MIN is negative, someone in the purchasing department must confirm that the number results from a prior credit and not an incorrect entry.

Figure 2.15 Using
@MIN to
determine the
lowest value

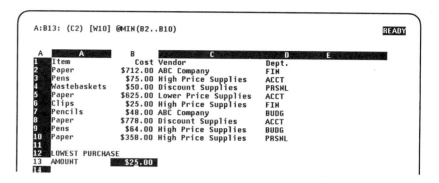

```
A:B13: (C2) [W10] @MIN(B2..B10)                                        READY

   A        A            B              C                  D          E
 1  Item               Cost  Vendor               Dept.
 2  Paper           $712.00  ABC Company          FIN
 3  Pens             $75.00  High Price Supplies  ACCT
 4  Wastebaskets     $50.00  Discount Supplies    PRSNL
 5  Paper           $625.00  Lower Price Supplies ACCT
 6  Clips            $25.00  High Price Supplies  FIN
 7  Pencils          $48.00  ABC Company          BUDG
 8  Paper           $778.00  Discount Supplies    ACCT
 9  Pens             $64.00  High Price Supplies  BUDG
10  Paper           $358.00  High Price Supplies  PRSNL
11
12  LOWEST PURCHASE
13  AMOUNT           $25.00
14
```

Other Applications

For a sales report that separates sales by salesmen, displaying the lowest
sales from any salesmen can be used as a motivational and performance
evaluation tool.

For a lengthy worksheet used to create a printed report, this function,
when combined with the @MAX function discussed later, can help you
judge how wide or narrow to make the column displaying sales numbers.
If a professor uses 1–2–3 to keep track of a class's grades, @MIN provides the lowest score for a graded assignment to pinpoint a student
whose performance needs improvement.

@MAX

The @MAX function provides the highest number in a list of entries.
You might use this number in another formula or to display the highest
cost in a group of expenses. The format of this function is @MAX(list).
Like all of the statistical functions, you can use a list of individual values,
ranges, cell addresses, or range names.

Example

You can use @MAX to determine the highest purchase amount shown
on a worksheet. In Figure 2.16, @MAX calculates the highest value
of the different items purchased. In the example, the information provided by @MAX can focus attention on expensive purchases. If the
result of @MAX is above a predetermined amount, someone in the
purchasing department can confirm that the number was correct. This
check can highlight an error or indicate that something purchased as
an office supply should have been a capital budget expense.

Figure 2.16 Using @MAX to determine the highest value

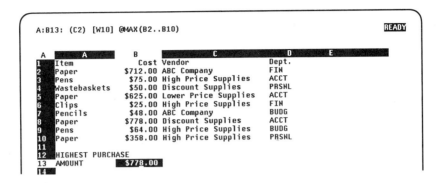

Other Applications

You can create a sales report that displays sales by salesperson and displays the highest sales amount for use as a motivational and performance evaluation tool.

When you create a report form, you can combine @MAX with @MIN to help you judge how wide or narrow to make a column of numbers.

A teacher can use @MAX to display the highest score for a graded assignment to obtain one measure of class performance.

MEASURING DISPERSION

The last four functions described in this chapter handle the dispersion of data. The concept of dispersion is a little more difficult than the concepts of the other statistical functions. An illustration will clarify the concept. Once you understand the concept of dispersion, you can apply the concept to several cases and use the @STD and @VAR functions to help you compute the dispersion of your data.

Definition of Dispersion

Dispersion is the degree to which data is distributed in a range. Figure 2.17 shows the grades of students for two tests with scores ranging from 50 to 100, with an average of 75. In the first test, the grades are scattered widely with several scores in the 90's and 50's. Any particular grade may range anywhere from 50 to 100 due to the wide dispersion. In the second test, which has a narrow dispersion, the grades are grouped closer together. There is an occasional score in the 50's or 90's, but most of the grades are in the 70's. As these two examples illustrate, dispersion is the way in which the data is spread across the range of values.

Figure 2.17
Examples of
dispersion

```
A:C3: [W10]  75                                                          READY

    A                  A              B          C          D        E        F
    1  Student Names       Number       Test #1    Test #2
    2
    3  Tripp, Donald       111-11-1111       75        75
    4  Jacobs, Jim         222-22-2222      100        74
    5  Sommers, John       333-33-3333       59        78
    6  Charles, Susan      444-44-4444       63        70
    7  Smith, Mark         555-55-5555       69        79
    8  Howe, Jason         666-66-6666       75        76
    9  Miller, Mike        777-77-7777       64        77
   10  Wells, Ann          888-88-8888       86       100
   11  Mayer, Karen        999-99-9999       59        73
   12  Prescott, Mike      101-51-9450       81        72
   13  Stevens, Andy       565-46-1657       67        77
   14  Robbins, David      546-90-5605       85        50
   15  Jones, Walter       264-65-6505       72        79
   16  Hagan, Steve        569-87-1237       91        76
   17  Powers, Joe         895-45-6045       50        72
   18  Denk, Janice        566-45-7893       87        74
   19  Black, Jim          978-12-3519       73        77
   20  Johnston, Neal      456-90-7319       94        71
```

The concept of dispersion is important because it tells you something about the data distribution. For example, if you wanted to guess a particular student's grade within five points, it is easier to guess for the second test since most of the grades are in the 70's. If you guess 75, your guess is correct for sixteen out of the eighteen students. In the first test, if you guess 75, the guess is only correct for four of the eighteen students. Therefore, you know more about your data by knowing the dispersion.

Applications

Dispersion of data is important in many fields such as marketing and accounting. Often, the basis for an auditing test or a release of a product is a trial-sized sample. For example, an accountant bases his assessment of the number of invoices to check upon the dispersion of the sample. Or, a company uses market research data to determine the effectiveness of its marketing strategy. The company then uses the information about its product to determine the most effective product features. A market study of consumers buying the product may also measure the age or income dispersion of the sample to better focus advertising for the product.

@VAR Variance measures the degree to which the individual values in a group of data vary from the average of that group. The lower the variance, the less individual values vary from the average and the more reliable the average is as a representation of the data. Table 2.1 provides a step-by-step look at the calculation of variance values. The format for the variance function is @VAR(list). The options for the argument list are the same as for the other statistical functions.

TABLE 2.1: A STEP-BY-STEP LOOK AT VARIANCE COMPUTATIONS

This example computes the variance for each test in Figure 2.17.

Step 1: Compute the Average. The average for Test 1 data is 75.

Step 2: Subtract each value in the range from the average. This information appears in the Difference column.

Student Name	Grade for Test 1	Average	Difference	Difference Squared
Tripp, Donald	75	75	0	0
Jacobs, Jim	100	75	25	625
Sommers, John	59	75	−16	256
Charles, Susan	63	75	−12	144
Smith, Mark	69	75	−6	36
Howe, Jason	75	75	0	0
Miller, Mike	64	75	−11	121
Wells, Ann	86	75	11	121
Mayer, Karen	59	75	−16	256
Prescott, Mike	81	75	6	36
Stevens, Andy	67	75	−8	64
Robbins, David	85	75	10	100
Jones, Walter	72	75	−3	9
Hagan, Steve	91	75	16	256
Powers, Joe	50	75	−25	625
Denk, Janice	87	75	12	144
Black, Jim	73	75	−2	4
Johnston, Neal	94	75	19	361

Step 3: Calculate the squares of the differences computed in Step 2. In the table above, the numbers in the Difference column are squared. The results are stored in the Difference Squared column.

Step 4: Sum the numbers generated in Step 3. The total of the numbers in the fourth column is 3158.

(Continued)

TABLE 2.1: (Continued)

Step 5: Divide the number calculated in Step 4 by the number of values. The result is the variance. For Test 1, the variance is 175.

1–2–3 computes the variance for Test 2 in the same way. The variance for Test 2 is 76.11

Example

You can compute the variance for a sample or for an entire group or population. @VAR calculates the variance for an entire population and uses the n method (biased). For example, if you are finding the variances for all packages made, as shown in Figure 2.18, you would use this formula. In this example, 1–2–3 checks the weight for every package in the production run.

Figure 2.18 Using @VAR to compute the variance for an entire group

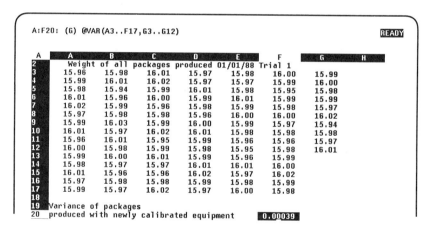

In some applications, the entire population is too large to include every one of its members in the variance computation. In this situation, you take a sample of the group and alter the computation. To calculate the variance for a sample of the population, use the n-1 method (unbiased). With Release 3, you can utilize the @VARS function described later. If you have an earlier version, you may still compute variances for sample groups by modifying the variance formula as follows:

$$@COUNT(LIST)/(@COUNT(LIST)-1)*@VAR(LIST)$$

This formula compensates for the bias in the @VAR function. An example of this formula is in Figure 2.19, which is taken from a survey that the manufacturer conducted with a sample of its customer base. To compute the variances for the survey questions, the manufacturer used the unbiased variance formula.

Figure 2.19 Using @VAR to compute the variance for a sample

```
A:F13:  @COUNT(A1..G10)/(@COUNT(A1..G10)-1)*@VAR(A1..G10)              READY

     A       A       B       C       D       E       F       G       H
     1       3      50       6      15      16      15      45
     2      38       5      35      20       3      20      10
     3      26      10      43      46      36      46       1
     4      39       1      18       6       5       6      37
     5       5      14      33      15      19      15      19
     6      49      25      23      15      23      15      20
     7      36      13      43      23      20       5      15
     8      45       4       6      22      15      25       9
     9      19      26      45      10       9      10      36
    10       5      25      10      13       9       4      45
    11
    12
    13   Variance of survey reponses in sample group    201.2373
    14
```

@VARS

You can use the @VARS function to compute the variance of a sample group. The special sample variance function is only available with Release 3. The sample variance function provides the same service as the population variance (@VAR), except it does so for a sample of the population instead of the entire population. This is useful when you either have a population that is too large to work with or you wish to narrow the focus of your variance calculation. The sample variance function will compute an unbiased measurement that takes into consideration that you are computing the variance for a limited group. This makes the computation more comparable to the whole. The format of the sample variance function is @VARS(list). The list argument follows the same pattern as other statistical functions.

Example

Figure 2.20 shows the variance computation for a sample within a population, such as the weight of cookie packages in a single production run. The function @VARS(A3..A13) produces this result. In this example, you are concerned only with the dispersion of the weights of the first column of cookie packages instead of the entire production run. The answer is unbiased. You can compare it to the rest of the population more easily than if you did not adjust the computation for the sample size.

Figure 2.20 Using
@VARS to compute
the variance for a
sample

```
A:F20:  (G) @VARS(A3..A17)                                        READY

  A        A          B          C          D          E         F          G        H
  1                           Crunchy Cookie Company
  2        Weight of all packages produced 01/01/88 Trial 1
  3        15.96      15.98      16.01      15.97      15.98     16.00      15.99
  4        15.99      16.01      16.02      15.97      15.97     15.99      16.00
  5        15.98      15.94      15.99      16.01      15.98     15.95      15.98
  6        16.01      15.96      16.00      15.99      16.01     15.99      15.99
  7        16.02      15.99      15.96      15.98      15.99     15.98      15.97
  8        15.97      15.98      15.98      15.96      16.00     16.00      16.02
  9        15.99      16.03      15.99      16.00      15.99     15.97      15.94
  10       16.01      15.97      16.02      16.01      15.98     15.98      15.98
  11       15.96      16.01      15.95      15.99      15.96     15.96      15.97
  12       16.00      15.98      15.99      15.98      15.95     15.98      16.01
  13       15.99      16.00      16.01      15.99      15.96     15.99
  14       15.98      15.97      15.97      16.01      16.01     16.00
  15       16.01      15.96      15.96      16.02      15.97     16.02
  16       15.97      15.98      15.98      15.99      15.98     15.99
  17       15.99      15.97      16.02      15.97      16.00     15.98
  18
  19       Variance of packages in Column A
  20       produced with newly calibrated equipment      0.000355
```

@STD

Another measurement of the dispersion of data is the standard deviation, which measures the degree to which the individual values in a group of data vary from the average of that group. The standard deviation is the square of the variance. The lower the standard deviation, the less individual values vary from the average and the more reliable the average as a representation of the data. @STD calculates the standard deviation for a list of data. The format for the standard deviation function is @STD(list). List follows the same rules used for the other statistical functions in this chapter.

Example

You can compute the standard deviation for a sample or an entire group or population. @STD calculates standard deviation when the values for an entire population are available. The standard deviation for a population uses the n method (biased). For example, if you are finding the standard deviations for all cartons made on a machine, as done in Figure 2.21, you can use this formula. In this example, you record the weight for every package in the production run.

Figure 2.21 Using
@STD to compute
the variance for an
entire group

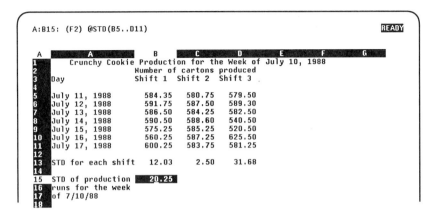

```
A:B15: (F2) @STD(B5..D11)                                              READY

A          A              B         C         D         E         F        G
1         Crunchy Cookie Production for the Week of July 10, 1988
2                        Number of cartons produced
3  Day                   Shift 1   Shift 2   Shift 3
4
5  July 11, 1988           584.35    580.75    579.50
6  July 12, 1988           591.75    587.50    589.30
7  July 13, 1988           586.50    584.25    582.50
8  July 14, 1988           590.50    588.60    540.50
9  July 15, 1988           575.25    585.25    520.50
10 July 16, 1988           560.25    587.25    625.50
11 July 17, 1988           600.25    583.75    581.25
12
13 STD for each shift       12.03      2.50     31.68
14
15  STD of production      20.25
16  runs for the week
17  of 7/10/88
18
```

If the population is too large to include every member in the standard
deviation computation, you must adapt the formula to use a sample.
To calculate the standard deviation for a sample of the population, use
the n-1 method (unbiased). If you have Release 3 you can accomplish
this by using the @STDS function described later in the chapter. Otherwise, you can modify the standard deviation formula to work for a sample
as follows:

$$@SQRT(@COUNT(LIST)/(@COUNT(LIST)-1))*@STD(LIST)$$

This formula compensates for the bias in the @STD function. Figure
2.22, which provides an example of this formula in use, uses the same
data as the variance example in Figure 2.19. The sample data is from
a survey that the manufacturer conducted with customers. Since it is
impossible for them to survey every customer, working with a sample
is the only option. Therefore, when computing the standard deviations
for the survey questions, the manufacturer uses the unbiased variance
formula.

Figure 2.22 Using
@STD to compute
the variance for a
sample

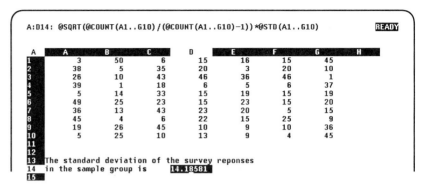

Figure 2.22 Using @STD to compute the variance for a sample

@STDS

With Release 3, you can compute the standard deviation of a sample with @STDS. This function is similar to @VARS and follows the same list format. You can use this function either to work with a population that is too large to handle, or to narrow your focus. Since this function provides for an unbiased result, it is a better representation of the group.

Example

You can calculate the standard deviation of a group within a population. For example, you might want to look at the standard deviation for a sample of cookie packages selected from a production run, as shown in Figure 2.23. This example uses the same data as Figure 2.18, except you are measuring the standard deviation rather than the variance. The result provides the standard deviation for the specific example.

Figure 2.23 Using @STDS to compute the variance for a sample

```
A:F20: (G) @STDS(A3..A17)                                    READY

A     A        B        C        D        E       F       G        H
1                       Crunchy Cookie Company
2     Weight of all packages produced 01/01/88 Trial 1
3     15.96    15.98    16.01    15.97    15.98   16.00   15.99
4     15.99    16.01    16.02    15.97    15.97   15.99   16.00
5     15.98    15.94    15.99    16.01    15.98   15.95   15.98
6     16.01    15.96    16.00    15.99    16.01   15.99   15.99
7     16.02    15.99    15.98    15.98    15.99   15.98   15.97
8     15.97    15.98    15.98    15.96    16.00   16.00   16.02
9     15.99    16.03    15.99    16.00    15.99   15.97   15.94
10    16.01    15.97    16.02    16.01    15.98   15.98   15.98
11    15.96    16.01    15.95    15.99    15.96   15.96   15.97
12    16.00    15.98    15.99    15.99    15.95   15.98   16.01
13    15.99    16.00    16.01    15.99    15.96   15.99
14    15.98    15.97    15.97    16.01    16.01   16.00
15    16.01    15.96    15.96    16.02    15.97   16.02
16    15.97    15.98    15.98    15.99    15.98   15.99
17    15.97    15.98    16.02    15.97    16.00   15.98
18
19    Standard Deviation of packages in Column A
20    produced with newly calibrated equipment      0.018848
FIG2F3.WK1
```

3

Logical Functions

1-2-3's logical functions are unparalleled for adding power to your models. One particular strength of this group is that many of the functions allow you to determine the value for a cell based on other entries in the worksheet. Other functions and formulas allow only one possibility for a cell entry.

THE NEED FOR LOGICAL CAPABILITIES

Most of the logical functions return one of two values. Thus, a logical function evaluates an argument and determines whether the argument is true or false. The type of entry used for logical function arguments is different from the other 1-2-3 functions; often logical functions will use logical conditions as an argument. For example, an argument might be to compare two cells and determine if the first one is larger than the second one, as in A3 > F3. If A3 is larger than F3, the condition evaluates as true. If the second cell entry is larger than the first, the condition evaluates as false.

1-2-3 lets you establish values based upon the result of these logical condition tests. Once you determine whether a condition is true, 1-2-3 can make decisions based upon the result of the condition.

APPLICATIONS FOR LOGICAL FEATURES

You can use logical functions in worksheets for different purposes, the most common of which is to control a cell entry based upon the contents of another cell. This feature effectively extends 1-2-3's abilities beyond the one formula per one cell rule. Using a logical function, 1-2-3 can perform calculations based upon the entry in another cell.

Another common use of logical functions is error prevention. For example, with a column of numbers that contains the result of a division, a logical function can prevent division by zero, thereby eliminating the error message that would appear from dividing by zero. A logical function can tell 1-2-3 to put a zero into the results column if the divisor equals zero.

Logical Operators

Logical functions have two kinds of operators: simple operators and complex operators. Simple operators are used for comparisons such as less than or equal to. Complex operators join or negate expressions. Simple logical operators are evaluated before the complex ones. For both types of operators, you can change the processing order through the use of parentheses. 1-2-3 always evaluates expressions in parentheses first.

1-2-3 uses simple logical operators to compare values or expressions. The simple operators available are equal to (=), greater than (>), less than (<), greater than or equal to (> =), less than or equal to (< =), and not equal to (< >). 1-2-3 evaluates the simple logical operators from left to right.

The logical operators are lower in precedence than the mathematical operators. Thus, when 1-2-3 evaluates the expression A3+10>F2-5, it performs the arithmetic operations first.

You can use the complex logical operators #AND#, #OR#, and #NOT# for joining two or more expressions. Although either lowercase or uppercase is allowed, you might wish to enter these operators in uppercase to distinguish them from the rest of the expression. Remember to use the # at the beginning and end of the word.

When you use the #AND# operator, the expression to the left and the right of this operator must be true for 1-2-3 to evaluate the expression as true. The entry F5=6#AND#D2>4 is not evaluated as true unless F5 is equal to 6 and D2 is greater than 4. The expression is false if either condition is false.

When you use the #OR# operator, either the expression to the left or the right must be true for the expression to be evaluated as true. The entry F5=6#OR#D2>4 is true if either of the two conditions is met.

The #NOT# operator negates the true or false value of the expression to its right. If the expression to the right of the #NOT# is true, the #NOT# will make it false. For example, the expression A2=6 is true if A2 is equal to 6. #NOT#A2=6 is false if A2 is equal to 6.

The #NOT# operator is evaluated before the #AND# or #OR#. The #AND# and #OR# operators are evaluated from left to right. 1-2-3 assigns a lower precedence to these complex operators than to the arithmetic or simple logical operators.

@TRUE & @FALSE

1-2-3 stores true and false values as a number. The @TRUE function provides a value of 1. The @FALSE function provides a value of 0.

While both of these functions can be replaced by a 1 or 0, they are used in other functions for their self-documenting properties. When you see an @TRUE or @FALSE, you know what the functions mean, but if you see a 1 or a 0, it is not clear what those numbers represent. You can combine these two functions with the @IF function to create many types of condition tests.

Example

Besides using @TRUE and @FALSE for documentation purposes, you can use their values of 1 or 0 in other formulas. For example, in Figure 3.1, each salesperson who meets a sales quota receives a $1,000 bonus; the sales personnel who do not meet their quota receive no bonus. The model combines the @TRUE and @FALSE functions with the @IF function covered later in the chapter. If the sales are greater than or equal to the quota, the @TRUE value of 1 is multiplied by the $1,000 resulting in a $1,000 bonus. If the sales are less than the quota, the @FALSE value of 0 will be multiplied by the $1,000 resulting in a $0 bonus.

Figure 3.1 Using
@TRUE and
@FALSE functions
to determine a
bonus

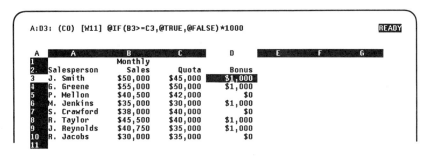

The @TRUE and @FALSE functions also can be used for error checking. In Figure 3.2, any purchase order that has a backorder shows a 1. The model places the 1 in the cell with an @IF function that contains @TRUE if the condition check is true. The orders that do not have a backorder display a 0. Another option would be to show the 0, or @FALSE value, for a false condition and to supply the label "Backorder" for the true condition. This focuses more attention on the backorder status of the entry.

Figure 3.2 Using
@TRUE and
@FALSE functions
to determine
backorder status

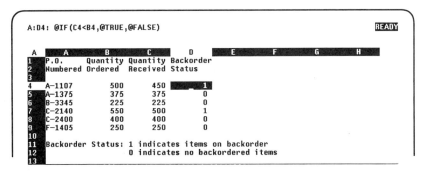

@IF

The @IF function is the most frequently used logical function. This function evaluates a condition and chooses one of two values. 1–2–3 chooses the first value if the condition is true and the second value if the condition is false. Although one @IF statement is limited to a single condition test, you can use nesting to expand the possibilities.

The format of the @IF function is @IF(condition,value if condition is true, value if condition is false).

The **condition** is an expression or group of expressions joined by operators. 1-2-3 evaluates the expression to determine whether it is true or false. The condition can contain values, strings enclosed in double quotes, cell references, range names, operators, and functions.

If 1-2-3 determines that the condition is true, it uses the **value if condition is true** for the result of the function. This value can consist of a value entry, a string enclosed in double quotes, the ampersand (&) for joining strings, cell references, range names, and other functions, including another @IF function.

If 1-2-3 determines that the condition is false, it uses the **value if condition is false** for the function result. This value can contain values, strings enclosed in double quotes, ampersands (&) for joining strings, cell references, range names, and other functions, including another @IF function.

Example

You can use @IF to compute the delivery charges for different purchases. Delivery charges can be simple or complex calculations. The following example takes a simple situation and makes it more complex through nested @IF functions. First, Figure 3.3 displays the delivery locations and purchase amounts, which are then used to compute the delivery charge. In this example, anything delivered in Akron has free delivery. Deliveries outside of the Akron area incur a $5 charge. @IF determines if the city is Akron. If so, a 0 displays in column G. If the city is not Akron, a value of 5 displays in column G. If you would prefer not to see the zero entries, use /Worksheet Global Zero to display zero entries as blank in Release 2 and above. With Release 3, you can use the Label option in this command to display a label such as FREE when the entry evaluates as zero.

Figure 3.3 Using @IF to compute delivery charges

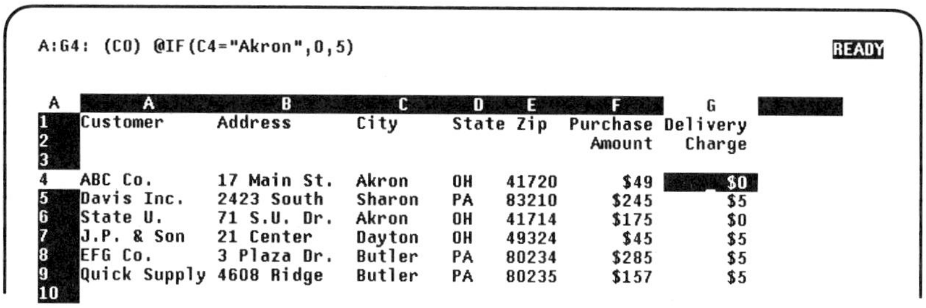

```
A:G4:  (C0)  @IF(C4="Akron",0,5)                              READY
```

	A	B	C	D	E	F	G
1	Customer	Address	City	State	Zip	Purchase	Delivery
2						Amount	Charge
3							
4	ABC Co.	17 Main St.	Akron	OH	41720	$49	$0
5	Davis Inc.	2423 South	Sharon	PA	83210	$245	$5
6	State U.	71 S.U. Dr.	Akron	OH	41714	$175	$0
7	J.P. & Son	21 Center	Dayton	OH	49324	$45	$5
8	EFG Co.	3 Plaza Dr.	Butler	PA	80234	$285	$5
9	Quick Supply	4608 Ridge	Butler	PA	80235	$157	$5
10							

To make this example a little more complex, change the delivery rate so that the delivery charge is free in Akron, $5 outside Akron but within Ohio, and $15 outside of Ohio. While the @IF function allows only two choices, you can create a nested @IF function that expands the choices to three. In Figure 3.4, the first @IF function computes a delivery charge of 0 for Akron deliveries. For deliveries outside Akron, the second @IF checks the state in column D. The delivery charge is $5 for Ohio and $15 outside of Ohio.

Figure 3.4 Using nested @IF functions to compute delivery charges

```
A:G4:  (C0) @IF(C4="Akron",0,@IF(D4="OH",5,15))                    READY
```

	A	B	C	D	E	F	G
1	Customer	Address	City	State	Zip	Purchase	Delivery
2						Amount	Charge
3							
4	ABC Co.	17 Main St.	Akron	OH	41720	$49	$0
5	Davis Inc.	2423 South	Sharon	PA	83210	$245	$15
6	State U.	71 S.U. Dr.	Akron	OH	41714	$175	$0
7	J.P. & Son	21 Center	Dayton	OH	49324	$45	$5
8	EFG Co.	3 Plaza Dr.	Butler	PA	80234	$285	$15
9	Quick Supply	4608 Ridge	Butler	PA	80235	$157	$15
10							

You can add additional conditions to this model. In Figure 3.5, the delivery charge is free for deliveries in Akron. Deliveries are free in Ohio if the purchase amount exceeds $50. The delivery charge is $5 outside of Akron in Ohio if the purchase amount is $50 or less. The delivery charge is free outside Ohio with a purchase amount of more than $200. Without the $200 purchase, the delivery charge outside Ohio is still $15. You can create a model to handle these situations if you use nested @IF statements.

Figure 3.5 Adding complexity to the delivery charge computations

```
A:G4:  (C0) @IF(C4="Akron",0,@IF(D4="OH",@IF(F4>50,0,15),@IF(F4>200,0,15)))  READY
```

	A	B	C	D	E	F	G
1	Customer	Address	City	State	Zip	Purchase	Delivery
2						Amount	Charge
3							
4	ABC Co.	17 Main St.	Akron	OH	41720	$49	$0
5	Davis Inc.	2423 South	Sharon	PA	83210	$245	$0
6	State U.	71 S.U. Dr.	Akron	OH	41714	$175	$0
7	J.P. & Son	21 Center	Dayton	OH	49324	$45	$15
8	EFG Co.	3 Plaza Dr.	Butler	PA	80234	$285	$0
9	Quick Supply	4608 Ridge	Butler	PA	80235	$157	$15
10							

Other Applications

You can use @IF to select a cell value from among several entries. For example, @IF can create messages relating to the model status. You can modify the earlier example used with the @TRUE and @FALSE functions to provide a clearer message. You can also change the @IF function so that a message appears when there is a backorder. The same @IF function leaves the cell blank when the ordered and received quantities are the same.

@IF also prevents division by zero, by eliminating the computation and displaying an error message. You might type @IF(A3 = 0,"CANNOT DIVIDE BY ZERO", + A4/A3) to remind users that they cannot divide the number in cell A4 by zero in cell A3. If the condition is false, 1–2–3 will evaluate the expression.

You can use @IF to limit the area in which an error condition in the worksheet displays. Normally ERR displays in any cell that references a formula returning ERR. You can use a condition check to leave some of the cells blank if another cell caused the error condition. You might type @IF(D1 = "ERR"," ",A1/A2) so that an error message will not be displayed in cell D1 if cell A2 contains a zero and 1–2–3 cannot evaluate the expression.

Since the @IF condition is flexible, you can use it for string or number comparisons, as in @IF(A3="Dallas",B3*2,B3*7). Also, you can use @IF with the date and time functions described in Chapter 5 to emphasize which items are past due, as in @IF(DUE__DATE < @DATE (89,12,30),F4*.1,0).

You can also use @IF to test for conditions that must be met before 1–2–3 evaluates a nested @function. You can nest any combination of @functions within an @IF statement to check and test data using a variety of conditions. For example, to discover the average sales for employees with greater than five years experience, use @IF to test for years of experience and perform the calculation if the five-year condition is true. The formula entry might look something like @IF(C7 > =5, @AVG(E7..H7)," "). The calculation is not performed for employees with less than five years experience.

When testing two numbers for equality, you may obtain unexpected results if one or more of the numbers are computed. 1–2–3 sometimes produces a slightly different number for one of the values, thus resulting in a comparison that is different than you might expect. This difference occurs because of the way that computers store numbers. Although you do not see them, the computer maintains several digits to the right of the decimal point. Since two numbers must be exactly equal for 1–2–3 to treat them as equal, a difference as small as .00000001 will prevent 1–2–3 from treating the numbers as equal. You can compensate for this feature if you wish. For example, if your @IF function is comparing two values, A3 and B4, you can check to see if they are almost equal by typing @IF((@ABS(A3–B4))<.000001,@TRUE,@FALSE) instead of @IF(A3=B4,@TRUE,@FALSE).

By using 1–2–3 Release 2.2 and Release 3 on a network, you can access shareable files once they have been updated with the current month's data. You may have a macro to run final month-end reports once the files are updated, but you will not want to execute the macro until the files have been updated. @IF can examine information in another worksheet and indicate whether the field has been updated for the current month. You can then execute your macro.

Release 3 allows use of the linked data directly within the @IF function. Release 2.2 supports a cell-to-cell link, which requires you to store the external data in the current worksheet and reference the cell there to check the value of the external data. If your ability to produce a final report is dependent on a cell in the external file being equal to the current month, type this @IF statement in Release 3: @IF(@MONTH (@TODAY)=<<ACCT.WK3>>CURRENT_MO,"Run final report","Do not run final report"). The appropriate message will display in the current cell to tell you the appropriate action. With Release 2.2, type +<<ACCT.WK3>>CURRENT_MO in one cell on the current worksheet and reference this cell in the @IF function. For both releases, you can refresh links to external files before checking the status of the key information by using the command /File Admin Link-Refresh.

Error Checkers

1-2-3 provides several functions that can prevent an error condition from spreading over the entire worksheet. These functions can prevent the functions @NA (not-available) and @ERR from interfering with other calculations.

@ISERR

The function @ISERR determines if the value of its argument is an error by checking for the error value that is equivalent to @ERR. Although you can generate the error value with the @ERR function, the errors you are looking for are usually the result of a calculation.

You normally use @ISERR in conjunction with other formulas. For example, you can combine it with @IF to provide two options based on the result of a condition test. The format of the function is @ISERR (argument). 1-2-3 determines if **argument** is equal to ERR. The argument can be a value, formula, range name, or cell reference.

Example

You can use @ISERR to determine the location of an error. In Figure 3.6, a division by zero error causes problems in adding unit prices. @ISERR in column E will determine which item is causing the problem. The item with the value ERR displays a 1 in column E. 1-2-3 generates the 1 since the value of the @ISERR function is true. Although using @ISERR in this manner may seem unnecessary here, it is extremely useful when your worksheet is too large for you to see the error quickly.

Figure 3.6 Using @ISERR to determine items with errors

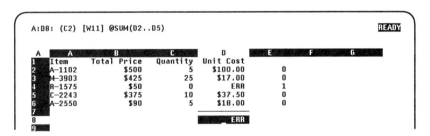

You can use @ISERR to remove the error from the calculation of a total. For example, in Figure 3.7, the formula incorporates both an @IF and a @ISERR function. This formula places a 0 rather than ERR in the cell when 1-2-3 encounters an error.

Figure 3.7 Using @ISERR and @IF to display items that contain ERR

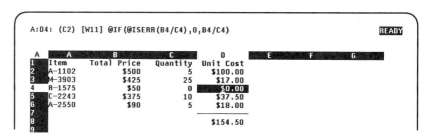

Other Applications

@ISERR can help you find the location of an ERR or prevent one from interrupting other worksheet calculations. For example, you might use this function to process statistical data when you do not want cells containing error messages to be included in the calculations.

@ISNUMBER

The @ISNUMBER function determines if an entry is a number. This function is used in conjunction with other formulas, primarily the @IF function. The format of the function is @ISNUMBER(argument). The argument can be a value, formula, or cell reference. 1-2-3 views @ERR and @NA, which are discussed in Chapter 8, as numeric.

Example

You can use @ISNUMBER to determine why a column of numbers does not sum properly. In Figure 3.8, the total of the numbers should be 196,000, but since three of the numbers are entered as labels, the total is incorrect. After @ISNUMBER is used in column D to determine which items are causing the problem, each salary entered as a label will display a 0 in column D. Note that label and currency entries look the same. Thus, without @ISNUMBER you cannot identify the entry $32,000 as a label without looking at each entry.

Figure 3.8 Using @ISNUMBER to find salaries entered as strings

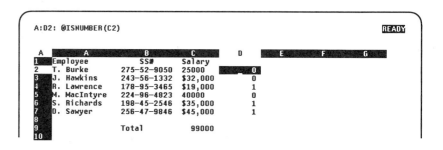

You can make @ISNUMBER more understandable by combining it with @IF, as in Figure 3.9. In this figure, employees whose salaries have been incorrectly entered as text have an error message in column D. Employees whose salaries have been correctly entered display a blank.

Figure 3.9 Using @ISNUMBER and @IF to find salaries entered as strings

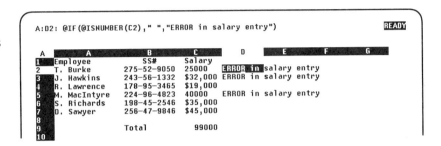

Other Applications

You can use @ISNUMBER to find out how many numbers there are in a column with both value and label entries. You can also determine the number of cells with entries using the @COUNT function, although @COUNT will not tell you how many of these entries are numbers or labels. If you enter @ISNUMBER in a column, you can add the results to get the total number of values in the column. This type of application is used to perform statistical computations on a table of numbers that has a few cells containing characters.

@ISSTRING

@ISSTRING determines if an argument in an entry is a string. This function is used in conjunction with other formulas such as the @IF function. The format of the function is @ISSTRING(argument). The argument can be a value, formula, or cell reference. 1–2–3 treats @ERR and @NA as numeric entries and returns the value false if you use @ISSTRING to check a cell that contains these entries.

Example

You can use @ISSTRING to probe a display of entries that should be labels. You might use this function to determine why some numbers in a column of social security numbers look incorrect. In Figure 3.10, the first social security number looks different from the others. The @IF and @ISSTRING functions used in column D indicate that the first entry is a social security number that is entered incorrectly as a value. Note that certain types of numbers such as social security numbers and phone numbers must be entered as strings. If you enter these numbers as values, 1-2-3 interprets the dashes as minus signs instead of hyphens and subtracts the various components rather than displaying the entire entry. For example, if you enter 275–52–9050, 1-2-3 subtracts 52 from 275, and then subtracts 9050 from the result.

Figure 3.10 Using @ISSTRING to find social security numbers entered as values

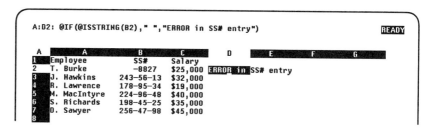

Combining the @IF function with the @ISSTRING function makes the worksheet easier to understand. If you combine the two functions, you can display a message rather than a 0 or a 1. With the combined function, it is not necessary to know what the 0's and 1's mean to find the social security number that is causing the problem.

Other Applications

You can use @ISSTRING to find out how many labels in a column contain both numbers and labels. If you use @ISSTRING in a column, you can add the results to determine the total number of strings in the column. The entries that return a true condition will increment the sum by 1.

@ISNA

The @ISNA function determines if an entry is equivalent to @NA, which indicates that data is not available. If you use @NA to indicate a piece of missing data, any cell that refers to the cell containing @NA displays the value NA. Chapter 8 covers @NA in more detail.

You can use @ISNA to check for the presence of NA. @ISNA returns a 0 if the cell is not equal to NA and a 1 if it is. You can use this function in conjunction with other functions like @IF function to prevent the @NA value from affecting other calculations. The format of the function is @ISNA(argument). 1-2-3 checks the argument to determine if it is equal to NA. The argument can be a value, formula, range name, or cell reference.

Example

You can use @ISNA to locate entries that are missing information. In Figure 3.11, several pieces of vendor information are missing. To find out which vendors require additional entries, use @ISNA in combination with @IF in column E. If you use the #OR# operator, you can check for multiple cells that are missing data. The function entry places a Missing Data string in column E for any vendor that has a @NA for their phone number or contact. This function is particularly useful with larger worksheets.

Figure 3.11 Using @ISNA to determine which vendors have missing information

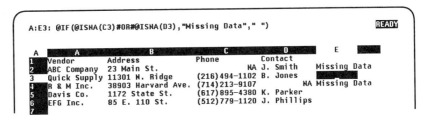

Other Applications

@ISNA can help you find out the location of an @NA entry or prevent an NA entry from interrupting other worksheet calculations. For example, @ISNA can prevent a sum from becoming @NA if one of the values in the sum has a value of @NA. The formula can incorporate both an @IF and a @ISNA function to place a zero rather than @NA in a cell.

@ISRANGE

Using a nonexistent range name in a formula produces an error condition in releases prior to Release 3. 1–2–3 allows you to check the validity of a range name with the @ISRANGE function.

This function checks a character string to see if it matches an existing range name. The format of the function is @ISRANGE(string). The **string** is a string, a string formula, or a reference to a cell containing a string or a string formula.

The @ISRANGE function returns a 1 representing true if 1–2–3 finds the argument in its list of valid range names. The function returns a 0 if the string does not match any of the existing range names.

Example

You can use @ISRANGE to ensure the integrity of range names before using them in calculations. When combined with the @IF function, @ISRANGE provides a flexible method for dealing with varying data values. If you reference a range named Interest in a calculation and that range name does not exist, you may want to substitute a number in the calculation.

Figure 3.12 presents the @ISRANGE function used to select an interest rate. The function entry is

@IF(@ISRANGE(INTEREST),INTEREST*C3,.105*C3)

If the range name you want to check is in another file named DATA, your entry might look like

@IF(@ISRANGE(<< DATA >> INTEREST), << DATA >> INTEREST*C3,.105*C3)

Figure 3.12 Using @ISRANGE to determine if a string is a defined range name

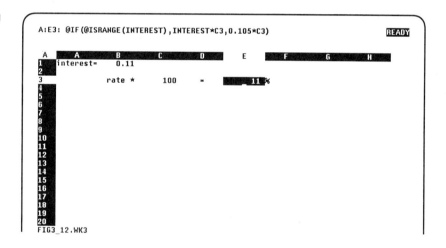

```
A:E3: @IF(@ISRANGE(INTEREST),INTEREST*C3,0.105*C3)                    READY

 A     A         B         C         D        E        F         G         H
1    interest=      0.11
2
3              rate *       100        =              11 %
4
5
6
7
8
9
10
11
12
13
14
15
16
17
18
19
20
FIG3_12.WK3
```

RELEASE DIFFERENCES

Release 2.2 offers two new logical @functions. @IFAFF(name) tests to see if name is a valid add-in @function, as in @IFAFF(''liter''). @IFAPP(name) checks to see if name is an attached add-in, as in @IFAPP(''allways''). Both return 0 if false and 1 if true. @IFAFF is itself an add-in @function.

4

Math Functions

Although most of 1–2–3's functions perform some type of mathematical computation, there is a separate category of functions for basic mathematical features. These features are organized into three distinct groups. One group focuses on basic mathematical capabilities such as absolute value and rounding. A second group handles the logarithmic capabilities that provide a quick way to perform complex calculations, and the third group focuses on the trigonometric functions that relate to the properties of angles. You can use these functions to determine distances like the height of a mountain or the angle required to focus a laser beam.

1–2–3's BASIC MATH FUNCTIONS

1–2–3 has seven functions that perform basic calculations or provide numbers that you can use in calculations. Since the features of these functions provide elementary capabilities such as rounding, absolute value, extracting the integer portion of a number, or the constant that represents π (pi), these functions are normally used as part of a larger formula.

@ROUND   The @ROUND function rounds a number to a specified place to the left or right of the decimal point. This function is essential for controlling the internal accuracy with which 1–2–3 stores numbers. The format is @ROUND(number,place). The **number** is the value to be rounded. You can use a number, a reference to a cell that contains a number or a formula, or a formula for the argument number.

The **place** is the position before or after the decimal where the rounding should take place. Positive place values cause rounding to the right of the decimal point. A value of 1 for place results in one decimal digit. As place increases, the number of decimal digits retained increases. For example, @ROUND(150.46517,2) equals 150.47 and @ROUND (150.46517,4) equals 150.4652. If 0 is entered for place, the result will be a whole number. Negative values for place cause rounding to the left of the decimal point. For example, @ROUND(32.6,−1) equals 30 and @ROUND(2517.03,−3) equals 3000. Notice that 1–2–3 follows the convention of rounding to the next higher digit if the number to the right of place is 5 or greater.

In addition to affecting the display of a number, rounding affects the internal storage of the value. Formatting a cell affects only the display and leaves the internal accuracy of the number unchanged.

Example

Some 1–2–3 users mistakenly believe that @ROUND produces that same result as the Fixed Decimal format. Note that if you round 15.34 to one decimal place, the number is stored as 15.3. Using a Fixed Decimal format with one decimal digit on a cell containing 15.34 will display as 15.3 but the value is still stored as 15.34. Consequently, when performing calculations, 1–2–3 uses 15.34, not 15.3. This feature of @ROUND makes it very useful in worksheets that require computing column or row totals.

Another example of the potential problem created by the disparity between stored values and displayed values is a column of interest calculations with a total at the bottom of the column. If you format the interest computations with two decimal places, the total at the bottom of the column may appear inaccurate. To fix the accuracy, round the individual calculations.

Figure 4.1 displays purchase orders for office supplies. Column C contains the price per dozen for each item. Column D contains the unit quantity ordered. To compute a unit price, simply divide the price per dozen by 12. Formula +C11*D11/12 in E11 calculates the cost for thirty-five units of item #6398. In Figure 4.2, the same formula is combined with @ROUND to control the accuracy of the decimal places in the unit costs.

Figure 4.1
Worksheet with
unrounded
numbers

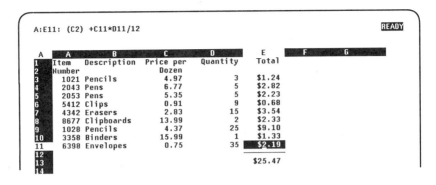

Figure 4.2
Worksheet from
Figure 4.1 with
rounded numbers

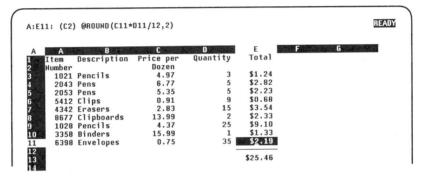

The format for column E in both worksheets is currency with two decimal places, and the formula in E13 for both worksheets is @SUM(E3.E11). Notice that when @ROUND computes the total cost, the grand total is $25.46; without @ROUND, it is $25.47. The one-cent difference occurs because @ROUND stores the values in memory with two decimal places, but the values in the other worksheet display with two decimal places because of the format chosen. 1-2-3 stored them in memory with the full decimal accuracy permitted. When 1-2-3 performs calculations with these values, the number in memory, rather than the number displayed on the screen, is used.

Other Applications

Any formula using multiplication and division can create additional decimal digits, and you can choose how many of these digits to display. Your display choice does not affect the accuracy used for the storage of these items.

These applications involving multiplication and division include mortgage payment schedules, project costing, financial statements, budgeting, and a variety of other applications.

@INT

The @INT function returns the integer portion of a number and drops any digits after the decimal point. The format is @INT(number). The **number** is the number you wish to truncate. It can be an actual number, a reference to a cell containing a number or a formula, or a formula.

Example

@INT is useful for determining the number of complete products that are available for shipment. If a plant produces 500.5 products, only 500 are ready for shipment. @INT will produce the correct result.

Some 1-2-3 users mistakenly believe that @INT produces that same result as using the Fixed Decimal format with zero decimal places. This is incorrect. If you enter @INT(15.34), the number is stored as 15. If you use a Fixed Decimal format with zero places on a cell containing 15.34, 1-2-3 displays the entry as 15. 1-2-3 stores the value as 15.34 and it uses the stored value in computations.

The difference between @INT and @ROUND is significant: @INT ignores the numbers to the right of the decimal point, and @ROUND uses the numbers to the right of the decimal point to round the number up or down.

Example

Figure 4.3 is a production schedule for music box parts. This type of music box has six parts. To compute the number of music boxes completed, divide the number of parts by six. Since you cannot have a fraction of a music box completed, the number of completed music boxes is the integer portion of the calculation. @ROUND will not work since you do not want any of the numbers rounded to the next highest number. The formula in B3 determines the number of music boxes finished as @INT(A3/6). Suppose the cost to produce each music box is $2.50 and you want the total cost of the completed boxes, rounded to the nearest dollar. You can use the formula in C3 to multiply the number of completed boxes by the production cost for each box. Use the @ROUND function to round the total cost to the next highest whole number.

Figure 4.3 Using @INT to determine the number of music boxes produced

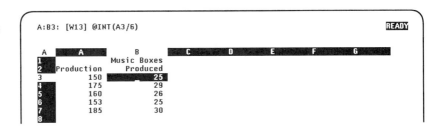

@MOD   The @MOD function finds the remainder when a number is divided by a divisor. 1–2–3 refers to the remainder as the modulus, from which the function name is derived. The format is @MOD(number,divisor). The **number** is the number that you want to divide. The **divisor** is the value divided into number. You can use any value as the arguments except that divisor cannot be zero. You can enter the values for the arguments directly in the function, as a formula, or as a cell reference.

Example

Figure 4.4 shows how @MOD can determine the square feet of raw material left over in a cushion manufacturing process. The hides used in making the leather cushions are available only in the sizes specified in column B for each of the colors listed in column A. Each cushion requires 3.3 square feet of leather. The manufacturing process is the same for each color, but because of the varying sizes of the hides there is more waste for some colors than others. Since the color with the most waste per cushion costs the most to manufacture, you can use the waste calculations to adjust prices for each color accordingly. @INT(B2/3.3) is entered in C2 to determine how many complete cushions can be made from one blue hide.

Figure 4.4 Using @MOD to determine the scrap from different pieces of leather

```
A:D2: [W13] @MOD(B2,3.3)                                    READY

    A        A          B              C                D         E       F
  1                  Sq. Ft.   No. of Cushions     Leftover
  2      Blue Hide     12             3                2.1
  3      Grey Hide     14             4                0.8
  4      Red Hide      13             3                3.1
  5      Green Hide    11             3                1.1
  6      Black Hide    10             3                0.1
  7      Brown Hide    15             4                1.8
  8
```

To determine the amount wasted in each blue hide, type @MOD(B2,3.3) in D2. You can follow the detail behind the @MOD calculation if you multiply three complete cushions per blue hide by 3.3 square feet per cushion. The material used is 9.9 square feet. Since the hide is twelve square feet, the leftover footage is 2.1 square feet (12 sq. ft. – 9.9 sq. ft.).

Other Applications

Use @MOD to find the remainder of a division operation. You can also use @MOD in an application to compute the number of music boxes completed, as discussed above. @INT provides the number of completed boxes, and @MOD returns the number of parts available for production the next day. To determine the number of parts remaining, use @MOD(Number_produced,6).

You can use @MOD to determine the day of the week for any date. The formula @MOD(@DATE(YY,MM,DD),7) returns a number from 0 to 6. This number is the remainder from the division but also represents the day of the week. When the result is 0, the day is Saturday; 1 when the day is Sunday, and so on to 6 when the day is Friday. To create a lookup table, the first column would contain entries from 0 to 6, and the next column would contain the days of the week. A revision to the original formula returns the day of the week rather than the number. The formula is

@VLOOKUP(@MOD(@DATE(YY,MM,DD),7),TABLE_LOC,1)

@ABS The @ABS function returns the absolute value of a number. The absolute value is a number's absolute distance from zero whether the number is positive or negative. The format is @ABS(number). The **number** is the value for which you want the absolute value. If the number is a positive value, the number returned will match the argument supplied. If the number is a negative value, the number returned will equal the argument supplied, multiplied by −1. The number can either be a value or a cell reference to a value.

Example

Figure 4.5 is a schedule for the measurement of different samples of 42-inch beams produced. This sample determines the deviation of the beams from their 42-inch ideal measurement. Since you are interested in the amount of the difference for each sample beam rather than whether it is over or under 42 inches, you can use @ABS to provide the absolute difference between the actual and ideal length. Without @ABS, the total at the bottom would be smaller since the smaller beams would offset the larger ones. You can use the absolute value to determine whether you need to make changes in the production process to correct irregularities in the length of beams.

Figure 4.5 Using @ABS to determine absolute deviations of 42-inch beams

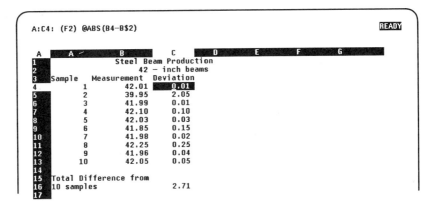

```
A:C4:  (F2)  @ABS(B4-B$2)                                            READY

     A      A          B          C        D       E       F       G
1                            Steel Beam Production
2                              42 - inch beams
3          Sample  Measurement  Deviation
4             1        42.01       0.01
5             2        39.95       2.05
6             3        41.99       0.01
7             4        42.10       0.10
8             5        42.03       0.03
9             6        41.85       0.15
10            7        41.98       0.02
11            8        42.25       0.25
12            9        41.96       0.04
13           10        42.05       0.05
14
15     Total Difference from
16     10 samples                 2.71
17
```

Other Applications

You can use @ABS within other functions. One application ensures that a value used in or produced by a function is positive. For example, to take the square root of the result of a formula, use the absolute value of the formula to ensure that the value is positive.

@RAND

The @RAND function generates a random number between 0 and 1. The function does not require arguments and is entered as @RAND.

Even though the @RAND function creates numbers between 0 and 1, you can change the range of the random numbers generated. To create these numbers, use @RAND as part of a formula. If you want the range to start at 0 and end at a number larger than 1, multiply the @RAND by the largest number in the desired range. For example, entering @RAND*50 allows you to generate random numbers between 0 and 50.

If you want one end of the range to be 0 and the other end of the range to be a negative number, multiply @RAND by the lowest number in the range. For example, @RAND*−50 generates random numbers between 0 and −50.

To begin the range with a number other than 0 and continue to a higher number, reduce the higher range by the number you want to use for the beginning of the range. Next, multiply by the @RAND function. Finally, add the intermediate result to the starting range number. For example, @RAND*100+100 generates random numbers between 100 and 200.

Example

You can use @RAND to create a random number table for queuing studies, audit selections, or other applications. An auditor uses a random number table to determine a sample of invoices to check to determine if the invoicing system functions correctly. Choosing the invoices randomly guarantees that the invoices checked represent the group of the invoices as a whole.

To determine which invoices to check, the auditor creates a random table like the one in Figure 4.6. In this table, each cell with a number in it ranges from 0 to 10,000. These entries represent the range of invoice numbers. The auditor creates the table entries by multiplying the result from the @RAND function by 10,000. Since the auditor wants to check one hundred of these invoices, the auditor copies the formula to one hundred cells. You could format these entries as fixed with zero decimal places or use the @ROUND function with @RAND. Since it is just as easy to tell the auditor to use the whole number portion of the entry for invoice selection, no changes were made. For every number in the random number chart, the auditor checks the corresponding invoice. According to the table entries, the first three invoices the auditor checks are 1794, 4175, and 2789.

Figure 4.6
Using @RAND to
generate a random
number table

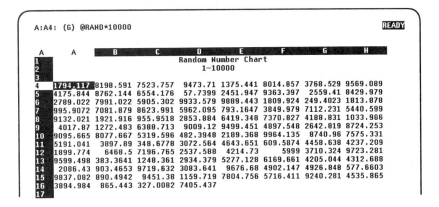

Once you compute the random numbers, you can do several things to them. For example, you can combine the results with the @ROUND function to round each of these numbers to the nearest integer. If you need to regenerate another set of random numbers, pressing the F9 key tells 1-2-3 to regenerate all of the random numbers. Editing any of the cells has the same effect. In the early releases, 1-2-3 recalculated the entire spreadsheet when you modified any cell entry. Release 3 introduced minimal, intelligent, background recalculation that updates only the cells affected by a worksheet entry and certain functions like @RAND and @NOW. When you press F9 (Calc), the recalculation is not done in the background and you must suspend other spreadsheet work while you wait.

@PI

The @PI function produces the value of pi, which is approximately equal to 3.14159. You will use this function primarily with other formulas and functions. A major application area for the function is computations relating to circles and cylinders. This function does not require arguments. Its sole purpose is to return the value of pi.

Example

You may occasionally need to compute the area of circles. For example, if you want to apply gold plating to some old plates, you need to know the size of the area that you are plating. You can multiply the cost of gold plating a square inch of material by the number of square inches in the area of the plate to determine the cost. To determine the area, you use a formula like the one in cell B4 in Figure 4.7. The formula uses the radius, which is the distance between the center of the plate and the edge, and multiplies it by pi. Once you have the area for one plate, you can multiply the formula times the cost per square inch of plating to produce the results in column C.

Figure 4.7
Using @PI to
determine cost for
gold-plating

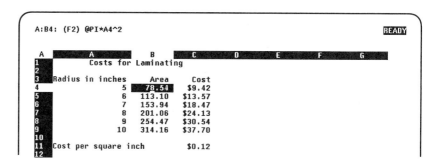

Other Applications

Another use of pi is the perimeter calculation. The perimeter is the distance around the edge of the circle. You can use the perimeter to determine the number of yards of fencing materials required to enclose a circular garden.

@SQRT

The @SQRT function computes the square root of a number. The square root of a number is the number which when multiplied by itself produces the original number. The format of the SQRT function is @SQRT(number). The **number** is the number for which you want the square root. You must use a positive number for the argument.

You can compute a square root by raising the number to the .5 power as an alternate method. For example, @SQRT(64) and 64^.5 produce equivalent results.

Example

Figure 4.8 displays the square root function used to determine the period, which is the number of seconds per cycle for a sample of grandfather clocks. Since accuracy is a desirable characteristic of clocks, it is important that the period be the same for all clocks.

Figure 4.8 Using @SQRT and @PI to determine period for one cycle

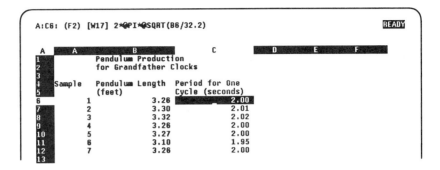

```
A:C6:  (F2)  [W17]  2*@PI*@SQRT(B6/32.2)                        READY

  A    A              B              C           D    E    F
  1              Pendulum Production
  2              for Grandfather Clocks
  3
  4    Sample   Pendulum Length   Period for One
  5              (feet)            Cycle (seconds)
  6       1            3.26            2.00
  7       2            3.30            2.01
  8       3            3.32            2.02
  9       4            3.26            2.00
  10      5            3.27            2.00
  11      6            3.10            1.95
  12      7            3.26            2.00
  13
```

You can determine the period of each clock by its pendulum length by using a standard physics formula. Divide the pendulum length by 32.2, take the square root of the result, then multiply by pi times 2.

1–2–3's LOGARITHMIC FUNCTIONS

1–2–3's three logarithmic functions are @LN, @LOG, and @EXP. You can use these functions in problems involving compound growth such as populations studies. A logarithm is defined as the power to which a number, called the base, must be raised to result in a specified number. The mathematical expression for a logarithm is

$$\log_b y = x$$

This is read as ''the logarithm of y to the base b is x. This formula can be expressed as

$$b^x = y$$

This is read as ''b raised to the power of x is y.'' This formula expresses the same relationship as an exponential relationship.

The base **b** can be any number greater than 0, excluding 1. The most widely used bases are base 10 and base e. (The number represented by e is a real number approximated by 2.7182818285) When you use a base of 10, the logarithm is called a common logarithm or base 10 logarithm. If a base is not specified, as in

$$\log 100 = 2$$

the base is assumed to be 10. When you use a base of e, the logarithm is called a natural logarithm.

@LN

The natural logarithm is written as

$\log_e y = x$ or $\ln y = x$.

The format for the natural log function is @LN(number). The **number** is the number for which you want to find the natural log. Number is any value greater than zero. ERR displays in the cell if an invalid value is used. You can enter the value directly, as a formula, or by referencing the appropriate cell.

Example

You can use the natural log to determine how long it will take a region to reach a desired population. Weston Inc. is a growing company that wants to expand into region A. At the present time, region A has a population of one million, but their marketing management does not feel that expansion is possible until the population of the region reaches 1.2 million. The population now and the desired population are entered in B1 and B2, respectively, in Figure 4.9. The approximate growth rate of 6 percent, estimated from past population data, is entered in B3. The formula in B6 for finding how many years are needed to reach the desired population is @LN(B2/B1)/B3. This formula is combined with @ROUND to provide an estimate of the year.

Figure 4.9 Using @LN and @ROUND to determine years of exponential growth

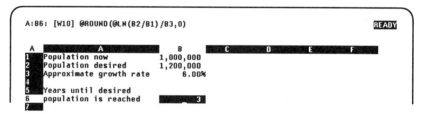

@LOG

The @LOG function determines the base 10 log of a number. The format for this function is @LOG(number). The **number** is the number for which you want to know the log. Any number greater than zero is acceptable. If you use a negative number, ERR displays in the cell. The argument can be entered directly in the function, as a formula, or as a cell reference.

Example

1–2–3 provides a built-in function for calculating the square root of a number, but it cannot directly calculate the cube root of a number. Figure 4.10 shows how to calculate the cube root of a number using @LOG. B1 contains the number 15625. The formula in D1 is $10^\wedge(@LOG(B1)/3)$ and results in 25. The formula +D1$^\wedge$3 in cell D3 provides a quick check for the answer.

Figure 4.10 Using @LOG to determine cube root of 15625

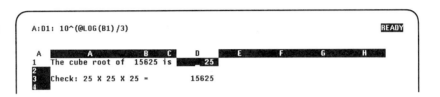

Other Applications

You can use @LOG to find other roots. The only change to make to the formula $10^\wedge(@LOG(B1)/3)$ in D1 of Figure 4.10 is to replace the 3 with the number corresponding to the root that you want to find. For example, if cell B1 contains 15625 and you want to know its cube root, use the formula $10^\wedge(@LOG(B1)/3)$ to obtain an answer of 25. To check the answer, raise it to a power of 3.

@EXP

The result of the @EXP function is the number e, approximated by 2.718281828, raised to a specified power. The format is @EXP(number). The **number** is the power to which e is raised. You can enter the value directly, as a formula, or as a cell reference.

Example

Figure 4.11 compares the maturity value of a Certificate of Deposit with interest compounded quarterly to the maturity value of the CD with interest compounded continuously. While the interest on most CDs is compounded monthly or quarterly, continuous compounding is also presented to show how it compares with conventional monthly compounding of interest.

Figure 4.11 Using @EXP to determine value of CD for continuous compounding and monthly compounding

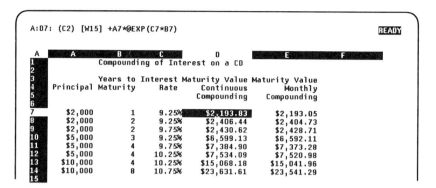

To create the model, enter the principal for a CD in column A and the years to maturity and the interest rate in columns B and C respectively. In D7, type the formula for continuous compounding, +A7*@EXP(C7*B7). Copy this formula down column D. Next, type the formula for monthly compounding, +A7*(1+C7/12)^(B7*12), in E7 and copy it down column E. As expected, continuous compounding results in higher maturity values. The difference between the maturity value for continuous versus monthly compounding increases as the principal, years to maturity, and/or interest rate increases.

1–2–3's TRIGONOMETRIC FUNCTIONS

The six trigonometric functions, sine, cosine, tangent, secant, cotangent, and cosecant, involve the relationships of the sides and angles of triangles. Early astronomers used these computations in determining distances that were otherwise unmeasurable. Astronomers gauged these unmeasurable distances by information already known about angles and sides of a triangle. With that information, they determined the length of the unknown side of the triangle in the sky.

1–2–3 has seven trigonometric functions. Included are the three basic functions, sine, cosine, and tangent, as well as several inverse functions, which are based on an inverse relationship for some of the basic functions. All of these inverse functions are arc functions. They include the arcsine, arccosine, arctangent, and arctangent-2. Ratios form the basis for each of these trigonometric functions because they measure angles. You can compute the secant, cosecant, and cotangent by combining simple formulas with the trigonometric functions.

Basic Trigonometric Ratios

Inscribing an angle in one of the four quadrants of a circle creates a diagram that is helpful in explaining trigonometric concepts. Figure 4.12 provides an example of this figure. The angle XYZ is the angle of interest in this diagram. Following the naming conventions for angles, you can describe this angle by listing the letters representing the points on the two lines that create the angle. The center letter is the pivot point for the two lines that form the angle. Angle XYZ is created by the rotation of the line XY to point Z on the circle's circumference.

Figure 4.12
Inscribed angle

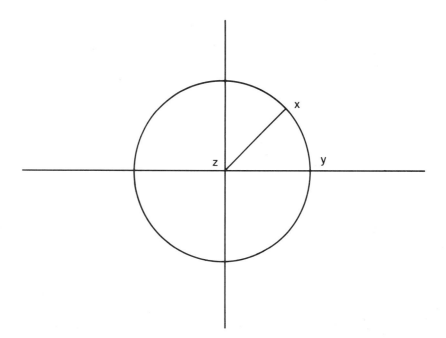

Key measurements for the trigonometric calculations are the distance of point Z from the vertical and horizontal axes. The axes are the lines that split the circle into quadrants. The distance from the vertical line is b and the distance from the horizontal line is a. The other important measurement for the ratio computations is r, the distance from point Y to point Z. The length of r does not affect these ratios because larger and smaller circles have triangles that are proportional. However, an angle of a different size affects the ratios since the a and b values change as r remains the same as shown in Figure 4.13.

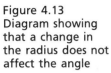

Figure 4.13
Diagram showing
that a change in
the radius does not
affect the angle

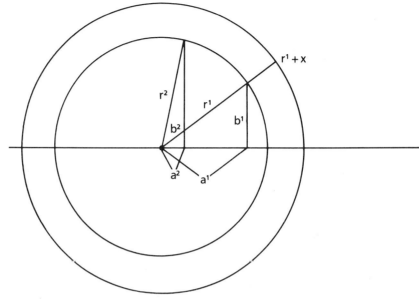

r¹ = r² but angles differ

r¹ ≠ r¹ + x but angles are the same

You can find tables that determine the sine, cosine, and tangent of various size angles in any math book that covers the trigonometric functions; the tables support both positive and negative ratios. However, with 1-2-3 you can automatically calculate these ratios without consulting a table. You can also use these ratios in computations to solve for unknowns such as the height of a building or the distance across a river.

Measuring Angles

There are two widely accepted ways of measuring angles. One method uses degrees with a complete revolution around the central point of the circle representing 360 degrees. In advanced mathematical calculations, the radian (equal to approximately 57.296 degrees) is the more commonly accepted measure. One revolution around the circle is 2 ~ radians; a revolution through one quadrant of the circle is ½ radian. A positive angle is measured counterclockwise starting from the positive x-axis; a negative angle is measured clockwise from the positive x-axis.

Converting Between Degrees and Radians

1–2–3 assumes that the angles specified for the trigonometric functions are measured in radians. Thus, if you prefer to use degrees, you must use the conversion factor, which multiplies the radians by 180/@PI. Conversely, multiply degrees by @PI/180 to change from degrees to radians.

@SIN

The @SIN function provides the sine of an angle, which is the ratio of the side opposite the acute angle of a triangle to the hypotenuse of the triangle. The acute angles in a right triangle are the angles that are less than 90 degrees. The hypotenuse of a triangle is the side opposite the right or 90 degree angle.

The format for this function is @SIN(angle). **Angle** is the angle measured in radians. The value can be entered directly, as a formula, or referenced by a worksheet cell.

Example

As shown in Figure 4.14, you can use the sine function to determine the length of the hypotenuse of a right triangle. The problem presented in the example is a dilemma faced by Mike Jones in driving to work. Mike drives from B to A then from A to C to get to work. Recently a new road has been built that will allow him to drive directly from B to C.

Figure 4.14 Using @SIN to determine distance of the new road

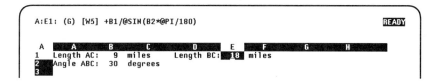

Using a map and his existing knowledge, Mike can approximate his distance with the new road. Mike knows that the distance AC is nine miles. This value is placed in cell B1 in Figure 4.14. The value in cell B2 is 30 degrees, the angle at which the new road intersects AB. The ratio for finding the sine of an angle is Sin(angle)=Opposite/Hypotenuse, where Opposite is the side opposite the angle for which the sine is being determined. Since Mike wants to know the distance of the hypotenuse, the formula to use is B1/@SIN(B2*@PI/180). The angle is multiplied by @PI/180 to convert from degrees to radians.

@COS

The @COS function determines the cosine of a given angle, which is the ratio of the adjacent side of the acute angle of a triangle to the hypotenuse of the triangle. The format is @COS(angle). **Angle** is the angle, measured in radians, for which the cosine is to be determined. The value for angle can be entered directly in the function, as a formula, or a reference to a worksheet cell.

Example

A surveyor can use @COS to measure side AB of the tract of land shown in Figure 4.15. The land is in the shape of a right triangle. The ratio for finding the cosine of an angle is Cosine(angle)=Adjacent/ Hypotenuse. The adjacent side (AB) is the side that makes the angle (ABC) with the hypotenuse (BC). Side BC is 75 feet and is entered in cell B1. The angle ABC is 30 degrees and is entered in cell B2. You can determine the length of AB by manipulating the cosine formula, @COS(B2*@PI/180)*B1. Notice that the value for the angle is converted to radians.

Figure 4.15 Using @COS to determine length of one side of the land

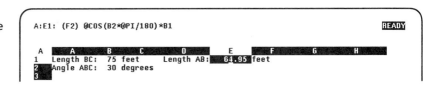

@TAN

The @TAN function determines the tangent of an angle, which is the ratio of the side opposite the acute angle of a triangle to the side adjacent to the acute angle. The format is @TAN(angle), where **angle** is measured in radians. The value for angle can be entered directly, as a formula, or referenced by a worksheet cell.

Example

Figure 4.16 shows how @TAN can be used to determine the length of the side of a right triangle. A man rows directly from B to A. He wants to know how far west point A is from point B if point C is 400 meters south of point A and AB meets BC at a 60 degree angle. Since the ratio for finding the tangent of an angle is Tangent(angle)=Opposite/ Adjacent, the formula @TAN(B2*PI/180)*B1 can be used to determine how far west A is from B.

Figure 4.16 Using
@TAN to determine
distance from point
A to point C

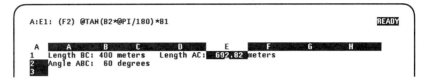

THE INVERSE TRIGONOMETRIC FUNCTIONS

The four remaining trigonometric functions are inverse functions. This means that these functions require a ratio rather than an angle for their argument, but they return an angle rather than a ratio. For example, the function @ASIN(angle) returns the inverse sine (or arcsine) of the angle. Recall that in Figure 4.14, the sine of angle XYZ is the ratio a/r, where a is the opposite and r is the hypotenuse. If you know the value of a/r you can take the arcsine of a/r and the result is the angle XYZ. Similarly, the arccosine of b/r and the arctangent of a/b would result in angle XYZ.

@ASIN

The @ASIN function finds an arcsine. The format is @ASIN(ratio), where **ratio** is the sine of an angle. The ratio must be in the range −1 to 1. The sine of an angle is always in this range because the ratio opposite/hypotenuse is always less than or equal to one. The result is the angle measured in radians.

Example

Figure 4.17 shows a 60-foot tower with a 120-foot guide wire attached. Figure 4.18 shows how @ASIN can be used to find the angle between the ground given the data shown in Figure 4.17. The formula @ASIN (B2/B1) provides the answer in radians. (Multiplying by 180/@PI converts the result to degrees.)

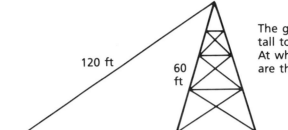

Figure 4.17
Diagram showing a
tower and guide
wire

The guide wires for a 60 ft
tall tower are 120 ft long.
At what angle to the ground
are the guide wires installed?

$$@ASIN \left(\frac{60}{120} \right)$$

Figure 4.18 Using
@ASIN to determine
angle between
guide wire and
ground

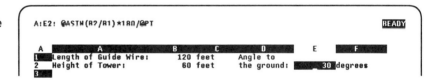

@ATAN

The @ATAN function finds an arctangent. The format is @ATAN(ratio).
The **ratio** is the tangent of an angle and can equal any numeric value.
The result is an acute angle in the first or fourth quadrant, measured
in radians (in other words, an angle in the range $-\frac{1}{2}$ to $\frac{1}{2}$). This always
returns an acute angle.

Example

@ATAN can determine the angle from the horizontal at which a road
rises. A road stretches 100 meters from A to B. This value is entered
in cell B2 in Figure 4.19. The value in B1 is 6 meters, the overall rise
of the road. Given this information, the formula @ATAN(B1/B2)*180/@PI
can be entered in cell E1 to find the angle. The result is in degrees
because @ATAN was multiplied by 180/@PI.

Figure 4.19
Using @ATAN to
determine angle of
the road from the
horizontal axis

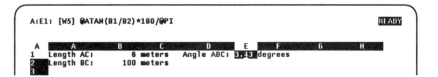

Other Applications

The @ATAN function can be used to solve other problems. For example, the information computed with the @ATAN function can be used to determine how much land must be moved if a construction company is building a new road in place of the old road and plans to level the land first.

@ATAN2

The @ATAN2 function is similar to @ATAN because it calculates an arctangent. @ATAN2 differentiates between angles in the four quadrants by returning an angle in the range −1 to 1. Angles in the first quadrant are in the range 0 to ½, angles in the second quadrant are in the range ½ to 1, angles in the third quadrant are in the range −1 to −½, and angles in the fourth quadrant are in the range −½ to 0. All angles start from the positive x-axis; you measure negative angles clockwise and positive angles counterclockwise.

The format for @ATAN2 is @ATAN2(X,Y). **X** is the x-coordinate of the angle and **Y** is the y-coordinate of the angle. If X and/or Y is negative, the negative sign must be entered. The sign of the arguments is very important when calculations involving directions are being performed. X and Y can be any numbers, including zero, but they cannot both be zero in the same application because (0,0) does not correspond to an angle. The values for the arguments can be entered directly in the function, as a formula, or by referencing a cell in the worksheet.

Example

Figure 4.20 shows the relationship between the sign of the argument and the angle returned. You enter the x-coordinates in column B and the y-coordinates in column D. The formula in F3 is @ATAN2(B3,D3). You can copy it down the column. Notice that the absolute value is 3 for all the x's, and 4 for all the y's. The results differ because the negative signs place each point in a different quadrant.

Figure 4.20
Using @ATAN2 for different angles in each quadrant

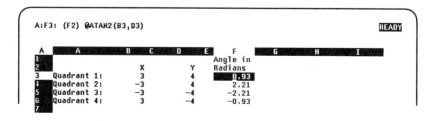

@ACOS

The @ACOS function finds an arccosine. The format is @ACOS(ratio), where **ratio** is the cosine of an angle. The ratio must be in the range −1 to 1. The cosine of an angle is always in this range because the absolute value of the ratio adjacent/hypotenuse is always less than or equal to one. The result is the angle measured in radians. You can enter the value for ratio directly in the function, as a formula, or by reference to a worksheet cell.

Example

The @ACOS function is useful when you know the hypotenuse and one other side of a right triangle and you need to find the angle between the two sides. Figure 4.21 illustrates how @ACOS can be used. Cell B2 contains the value 500 meters, the distance covered by a runner on a hill. Cell B5 contains the value 495 meters, which is the distance covered by a runner on flat ground. This is also the horizontal distance the runner on the hill has covered. The extra five meters the runner travels can be attributed to the slope of the hill. The formula @ACOS(B5/B2) computes the angle the hill forms with the horizontal. Multiply 180/PI to convert to degrees.

Figure 4.21
Using @ACOS to
determine angle
of hill

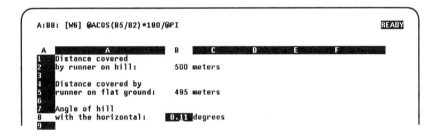

5

Date and Time Functions

1-2-3's date and time functions add the power of date and time calculations to your worksheet models. The date functions allow you to date stamp the models you create as well as to perform calculations that involve computing the difference between any two dates. This means you will be able to determine the date a report was printed, age your receivables, calculate the interest due on a loan, or determine what date the next bond payment is due.

1-2-3's time functions allow you to record the hour, minute, and second for an exact time stamp. They also provide the same type of arithmetic capabilities as the date functions so that you can calculate the amount of time that should be billed to a client, the elapsed time for a production run, or the overnight delivery times for the various couriers which you use.

The date and time functions are extremely easy to use once you understand the mechanics 1-2-3 uses for the storage of date and time entries. The first step is examining the unique numbers that 1-2-3 uses to represent every date and time between January 1, 1900, and December 31, 2099.

1-2-3'S DATE AND TIME SERIAL NUMBERS

The numbers stored for 1-2-3's date and time entries do not match the typical display of a date and time. After familiarizing yourself with the displays, you will need to learn how to manipulate the display through the use of the global or range format commands so that they will display to your liking. With Release 3, formatting date and time entries is easy. All you need to do is format the cells that will contain these entries with /Range Format Other Automatic. All your date and time entries will be properly formatted without having to use the date and time functions to enter them as date and time serial numbers. Once you have used the automatic format, Release 3 supports the entry of any date or time that uses one of 1–2–3's valid date or time formats. This means that you can enter a date as 13-Apr-90 or as 4/13/90. You can enter a time as 12:00:00 or 9:30 AM. In addition, Release 3 still supports the use of all the existing date and time functions. You will still find many uses even for the functions that create basic date and time entries, since they allow you to enter function arguments by referencing data in other locations.

DATE ENTRIES IN THE WORKSHEET

1–2–3 supports the entry of dates from January 1, 1900, through December 31, 2099. This range of dates is adequate for tracking historical transactions and future events. It is possible to compare historical prices to determine how much of an increase there has been each decade; it is also possible to record transactions for 20-year bonds or 99-year leases.

Each of the dates is represented by a serial number with 1 assigned to the first date handled by the package, January 1, 1900. Each succeeding day is represented by an increment of 1 until the final number is reached. The highest serial date number supported is 73050 corresponding to December 31, 2099. Although 1–2–3's serial date concept may seem a little strange at first, you will learn to appreciate how quickly 1–2–3 handles date computations.

Serial date numbers provide all the date arithmetic capabilities. Without the serial date numbers assigned, it is impossible to determine the number of days separating two dates easily. For example, there is no easy way to subtract 12/31/83 from 1/15/88. You would first have to determine how many days were in each month and if any leap years were involved. The process would be very error prone because of the number of calculations involved.

1–2–3's date arithmetic feature can handle this and other calculations with ease. Thus, you can compare two dates to see if a loan due date has been reached or to subtract two dates to determine how many days separate them so that you can determine interest earned.

Some of the date functions like @NOW, @DATE, and @DATEVALUE generate serial date numbers. Although you could type a serial date number into a cell directly, normally you will not know the serial number associated with a date and will choose one of these functions to generate one for you. Other functions like @YEAR, @MONTH, and @DAY expect a serial date number for an argument and extract one component of the date for use in the worksheet. Whether you work with a function that creates a serial date number or expects one as an argument, you will need to format serial dates if you expect to interpret the date they represent. Without formatting, serial date numbers have no resemblance to a date.

The serial date number feature also allows you to sort a column of dates and have them returned in an chronological order. Since each date serial number is 1 greater than the day before it, 1–2–3 sorts by this number to order the dates from earliest to latest.

Formatting Date Entries

Most worksheet entries can be used without special formatting since it is easy to tell what the entry represents even if it does not have the optimal format. However, date entries are different since it is not easy to tell what date a serial date number represents. Thus, you should either pre-format the cells where you plan to make date entries or format the cells after your date entries have been completed. The same commands are used in both methods.

1–2–3 offers two commands for formatting worksheet entries. Your selection will be determined by the number of cells you want to format. The /Worksheet Global Format command is the choice when you wish to select a format for most of the worksheet. The /Range Format command is the better choice when a more limited section of the worksheet must be formatted. The formatting options are the same for both commands. You will select Date from the format menu to see the selections in Figure 5.1.

Figure 5.1 Date format options

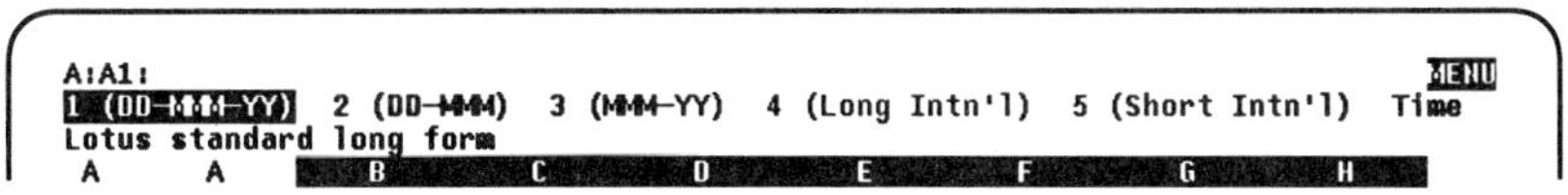

```
A:A1:                                                              MENU
1 (DD-MMM-YY)  2 (DD-MMM)  3 (MMM-YY)  4 (Long Intn'l)  5 (Short Intn'l)  Time
Lotus standard long form
  A      A        B          C           D            E         F         G         H
```

A serial date number of 32839 representing 11/27/89 can be displayed with any of the options from the date menu. Table 5.1 shows how each format option displays the date. It also shows the format indicator that appears in the control panel when a cell's date format is assigned with the range format command.

TABLE 5.1: DATE DISPLAYS OF /RANGE FORMAT DATE COMMAND

Format	Example
DD-MMM-YY	27-NOV-89
DD-MMM	27-NOV
MMM-YY	NOV-89
Long International	11/27/89 (default Long International)
Short International	11/27 (default Short International)

Additional changes are possible with the long and short international date formats. Both of these selections can be further customized by selecting /Worksheet Global Default Other International Date. Given the various international selections, you can choose any of the display formats in Table 5.2. The default selection automatically available to you is the first selection in the table.

TABLE 5.2: DATE DISPLAYS FOR LONG AND SHORT INTERNATIONAL DATES

Option	Long Format	Example	Short Format	Example
A	MM/DD/YY	08/15/90	MM/DD	08/15
B	DD/MM/YY	15/08/90	DD/MM	15/08
C	DD.MM.YY	15.08.90	DD.MM	15.08
D	YY-MM-DD	90-08-15	MM-DD	08-15

Since some of the date format options require more than the default nine-character column width to display the entry, you may also need to extend the width of the column to see the formatted date. The column width can be changed with either /Worksheet Column Set-Width, /Worksheet Column Column-Range Set-Width (in Releases 2.2 and 3.0), or /Worksheet Global Column-Width. The date entries will each display as * if the column is not wide enough for the format selected.

Date Arithmetic

Calculations with dates can take several forms. For example, you can add a fixed number of days to a date serial number to generate a date serial number representing a date that number of days in the future. If cell A1 contains a date entry, the formula +A1+5 in B1 generates the serial date number for the date five days after the date represented in A1.

Another application for date arithmetic is determining the number of days between two dates. For example, a date in A1 might represent the date that a piece of equipment was borrowed from a rental store, and B1 might contain a date serial number representing the date that the item was returned. If +B1−A1 is entered in C1, the result is the number of days that the equipment was borrowed.

Dates can also be used in logical formulas. You might have a date serial number for the date a loan is due. This date serial number can be compared against the serial date number for today's date. If today's date is greater than the due date, the loan is considered overdue.

TIME ENTRIES IN THE WORKSHEET

In addition to recording the date, Release 2 can also record the time of the day. Each second within the day is represented by a unique time serial number, expressed as a decimal fraction. The decimal fraction .00000 represents midnight, .25 represents 6 AM, .5 represents 12 noon, .75 represents 6 PM, and .999999 represents a time shortly before midnight. Every second of the day has a unique decimal fraction which remains constant for all dates.

Since time is represented by a decimal fraction, you can have both a date and a time stored in one worksheet cell. The number 32507.5 represents noon on December 30, 1988, and 32508.5 represents noon on December 31, 1988. Because you must choose to use either a date or a time format for a cell and no format exists to show both entries in one cell, once you select a date or a time format you will be telling 1-2-3 to focus on either the whole number representing the date or the decimal fraction that represents time. The other portion of the number remains in memory and will be used in any calculations that reference the cell, even though it appears by its format to consist of a date or a time alone.

As with the date functions, there are two types of time functions. The @NOW, @TIME, and @TIMEVALUE group generate time serial numbers. The @HOUR, @MINUTE, and @SECOND group expect a time serial number for an argument and examine the component parts of the time serial number that you supply.

Formatting Time Entries

Time entries can be formatted after they are entered or by entering them into cells that already have one of the time formats. The time format options are invoked with the same commands as date formats using either /Worksheet Global Format or /Range Format. The options for time formats are a little more difficult to find since you must first select Date from the format option menu. The last option in the menu presented is Time. Once this is selected the time formats as shown in Figure 5.2 will be displayed.

Figure 5.2 Time formatting options

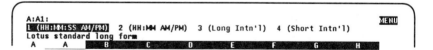

The effect of each of the time formats on a time serial number of .65353 is shown in Table 5.3. The format code used in the control panel when the format is assigned with a range command indicates that each of these entries are dates since they are found under the date menu. As with date formats, many time formats require that you expand the column width to avoid the display of *'s.

TABLE 5.3: TIME DISPLAYS OF /RANGE FORMAT DATE TIME COMMAND	
Format	Example
HH:MM:SS (AM/PM)	03:41:05 PM
HH:MM (AM/PM)	03:41 PM
Long International	15:41:05 (default Long International)
Short International	15:41 (default Short International)

Just as you can customize the international date formats, you can also customize international time formats. The command used to change the format is /Worksheet Global Default Other International Time. Table 5.4 shows the available options.

TABLE 5.4: TIME DISPLAYS FOR LONG AND SHORT INTERNATIONAL TIMES				
Option	Long Format	Example	Short Format	Example
A	HH:MM:SS	15:41:05	HH:MM	15:41
B	HH.MM.SS	15.41.05	HH.MM	15.41
C	HH,MM,SS	15,41,05	HH,MM	15,41
D	HHhMMmSSs	15h41m05s	HHhMMm	15h41m

Time Arithmetic

Time calculations follow the same pattern as date calculations. Thus, you can add a decimal fraction to an existing time serial number to generate a new time serial number. To add six hours to a time entry in A1, type +A1+.25. Adding twelve hours doubles the amount added to .5; halving it reduces the amount added to .125 for an addition of three hours. If the time generated by these additions is for the following day, the whole number portion of the entry will be increased by one. Any entry originally without a whole number portion has a day number of 0.

Time serial numbers can also be used in logical formulas. In this situation, time entries will be compared against the current or future time. An auto repair shop might use these features to monitor which vehicles do not have their repairs completed by the time they were promised to the customer. The scheduled completion time could be stored in a column of the model and compared against the current time. If the scheduled time is less than the current time, the job is late, and a new estimate may be required.

Some time functions do not produce time serial numbers. Functions such as @HOUR, @MINUTE, and @SECOND produce numeric values that can be used in calculations, although they are not time serial numbers.

THE DATE FUNCTIONS

There are eight unique date functions, four of which create serial date numbers that can be used in date arithmetic or to provide a date stamp on your worksheet. Three other functions allow examination of an existing date serial number to determine a specific component of the date. A new function in Release 3 computes the difference between two dates, using a 360-day year instead of a 365-day year.

@NOW and @TODAY

Prior to Release 2, the @TODAY function provided a date stamp for worksheets. With the addition of time features to Release 2, the package provides an @NOW function that includes both a date and a time stamp with one function. Release 3 uses both functions.

With @NOW, the format chosen for the cell determines whether the date or the time provided by the function will display. When you enter @TODAY in Release 2.0, 2.01, or 2.2, 1-2-3 converts your entry to @INT(@NOW) to look at just the date portion of the @NOW entry as shown in Figure 5.3. (Note: Release 3 leaves @TODAY as @TODAY.)

Figure 5.3
Release 2.0, 2.01,
or 2.2 converting
@TODAY to @INT
(@NOW)

A:B1:   (D4) @NOW   READY

A   A   B   C   D   E   F   G   H
1   03/28/89
2

The same thing occurs when you use Release 2.0, 2.01, or 2.2 to retrieve a worksheet that contains the @TODAY entry in a worksheet cell.

With both the @NOW and the @TODAY functions, the information accessed is the current system date and/or time. If you do not have a clock card in your system and do not respond to the operating system prompts with the correct information, the date and time stamps that you generate with these two functions will be useless.

Example

In Figure 5.4, the @NOW function was entered in D1 and D2. The /Range Format command was used to format D1 as date format 4 and D2 as time format 2. The entries in C1 and C2 enhance the @NOW function by providing an appropriate label for each of the entries.

Figure 5.4 Using @NOW for time and date stamps

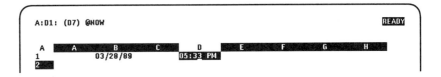

The @NOW function can be used in more sophisticated applications as well. When combined with @VLOOKUP and @MOD, it can determine the day of the week. @MOD provides the remainder when a number is divided by another number. To determine the day of the week, the date serial number is divided by 7, as in @MOD(@TODAY,7).

When a 0 is returned, the day of the week is a Saturday; when a 6 is returned, it is a Friday. Each of the intervening days can be determined by incrementing the number by 1.

The result of @MOD must be converted from the number to a word representing the appropriate day of the week. The @VLOOKUP function described in Chapter 8 performs the conversion as shown in Figure 5.5. In this figure, B1 also contains @NOW formatted with date format 1.

Figure 5.5 Using
@NOW with @MOD
and @VLOOKUP to
determine the day
of the week

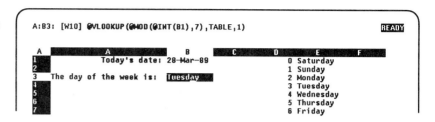

Other Applications

In addition to providing a date stamp that will be updated whenever you retrieve a worksheet, the @TODAY and @NOW functions can generate a permanent date in a worksheet. This static date or time stamp can be generated by entering the function, pressing F2 (EDIT), and then pressing F9 (CALC) to place a fixed number in the current worksheet cell.

This feature is useful for dating an entry for an order, the date or time a package was received, or the date a confirmation notice was received.

@DATE

The @DATE function is used whenever you wish to record a date in a worksheet cell and plan to use it in arithmetic calculations. 1-2-3 will take the year, month, and day that you provide as arguments to the function and convert the function to the serial date number that conforms to these entries.

The format for the @DATE function is @DATE(year,month,day). The **year** is any two or three digit year number. Years from 1900 to 1999 are represented by 00 to 99. The years in the twenty-first century are represented by 100 to 199.

The **month** is a number from 1 to 12 with 1 representing January and 12 representing December. The months from 1 to 9 can be entered with or without a preceding zero as in 2 or 02.

The **day** is a one or two-digit number representing the day of the month. The number 1 is the smallest number that can be used to represent a day and is used for the first day in a month, and the number 31 is the largest day number which is ever acceptable. Of course, the day entered must also be valid for the month and year entered. For example,

31 is not a valid entry for month 9 regardless of the year since September only has 30 days. The number of days that you can use for month 2 depends on whether or not a leap year is used for the year argument.

Invalid arguments for the @DATE function cause ERR to display in the worksheet cell. The one problem might be caused by using an invalid day number for the month and year arguments that you specify (for example, using a day number of 30 with a month number of 2). Entering a month number of 14 or a year number of 1988 rather than 88 also results in an ERR display. If you make this type of mistake, you will need to edit the function and change the entry for the argument causing the problem.

Example

In this section you will see an example that utilizes the @DATE function to record the date an order was placed as well as the date that it was received. Figure 5.6 shows three columns of information on the orders. The purchase order number is recorded in column A as a label entry, and the dates for the order and its receipt are shown in columns B and C respectively. Each date was recorded using the @DATE (year,month,day) pattern for the date function.

Figure 5.6 Using @DATE to enter a date

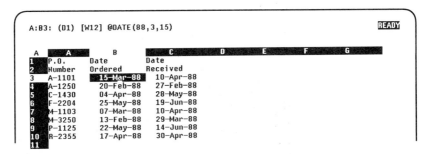

Date format 1 was selected for the display of the dates by using /Range Format Date 1 with a range of B3..C10. The width of columns B and C were also increased to 12 by using /Worksheet Column Set-Width 12 for each column. For Releases 2.2 and 3.0, the widths of columns B and C are set with /Worksheet Column Column-Range Set-Width.

The initial model can be expanded with the addition of another column as shown in Figure 5.7. After placing the label information in D1 and D2, a formula to compute the difference in the two dates, +C3−B3, is placed in D3. This formula is copied down the column to complete the calculation for each of the orders. This type of calculation is useful for rating various suppliers if there is a wide discrepancy between delivery times for the same items. (It is easy to add the additional data to the model if this comparison is required.) The use of the /Data Sort command to group the entries by elapsed days within item facilitates your comparison.

Figure 5.7
Using @DATE to
determine number
of elapsed days

```
A:D3:  +C3-B3                                                    READY

A       A           B           C           D       E       F       G
1   P.O.        Date        Date        Days
2   Number      Ordered     Received    Elapsed
3   A-1101      15-Mar-88   10-Apr-88       26
4   A-1250      20-Feb-88   27-Feb-88        7
5   C-1430      04-Apr-88   06-May-88       32
6   F-2204      25-May-88   19-Jun-88       25
7   M-1103      07-Mar-88   19-Mar-88       12
8   M-3250      13-Feb-88   25-Feb-88       12
9   P-1125      22-May-88   14-Jun-88       23
10  R-2355      17-Apr-88   30-Apr-88       13
11
```

Other Applications

The @DATE function is useful whenever you want to record dates. Alternatively, you can record dates as labels and convert them to serial date numbers with @DATEVALUE, but such an approach is inefficient when many calculations are required.

The @DATE function can record a loan due date, an appointment date, or hiring dates. Once these dates are recorded, it is possible to calculate late charges, the next scheduled appointment date, or employees with more than ten years of service. Additional dates can be generated by adding a number of days to an existing date recorded with @DATE or by combining @DATE with functions like @MONTH. You will explore this option later in the chapter.

@DATEVALUE

The @DATEVALUE function converts a label entry that looks like one of 1-2-3's date formats to a serial date number that can be used in calculations.

The format for the function is @DATEVALUE(date string). The **date string** is any label entry in one of 1-2-3's acceptable date formats. With a date of 12/31/88, a cell entry of '31-Dec-88 is acceptable since it corresponds with date format 1. Likewise, '31-Dec and 'Dec-88 are also acceptable since they conform to date formats 2 and 3. When @DATEVALUE is used with a date string in date format 2, the current year is used when the date serial number is computed. When a date string in date format 3 is used, the first day of the month is used in the computation.

Acceptable entries for date formats 4 and 5 vary depending on whether you have altered the default settings for the international date format. The acceptable date string formats for each of the international date settings are shown in Table 5.5.

TABLE 5.5: DATE STRING FORMATS FOR @DATEVALUE

Option A: MM/DD/YY and MM/DD Formats
Long: 11/09/90   Short: 11/09

Option B: DD/MM/YY and DD/MM Formats
Long: 09/11/90   Short: 09/11

Option C: DD.MM.YY and DD.MM Formats
Long: 09.11.90   Short: 09.11

Option D: YY-MM-DD and MM-DD Formats
Long: 90-11-09   Short: 11-09

You can check the current international date setting with /Worksheet Global Default Status. You can change the default setting for the current 1–2–3 sessions or permanently with /Worksheet Global Default Other International Date. Select Update from the Default menu before exiting to make this change permanent.

Example

In this section, you will look at several models that utilize @DATEVALUE. The model shown in Figure 5.8 is a variation of the example used for @DATE. Rather than enter the vehicle rental and return dates with @DATE, date strings were used for these entries in columns A and B of the model. Since these label entries match the format for date format 1, the @DATEVALUE function converts them to serial date numbers for calculations.

Figure 5.8 Using @DATEVALUE to determine rental charge

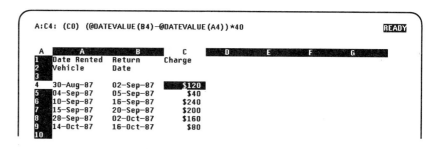

To complete the calculation for the model, you must determine the number of days between the rental and the return date. Charges are computed at $40 per day for the number of days the car was rented. Each date must be converted to a date serial number separately. You cannot use @DATEVALUE(B4-A4) because only one date string is acceptable as an argument and it is not possible to subtract one date string from another without converting them to date serial numbers.

The number of days is computed with @DATEVALUE(B4)–@DATEVALUE(A4). The number of days computed must be multiplied by 40. The parentheses around the @DATEVALUE computation is needed to ensure that the subtraction operation precedes the multiplication due to the priority sequence for arithmetic operations. To complete the model, the /Range Format command is used to format the rental charges as currency with 0 decimal places.

The second @DATEVALUE example produces a receivables aging report. The model shown in Figure 5.9 contains a reference to today's date with @INT(@NOW) or @TODAY placed in F1. The @INT function eliminates the decimal fraction that relates to the time of day and only the whole number representing the date remains. Column A contains the name of the customers, column B contains the amount due, column C contains the due dates stored as date strings, and column D computes the balances that are more than 30 days past due.

Figure 5.9 Using @DATEVALUE with @IF to create a receivables aging report

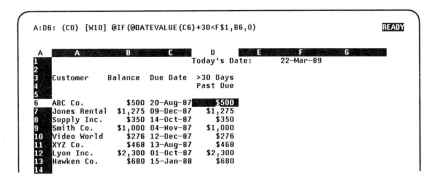

The formula used to compute the amount of the balances past due is complicated because it combines a logical formula comparison using @DATEVALUE with @IF. The logical formula that utilizes @DATE-VALUE is @DATEVALUE(C6)+30 < F$1. This formula adds 30 to the serial date number generated by @DATEVALUE and checks to see if this number is less than the serial date number that represents today's date. If it is less, the account is more than 30 days past due.

The @IF statement supplies a different value for D6, depending on whether the condition tests as true or false. If the condition is true, the cell displays the account balance; if it is false, a 0 displays. For more information on @IF, see Chapter 3.

The formula in D6 can be copied down the column for the remaining accounts. Columns B and D can also be formatted as currency with zero decimal places to improve the worksheet's appearance. If you are using Release 2 or above and prefer the $0 entries to display as blanks, use /Worksheet Zero Yes to suppress all the zeros on the worksheet.

This model can be expanded to include other receivable aging categories as shown in Figure 5.10. To make it easy to create formulas for both categories, use the $ selectively to control the formulas as they are copied. The entry placed in E6 is

@IF(@DATEVALUE($C6)+90 > =$F$1#AND#@DATEVALUE ($C6)+60 < $F$1,$B6,0)

This formula is copied down column E.

Figure 5.10 Using @DATEVALUE with @IF to create an expanded receivables aging report

```
A:F6: (C0) [W10] @IF(@DATEVALUE($C6)+90<$F$1,$B6,0)                    READY

A       A          B        C        D         E         F         G
1                                  Today's Date:           22-Mar-89
2
3     Customer    Balance  Due Date 30-60 Days 60-90 Days > 60 Days
4                                   Past Due   Past Due   Past Due
5
6     ABC Co.       $500 20-Aug-87      $0        $0        $500
7     Jones Rental $1,275 07-Sep-87      $0        $0      $1,275
8     Supply Inc.   $350 14-Oct-87      $0        $0        $350
9     Smith Co.    $1,000 05-Nov-87      $0        $0      $1,000
10    Video World   $276 01-Dec-87      $0        $0        $276
11    XYZ Co.       $468 13-Aug-87      $0        $0        $468
12    Lyon Inc.    $2,300 01-Oct-87      $0        $0      $2,300
13    Hawken Co.    $680 15-Jan-88      $0        $0        $680
14
```

Next the formula is copied to F6 and modified. Using F2 (EDIT) the formula in F6 is altered to read

@IF(@DATEVALUE($C6)+90<$F$1,$B6,0)

This formula is copied down column F and both columns are formatted as currency with zero decimal places to produce the results displayed.

Other Applications

The @DATEVALUE function is useful in applications where dates are stored as date strings that conform to one of the date formats. @DATEVALUE can provide a solution when you prefer to enter dates without the @DATE function. It can also be a quick solution when a worksheet contains date strings because you did not plan to perform calculations with the dates. Although it can be used in all of these situations, it is preferable to enter dates with @DATE when many calculations must be performed with a set of dates. With the @DATEVALUE approach, the date must be converted for every calculation.

@MONTH

The @MONTH function extracts the month number from a date serial number. @MONTH expects a date serial number as an argument and returns a number from 1 to 12 corresponding to the appropriate month number.

The format used for this function is @MONTH(date serial number). The **date serial number** can be any number from 1 to 73050. It can be placed directly within the function or stored in a worksheet cell and referenced by the function. To determine the month of a date string, combine @MONTH with @DATEVALUE as in @MONTH(@DATEVALUE (date string)).

Example

Although the month is shown in a complete display of dates, it is sometimes desirable to show it separately. One example is determining the anniversary date of employees. If you sort on the date of hire in Figure 5.11, the dates fall into chronological sequence and are not grouped by the anniversary month.

Figure 5.11 Using @MONTH to extract an employee's anniversary month

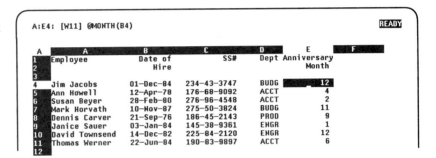

Column E was placed in the existing model to facilitate sorting by the month of hire. @MONTH(B4) is used to extract the first month number from the date serial number in B4. This formula can be copied down column E for the remaining employees.

Once the months are extracted, it is easy to sort the data by the contents of column E. This would put all the entries in sequence by the month of hire. A secondary sort of the date of hire would ensure that the records were in sequence by longevity within the anniversary month sequence.

Other Applications

The @MONTH function can generate dates. For example, you might want to generate a series of dates that are exactly one year apart. Simply reference the month number from an existing date and generate either new year or day numbers.

You can use @MONTH to create a text date entry. To do this, you could create lookup tables with words for the month, day, and year, and the month numbers could then be looked up in a table that matched month names.

@YEAR

The @YEAR function extracts the year number from a date serial number argument and returns a number from 0 to 199 corresponding to the appropriate year number. The numbers from 0 to 99 represent 1900 to 1999 respectively. The number 100 begins the years in the twenty-first century. The number 199 is the largest year number supported and represents 2099.

The format used for this function is @YEAR(date serial number). The **date serial number** can be any number from 1 to 73050. It can be placed directly within the function or stored in a worksheet cell and referenced by the function. To determine the year of a date string, combine @YEAR and @DATEVALUE as in @YEAR(@DATEVALUE(date string)).

Example

Figure 5.12 presents an example that uses the @YEAR function to extract a year from date serial numbers. It is used to complete the entries in column C as well as to complete a logical comparison for the @IF function in column D.

Figure 5.12 Using @YEAR with @IF to determine whether or not a warranty is in effect

```
A:D4: @IF(@YEAR(A4)<=83,"EXPIRED","EFFECTIVE")                    READY

A        A          B        C          D          E       F       G
1   Purchase    Car      Year of  Warranty
2   Date        Model    Purchase Effective
3
4   04-Apr-84   XM324       1984  EFFECTIVE
5   12-Oct-82   XS225       1982  EXPIRED
6   05-Jul-79   RS455       1979  EXPIRED
7   30-Nov-86   XM326       1986  EFFECTIVE
8   26-Nov-80   RS675       1980  EXPIRED
9   18-Jan-84   SL465       1984  EFFECTIVE
10  23-Mar-81   XS450       1981  EXPIRED
11  04-Sep-87   RS675       1987  EFFECTIVE
12
```

Column C is complete after you enter the purchase dates with @DATE and complete the car model numbers with label entries. The formula in C4 is @YEAR(A4)+1900. This formula is copied down for the remaining vehicles.

To determine at a glance whether the warranty features are still in effect, you must know if the car was purchased before 1983 (car models before that year are not covered under warranty). The comparison can be handled with @YEAR(A4)<=83, combined with @IF. When the logical

test is true, EXPIRED displays in column D; when it is false, EFFEC-
TIVE displays. The @IF statement shown in the control panel of the
example can handle the task.

Other Applications

The @YEAR function is effective for focusing on the year of a transaction. This is useful when displaying bond maturity dates or the date
of hire for employees since the year is frequently the most important
part of the date in these situations.

The @YEAR function is also useful for constructing a date using the
year from existing dates. To create the fixed holiday dates for 1988 when
the current date is in 1988, you might have an entry such as
@DATE(@YEAR(@NOW),12,25), which produces 25-Dec-88 when
the entry is formatted with date format 1.

@DAY

The @DAY function extracts the day number from a date serial number
argument and returns a number from 1 to 31 corresponding to the appropriate day number.

The format used for this function is @DAY(date serial number). The **date
serial number** can be any number from 1 to 73050. It can be placed
directly within the function or stored in a worksheet cell and referenced
by the function. To determine the day of a date string, combine @DAY
with @DATEVALUE as in @DAY(@DATEVALUE(date string)).

Example

In Figure 5.13, the @DAY function is combined with several other functions to generate a formula for a series of dates. The first entry is the
date that is placed in A1. Next, the formula is constructed in A2 to
increment the date by one month. The assumption is made that the
year will be 1988. The month number will be one more than the previous
month. @MONTH(A1)+1 and the day number will be equivalent to
the day number in the first date @DAY(A1). With Release 3, use /Data
Fill with a one month increment to implement this.

Figure 5.13
Using @DAY with
@MONTH and
@DATE to list dates
one month apart

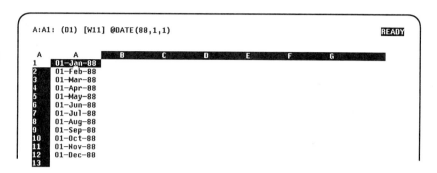

The date components are all joined together as @DATE(88,@MONTH
(A1)+1,@DAY(A1)). The formula entry for the date in A2 is copied to
A3..A12 to complete the date series for the entire year. Since the function does not contain the logic to check for month twelve and use special
processing, this formula is practical only when you mentally calculate
the range where a copy operation would be appropriate.

Other Applications

You may want to extract the date number from data for the purpose
of establishing a new appointment schedule, then use it to track the
number of sales or deliveries on a given day.

@D360

@D360 returns the number of days between two dates based on a 360-day
year. Financial institutions often use a 360-day year since, before pro-
grams like 1–2–3 told you the number of days to date, using the normal
calendar year was difficult due to the varying number of days in each
month. When you subtract two dates, 1–2–3 computes the number of
days between the two dates. If you use this result, especially in financial
applications, your computations may be different than if you had used
a 360-day year. (A 360-day year divides the year into 12 30-day months.)

The format for @D360 is @D360(start date, end date). The **start date**
is the earliest of the two dates between which you want to measure
the difference. The **end date** is the latter of the two dates. If you enter
the start date and end date in the wrong order, the function returns
a negative number. These arguments can be a date serial number, a
cell address, or a formula that evaluates to a date serial number.

Example

You can use this function to compute the proceeds from selling accounts receivable or notes payable. Companies will sell their accounts receivable or notes payable to receive immediate cash instead of waiting until the account or note is paid. When accounts receivable or notes payable are sold, the amount they are sold is discounted. The calculation to compute the proceeds often use a 360-day year. For example, suppose on September 15 you want to sell some accounts receivables due on November 1 totaling $100,000. If the bank charges 12% interest and uses a 360-day year, you can compute the discount that the bank charges by typing a formula like this:

@D360(@DATE(89,9,15),@DATE(89,11,1))/360*.12*100000

When you enter this formula, 1–2–3 returns a value of 1533.333. The difference between this number and $100,000 is the amount the bank will pay for the accounts receivable.

Other Applications

Since a 360-day calendar is primarily used in financial applications, this function is frequently used for applications such as determining if an account is overdue or in computing interest.

THE TIME FUNCTIONS

There are six unique time functions. Three of them create serial time numbers that can be used either in time arithmetic or to provide a time stamp on your worksheet. The other three functions allow you to examine an existing time serial number to determine a specific component of the time.

@TIME

The @TIME function is used to record a time in a worksheet cell. Using this function for the entry of a time will allow you to use it in arithmetic calculations. 1–2–3 will take the hour, minute, and second that you provide as arguments to the function and convert the function to the serial time number that conforms to these entries.

The format for the function is @TIME(hour,minute,second). The **hour** is a number between 0 and 23; midnight is 0, noon is 12 and the hours after noon add twelve to the hour. Thus, 1:00 PM is 13, 2:00 PM is 14, and so on. The **minute** is a one- or two-digit number from 0 to 59 representing the number of minutes in an hour. The **second** is a one or two-digit number from 0 to 59 representing the number of seconds in a minute.

Invalid arguments for the @TIME function cause 1–2–3 to display an error message in the worksheet cell. If, for example, you forget that 0 represents midnight and enter 24 as the hour, an error message will display. Entering a minute or second number greater than 59 also causes this problem. If you make a mistake like this, you will need to edit the function and change the entry for the argument causing the problem.

Example

The @TIME function is useful for computing the downtime on a production line. Simply record the time a machine on the production line breaks down and the time that it is put back into production. The two time entries can be subtracted to compute the downtime.

Figure 5.14 shows three columns of information that might be used to track machine downtime. The machine number is recorded in column A as a label entry. The time that the machine goes down is recorded in column B. The time that the machine is put back into production is recorded in column C. All of the time entries were recorded using the @TIME(hour,minute,second) format for the time function.

Figure 5.14 Using @TIME to track machine downtime

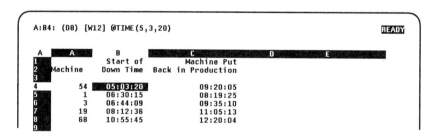

Time format 3, International Time format, was selected for the display of the times by using /Range Format Date Time 3 with a range of B4..C8. The width of column B is 12 and the width of column C is 20. These column widths were increased using /Worksheet Column Set-Width and the appropriate column width for each column.

The use of the @TIME function to record time entries allows you to perform time computations. After placing the information in B4 and C4, a formula to compute the difference in the two times, +C4−B4, is placed in D4 as shown in Figure 5.15. This formula is copied down the column with /Copy to complete the calculation for each occurrence of downtime. This type of calculation is useful for evaluating maintenance needs of different types of machines. The use of the /Data Sort command to group the entries by machine number facilitates your comparison. The database statistical function can be used to produce the total downtime or average downtime for each machine.

Figure 5.15
Expanding Figure
5.14 to calculate
machine downtime

A:D4: (D8) [W14] +C4−B4				READY
A	B	C	D	E
1	Start of	Machine Put	Elapsed	
2 Machine	Down Time	Back in Production	Time	
3				
4 54	05:03:20	09:20:05	04:16:45	
5 1	06:30:15	08:19:25	01:49:10	
6 3	06:44:09	09:35:10	02:51:01	
7 19	08:12:36	11:05:13	02:52:37	
8 68	10:55:45	12:20:04	01:24:19	

Other Applications

The @TIME function is useful whenever an application requires the recording of times. Although you can record times as labels and convert them to serial date numbers with @TIMEVALUE, that approach is less efficient when many calculations are required.

The @TIME function can be used for daily scheduling. For example, a lawyer can use the time features to record the amount of time spent on particular cases. Charges can be calculated once the start and stop times are recorded for each activity.

Another application of @TIME is projecting a completion time for an activity. The beginning time can be entered for an activity and an average time for the required task can be entered or obtained with @VLOOKUP. A completion time can then be calculated with a simple addition operation. You can use this capability to project a completion time for a customer leaving a car for repair.

@HOUR

The @HOUR function extracts the hour number from a time serial number argument and returns a number from 0 to 23 corresponding to the appropriate hour number using a 24 hour clock. The hour numbers greater than 12 represent hours after noon. When the hour number extracted is 8, the time is 8 in the morning; when the hour number extracted is 20, the time is 8 PM.

The format used for this function is @HOUR(time serial number). The **time serial number** can be any number from 0 to .999988. The hours function ignores the numbers to the left of the decimal place if a whole number is entered. The function only looks at the number after the decimal point. If the number has nothing after the decimal point, this function returns a 0, which is equivalent to 12 AM.

The time serial number can be placed directly within the function or stored in a worksheet cell and referenced by the function. To determine the hour of a time string, combine @HOUR and @TIMEVALUE as in @HOUR(@TIMEVALUE(time string)).

Example

The model in Figure 5.16 uses the @HOUR function to extract the hour from time serial numbers. It is used to show the hours of consultation calls to improve the scheduling of staff members.

Figure 5.16 Using @HOUR to extract hours from time of consultation

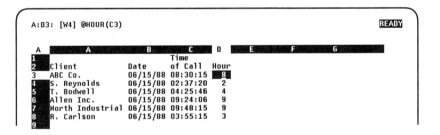

After entering the dates with @DATE or @NOW and entering the time with @TIME, the function @HOUR extracts the hour a staff member meets with each of their clients. If you have set the date with @NOW, you can reference that cell for the time as well.

To determine at a glance whether the staffing needs to be redistributed requires a frequency distribution like the one shown in Figure 5.17. From the output of the frequency distribution you can determine the hours when more staff members are needed. This will allow you to schedule your staff for these hours to better meet the needs of your clients. For example, after examining these results you may conclude that most of your clients need your services in the afternoon. You can then schedule your staff to use the mornings for non-client related tasks or reschedule the staff so that some individuals begin their day at noon and work later.

Figure 5.17 Using @VLOOKUP and @HOUR to create a frequency distribution

```
A:G3: 0                                                        READY

  A            A          B        C       D     E        F        G
1                                 Time
2      Client             Date    of Call  Hour       Frequency Distribution
3      ABC Co.            06/15/88 08:30:15  8              1        0
4      S. Reynolds        06/15/88 02:37:20  2              2        1
5      T. Bodwell         06/15/88 04:25:46  4              3        3
6      Allen Inc.         06/15/88 09:24:06  9              4        1
7      North Industrial   06/15/88 09:48:15  9              5        0
8      R. Carlson         06/15/88 03:55:15  3              6        0
9      R. Sanders         06/15/88 03:05:23  3              7        0
10     MR Graphics        06/15/88 08:35:22  8              8        2
11     D. Henderson       06/15/88 11:40:10 11              9        5
12     R.D.M.             06/15/88 10:05:16 10             10        2
13     G. Harris          06/15/88 09:15:03  9             11        1
14     J. Robertson       06/15/88 09:18:36  9             12        0
15     Powers Supply      06/15/88 03:12:05  3                       0
16     Gearson Inc.       06/15/88 09:30:19  9
17     M. Stapleton       06/15/88 10:55:23 10
18
```

Other Applications

The @HOUR function is effective for focusing on the hour of a transaction. For example, a rental car agency could use this information to compute billing on a hourly or daily basis.

The @HOUR function can also construct a time using the hour from an existing time entry. To create a time with the same hour as another cell entry, you might have entries such as @TIME(@HOUR(F23),12,25) to produce 12:25:25 when the entry is formatted with time format 3.

@MINUTE

The @MINUTE function extracts the minute number from a time serial number. @MINUTE expects a time serial number as an argument and returns a number from 0 to 59 corresponding to the appropriate minute number.

The format used for this function is @MINUTE(time serial number). The **time serial number** is the part of the date and time stamp that follows the decimal point. The time serial number is greater than or equal to 0 and less than 1, and can be placed directly within the function or stored in a worksheet cell and referenced by the function. To determine the minute of a time string, combine @MINUTE with @TIMEVALUE as in @MINUTE(@TIMEVALUE(time string)).

Example

Although the minute is shown in a complete display of the time, it is sometimes desirable to show it separately. One example is determining when different stations broadcast their news. If you sort on the time of news broadcast as in Figure 5.18, the times fall into chronological sequence and would not be grouped by the minutes after the hour that they are displayed.

Figure 5.18 Using @MINUTE to create a report of stations' news broadcast times

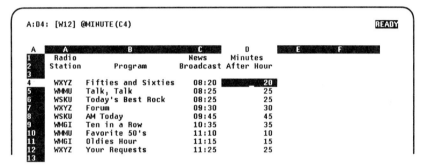

```
A:D4: [W12] @MINUTE(C4)                                              READY

A         A            B                C          D           E        F
1       Radio                          News       Minutes
2       Station      Program           Broadcast  After Hour
3
4       WXYZ         Fifties and Sixties   08:20        20
5       WMMU         Talk, Talk            08:25        25
6       WSKU         Today's Best Rock     08:25        25
7       WXYZ         Forum                 09:30        30
8       WSKU         AM Today              09:45        45
9       WMGI         Ten in a Row          10:35        35
10      WMMU         Favorite 50's         11:10        10
11      WMGI         Oldies Hour           11:15        15
12      WXYZ         Your Requests         11:25        25
13
```

Once the minutes are extracted, it is easy to sort the data by the contents of column D. This would put all the entries in sequence of the minutes after the hour that the news was broadcasted. A station not in this listing can use this information to determine when their station should broadcast their news.

Another concern of a radio station programmer is the length of time spent broadcasting the news. To determine this information, the station programmer can add a column for the time the news broadcast ended in column E. Column F could contain a formula to compute the difference between start and stop times.

Other Applications

The @MINUTE function can generate time entries. For example, you might want to generate a series of times that are a certain number of minutes apart. You can then reference the minute number from an existing time and generate a new time serial number. This is useful for generating a list of the news broadcast times as part of a report (as long as the broadcasts were a fixed number of minutes after the hour). The formula might resemble @TIME(H2+1,5,0). If the formula is placed in H3 and copied down the column, each entry will be for a broadcast time one hour after the previous time.

@SECOND

The @SECOND function extracts the second number from a time serial number argument and returns a number from 0 to 59 corresponding to the appropriate second.

The format used for this function is @SECOND(time serial number). The **time serial number** can be any number from 0 to .999988. It is the part of the serial number created with the @NOW function that is to the right of the decimal point. It can be placed directly within the function or stored in a worksheet cell and referenced by the function. To determine the second of a time string, combine @SECOND with @TIMEVALUE as in @SECOND(@TIMEVALUE(time string)).

Example

In Figure 5.19, the @SECOND function determines the number of seconds that each machine takes beyond two minutes. Column C displays the additional time that was used for each machine, thereby allowing comparison of machine performance. After reviewing this information, the maintenance department may decide to perform more preventative maintenance on machine B.

Figure 5.19
Using @SECOND to
calculate machines'
punching time

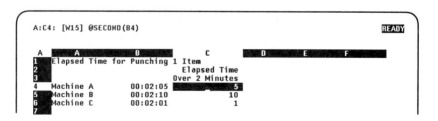

@TIMEVALUE

The @TIMEVALUE function converts a label entry that looks like one of 1-2-3's time formats to a serial time number that can be used in calculations. This function can be used in any application where labels that look like time entries are to be used in calculations.

The format for the function is @TIMEVALUE(time string). The **time string** is any label entry in one of 1-2-3's acceptable time formats. To record a time of eleven o'clock in the evening, a cell entry of '11:00:00 PM is acceptable since it corresponds with time format 1. Likewise, '11:00 PM is acceptable since it conforms to the second time format. If you do not specify AM or PM, 1-2-3 assumes that you are referring to a time before noon. Therefore, if time string '11:00 is used, @TIMEVALUE returns a time value that represents eleven o'clock in the morning.

Acceptable entries for time formats 4 and 5 vary depending on whether you have altered the default settings for the international time format. The acceptable time string formats for each of the international time settings are shown in Table 5.6.

TABLE 5.6: TIME STRING FORMATS FOR @TIMEVALUE

Option A: HH:MM:SS and HH:MM Formats
Long: 09:03:33   Short: 09:03

Option B: HH.MM.SS and HH.MM Formats
Long: 09.03.33   Short: 09.03

Option C: HH,MM,SS and HH,MM Formats
Long: 09,03,33   Short: 09,03

Option D: HHhMMmSSs and HHhMMm Formats
Long: 09h03m33s   Short: 09h03m

You can check the current international time setting with /Worksheet Global Default Status. You can change the default setting for the current 1-2-3 sessions or permanently with /Worksheet Global Default Other International Time. To make this change permanent, select Update from the Default menu before exiting.

Example

Figure 5.20 displays the time in and time out for several different employees. The person who entered these times did not know about the @TIME function and all time entries were recorded as text strings.

Since the current international time setting is HH:MM:SS and these label entries match the third time format, the @TIMEVALUE function can convert them to serial time numbers for calculations.

Figure 5.20 Using @TIMEVALUE to calculate hours worked

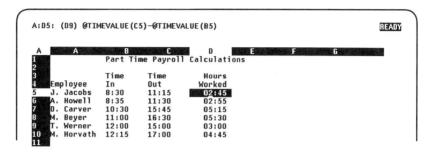

To complete the calculation for the model, it is necessary to determine the amount of time worked for each employee. You cannot use @TIMEVALUE(B4–A4) since only one time string is acceptable as an argument and it is not possible to subtract one time string from another without converting them to time serial numbers. The time worked by each employee is computed with @TIMEVALUE(B4)–@TIMEVALUE(A4).

Other Applications

The @TIMEVALUE function is useful in any application where time entries are stored as time strings that conform to one of the time formats. It can provide a solution when you prefer to enter times without the @TIME function or as a quick solution when a worksheet contains time strings because you did not plan to perform calculations with the time entries. Although it can be used in all of these situations, it is preferable to enter times with @TIME when many calculations must be performed with a set of times. With the @TIMEVALUE approach, the time must be converted for every calculation.

RELEASE DIFFERENCES FOR THE DATE AND TIME FUNCTIONS

Support for time entries was added to Release 2 of 1-2-3. Prior to Release 2, the @TIME, @HOUR, @MINUTE, @SECOND, @TIMEVALUE, and @NOW functions were unavailable. The @TODAY function was used to datestamp a worksheet and created a date serial number representing the current system date.

Entering @INT(@NOW) in a Release 2 worksheet is equivalent to entering @TODAY in a Release 1A worksheet since @INT drops the decimal fraction from @NOW. The whole number that remains is the date serial number for the current date. If you enter @TODAY in a Release 2 worksheet or retrieve a Release 1A worksheet which contains the entry, it will be converted to @INT(@NOW).

Release 3 supports the @TODAY function without converting it to @INT(@NOW). Although the result is the same, you will still see @TODAY if you look at the control panel when your cell pointer is in the cell containing the original @TODAY entry.

Release 3's other difference in this area is its ability to automatically convert date and time entries into date and time serial numbers. You can now enter date and time serial numbers in a cell without the need for @DATE or @TIME. If the cell format is automatic, an entry in any of 1–2–3's valid date and time formats will generate the date or time serial number and apply a permanent format to the cell that matches your original entry. The results are identical to entering @DATE and @TIME with appropriate Date and Time formats.

6

Financial Functions

1-2-3 provides an entire category of functions for financial calculations. These calculations provide features that support investment decisions, depreciation calculations, and loan payments. You can use financial functions for many different financial models. For example, you can use them for capital budgeting decisions that determine whether to purchase a new asset, to calculate depreciation expense, or to plan investment decisions. The financial functions are a tool kit of computations that will meet your needs in many areas.

1-2-3's financial functions use two financial concepts that may be new to non-business users: time value of money and depreciation. The time value of money concept states that a dollar today is worth more than a dollar tomorrow. Depreciation also has a time orientation in that an asset has a limited life. Thus, you should expense an asset over its useful life rather than at replacement. Depreciation allows you to compute an asset's loss in value over a given time interval. Rather than measuring how much an asset has produced against expected production, depreciation methods use time as the basis for the decline in the value of an asset.

AVOIDING HIDDEN TRAPS IN FINANCIAL FUNCTIONS

Many of the financial functions use time periods and interest rates in the calculations. Remember to express the interest rate with the same time basis as the time interval used in the calculations. Thus, if you express the time period in years, use an annual interest rate. If you use a different time period, use a rate of interest applicable for the time period. For example, to compute a monthly payment, use the monthly interest rate, or one-twelfth of the yearly rate. The solution is as easy as dividing the annual rate by 12, but many users forget to make the adjustment. Using a yearly rate of 12% is different than using a monthly rate of 1% due to compounding. For example, investing $10,000 for a year at 12% annually with annual compounding will earn $1,200.00 at the end of the year. Investing $10,000 for a year at a 12% annual rate, or 1% monthly rate with monthly compounding, will earn $11,268.25 at the end of the year. The difference in results due to compounding makes it important that you use the appropriate interest rate for the time period. 1–2–3 does not return an error message if you make this mistake and does not provide an indication of the error. Your only clue is a return value that seems unreasonable.

When you include an interest rate in a function, you have several choices for the format. You can either enter percentages with the percent symbol as in 10% or 15.5%, or enter the same percentage with decimal fraction entries of 0.1 and 0.155. To display these entries with a % symbol, you must format the cell as a percent. If you have Release 3, pre-format the cell as Automatic and 1–2–3 will convert the cell format to Percent. It will then multiply your entry by 100 and add a % symbol at the end of the entry.

If you inadvertently enter a whole number as a percentage, 1–2–3 interprets the entry as a whole number. Thus, an entry of 5 would be interpreted as 500% rather than 5%.

DEPRECIATION CALCULATIONS

Release 2 provides three different types of depreciation methods: straight-line, double-declining balance, and sum of the years' digits. Release 3 adds a variable-rate declining depreciation option.

The method that you use will depend on what you are using it for. Tax accounting frequently uses an accelerated depreciation method that depreciates most of the asset's cost in the beginning of the asset's life. The Internal Revenue Service determines which depreciation method can be used. Financial accounting, the type that you see in published financial statements, frequently uses straight-line, sum of the years' digits or double-declining balance to depreciate the asset more during the beginning of the asset's life. Straight-line is also used in financial accounting, although it is often used in cost accounting.

Selection of a depreciation method is based on a desire for accelerated depreciation and other factors. Each of the examples for the four depreciation methods uses the same assets and assumptions, thereby allowing you to contrast the results obtained for the different methods. If you are using Release 1A, you will not be able to access these depreciation calculations. Release 2 is the first release to support depreciation computations.

Varying amounts of depreciation occur over the life of the asset depending on the method used. Choosing a method and planning its tax savings implications over future financial periods is an important consideration for companies. If greater amounts of depreciation are recognized in the asset's early life, future tax savings will be reduced. Subsequently, future income will not benefit from these reduced tax savings. To maximize your tax savings in the current year, recognize as much depreciation as the tax laws permit.

@SLN

The @SLN function returns the straight-line depreciation for an asset. Straight-line depreciation assumes that a fixed amount of an asset's value is consumed every year. With this method, depreciation is a fixed amount for each period in life of the asset. The formula for straight line depreciation is

$$\frac{\text{Cost of asset} - \text{salvage value}}{\text{life of asset}}$$

The format of the @SLN function is @SLN(cost,salvage,life). The **cost** is the initial amount paid for the asset, and **salvage** is the amount that you expect to sell the asset for at the end of its useful life. For example, when you dispose of your car, you normally receive some financial compensation; this compensation is the car's salvage value. The salvage value received depends on the model and make of the car as well as its condition. With the depreciation calculations, you are estimating the salvage that you expect to receive for the asset at the end of its life. The calculated depreciation is then recorded in the company's books, and adjustments are made at the time of sale to account for any differences.

The **life** is the length of time that you expect to use the asset. Since it is impossible to determine the exact period of use, this is a "best guess" approximation. You can express these arguments as a number, formula, or cell reference.

Example

Figure 6.1 shows the depreciation calculations for different assets. Column B is the cost column, column C is the salvage column, and column E is the life column. The combined information in the three columns determines the depreciation. Since depreciation is evenly spread over the life of the asset, it is not important to know the period in the life of the asset for which you are computing depreciation.

Figure 6.1 Straight line depreciation of assets

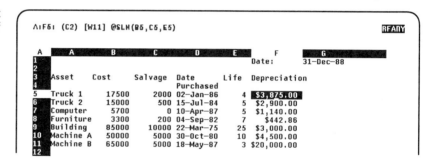

Other Applications

You can use depreciation calculations in capital budgeting decisions and cash flow analysis for purchasing assets. For example, you can deduct the calculated depreciation in computing taxable income, thus providing tax savings to the firm. For this reason, companies should evaluate the impact of the various depreciation methods before selecting one.

@SYD

The @SYD function returns the depreciation computed by the sum of the years' digits method, which is an accelerated depreciation method. Like other accelerated depreciation methods, the sum of the years' digits method assumes that a greater portion of the asset's worth is consumed at the beginning of the asset's life. Although this is an accelerated depreciation method, it does not depreciate the asset as quickly as the double declining balance method discussed later. The formula for sum of the years' digits depreciation is

$$\frac{(\text{Cost} - \text{salvage value})*(\text{life-period for depreciation expense}+1)}{(\text{life of asset}*(\text{life of asset}+1))/2}$$

The format of the function is @SYD(cost,salvage,life,period). The **cost** is the amount paid for the asset, and **salvage** is the amount that you expect to sell the asset for at the end of its useful life. If you expect to junk an asset at the end of its useful life, use 0 as the salvage value. If you feel that the asset will have some salvage value, you must estimate this to the best of your ability. The **life** is the length of time that you expect to use the asset. Since you do not know the exact life for the asset, you must approximate its life. The **period** is the year of the asset's life for which you are calculating the depreciation. Each of these arguments can be a number, a formula, a range name, or a cell reference.

Example

Figure 6.2 shows the depreciation calculations for the same assets using a straight-line depreciation model. In this example, the formula uses the sum of the years' digits depreciation function. The @SYD function uses the information in the cost, salvage, life, and period columns to determine the depreciation.

Figure 6.2 Sum of the years' digits depreciation of assets

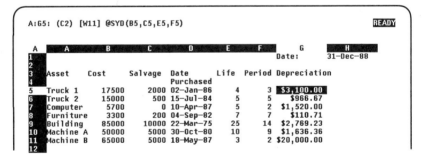

The second and third assets illustrate the impact of accelerated depreciation. The second asset is older and has a higher cost than the third asset. The depreciation is lower for the second asset because the third asset is newer. The third asset is being depreciated at a higher rate in its second year than the second asset which is in its fifth year.

Figure 6.3 presents the previous example with a few modifications. First, the formula uses a new period for computing the assets' depreciation. In addition, the formula in column G uses a half-year convention.

Figure 6.3 Sum of the years' digits depreciation of assets using the half-year convention

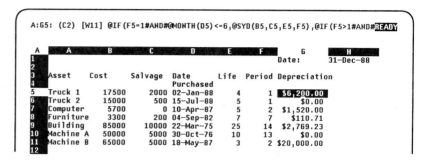

Before looking at the solution in 1–2–3, a more detailed explanation of the half-year convention is useful. Only the first and last years of depreciation calculations are affected by the half-year convention. If an asset is purchased in July, no depreciation is recorded in this year since it was owned for six months or less. This depreciation is recognized in period 6 for an asset with a five-year life. Figure 6.4 shows the recognition of depreciation for this asset.

Figure 6.4 Asset purchased in second half of year

7/89 purchase	Year 1989	No depreciation
	Year 1990	Full year depreciation
	Year 1991	Full year depreciation
	Year 1992	Full year depreciation
	Year 1993	Full year depreciation
	Year 1994	Full year depreciation

If you purchase an asset any time in the first half-year, the first year depreciation is for a full period. Figure 6.5 shows the periods that depreciation is recognized for this asset.

Figure 6.5 Asset purchased in first half of year

5/89 purchase	Year 1989	Full year depreciation
	Year 1990	Full year depreciation
	Year 1991	Full year depreciation
	Year 1992	Full year depreciation
	Year 1993	Full year depreciation
	Year 1994	No depreciation

Although the concept is straightforward, the new formula is more complex than the original formula. Nested IF statements compute the depreciation charge for all possibilities. Since you can enter the formula once and copy the remaining entries, it is not as difficult to use as it first seems. The formula in G5 is

@IF(F5=1#AND#@MONTH(D5)<=6,@SYD(B5,C5,E5,F5),
@IF(F5>1#AND#F5<=E5, @SYD(B5,C5,E5,F5),@IF(F5=(E5+1)
#AND#@MONTH(D5)<=6,@SYD(B5,C5,E5,F5),0)))

In this formula, @IF first checks to see if the period is 1 and the purchase month for the asset is before July. If both conditions are true, the formula computes the sum of the years' digits depreciation. If either condition is false, the second @IF checks the period to determine if it is greater than 1. If the condition is false, either the asset is fully depreciated or the asset was purchased after June. The half-year convention expenses a full year of depreciation for all assets purchased in the first half of the year and no depreciation for assets purchased in the second half of the year. Assets that you acquire after June do not have any first year depreciation. The first year's depreciation is taken at the end of the asset's life. Since you use a newly acquired asset only for a portion of the year, you should take depreciation only for the period that you use it. The half-year convention makes the assumption that you purchase assets uniformly throughout the year.

The third @IF function tests to determine if the asset is at the end of its life. A second condition determines if you expensed depreciation the year you acquired the asset. If these conditions are met, the formula computes another year of depreciation. If the condition is false, the entire formula has a value of 0. This happens when the purchase date of the acquired asset is after June or the asset is fully depreciated.

Other Applications

Figure 6.6 shows the computation for an asset that required major repairs in the third year of its life. Assuming the same useful life for the asset, the cost of the repairs are added to the book value and the new book value is depreciated over the remaining useful life for the asset. You can either construct an IF statement that recognizes the proper book value for each year or revise the depreciation computation at the time you incur the repair expense.

Figure 6.6 shows the formula used to compute the depreciation for the first two years. Subtracting the depreciation from the cost provides the current book value; the cost of repairs is added to this figure. Another option is to continue to depreciate the original cost of the truck over its five year life and to compute the cost of the repairs separately over three years. The first computation would use the salvage value and the second computation would use a salvage value of 0.

Figure 6.6
Calculating
depreciation after
a major repair

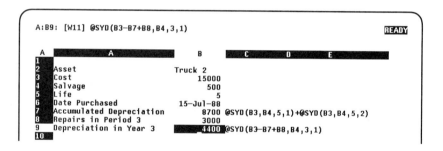

@DDB

The @DDB function returns the depreciation computed by the double-declining balance method. Double-declining balance is an accelerated depreciation method that assumes that a greater portion of the asset's worth is consumed during the beginning period of the asset's life. This accelerated depreciation method depreciates the asset faster than the straight-line and sum of the year's digits methods. Release 3 offers a variable-declining balance computation that supports faster depreciation schedules. The formula for double declining balance depreciation is

$$\frac{\text{book value} * 2}{\text{life of asset}}$$

Book value of an asset is the cost of the asset less all depreciation expensed at any point in time. @DDB is only available for Release 2.0 or higher.

The format of the function is @DDB(cost,salvage,life,period). The **cost** is the initial amount paid for the asset. The **salvage** is the value of the asset at the end of its useful life. The **life** is the length of time that you expect to use the asset. Since it is not possible to determine this time exactly, a "best guess" estimate is made. The **period** is the year of the asset's life for which you are calculating the depreciation. Each of these arguments is a number, formula, range name, or cell reference.

Example

Figure 6.7 shows the double-declining balance depreciation calculations for the same assets used in straight-line depreciation example. In this example, the function uses the information in the cost, salvage, life, and period columns to determine the depreciation. The addition of the period column is important since depreciation is not recognized evenly over each period in the asset's life. The calculations for the second and third assets illustrate accelerated depreciation. The second asset is older and has a higher cost than the third asset. The depreciation is lower for the second asset because the less expensive asset is in the second year of its life. The more expensive asset is in the fifth year of its life.

Figure 6.7 Double-declining balance depreciation of assets

```
A:G5: (C2) [W11] (@DDB(B5,C5,E5,F5))                              READY

   A        A        B       C        D        E     F      G          H
                                                          Date:    31-Dec-88
1
2
3      Asset    Cost    Salvage  Date       Life  Period Depreciation
4                                Purchased
5      Truck 1   17500    2000  02-Jan-86    4      3    $2,187.50
6      Truck 2   15000     500  15-Jul-84    5      5      $777.60
7      Computer   5700       0  10-Apr-87    5      2    $1,368.00
8      Furniture  3300     200  04-Sep-82    7      7      $125.22
9      Building  85000   10000  22-Mar-75   25     14    $2,300.12
10     Machine A 50000    5000  30-Oct-80   10      9    $1,677.72
11     Machine B 65000    5000  18-May-87    3      2   $14,444.44
12
```

@VDB

The @VDB function provides another alternative for computing depreciation. This function is only available on Release 3. The rationale behind variable-declining balance is similar to that of double-declining balance. The differences are that you can choose the rate, whether the function switches to straight-line depreciation when it is higher, and the number of periods for which the function calculates depreciation. The formula for variable-declining balance is

$$\frac{\text{book value * rate}}{\text{life of the asset}}$$

Book value equals the cost of the asset less any previous periods depreciation.

The format of this function is @VDB(cost, salvage, life, start-period, end-period, [depreciation factor], [switch]). The **cost** is the historical amount paid for the asset. The **salvage** is the expected value of the asset at the end of its life. The **life** is the estimated life of the asset. The **start-period** is the beginning of the period of the asset's life for which you want to compute depreciation. The **end-period** is the end of this period. You can use decimal values for portions of a year for the start-period and end-period arguments. For example, you can use .5 as the start-period and 1.5 as the end period when you have already depreciated the first year of the asset's life and want the following year's depreciation. The **depreciation factor** is the depreciation rate. Although you can choose any rate you wish or rely on its default value, a rate somewhere between 1 and 2 is the most widely accepted option.

If you do not enter the rate, 1–2–3 defaults to 200% (2.0). The switch is 0 (the default) to change from double-declining balance to straight-line toward the end of the asset's life when straight-line depreciation is higher, or 1 to use double-declining balance throughout the asset's life. A rate of 200% gives you the same result as double-declining balance. The variable-declining balance method is useful when double-declining balance is too rapid and straight-line is too slow.

Since depreciation is based upon a percent of the current book value because it is theoretically impossible to fully depreciate an asset, because each year you are only taking a smaller amount derived from a smaller base. An analogy would be to eat only one half of a piece of pie remaining in the pan. Each time you take one-half, a smaller piece results. But since you always leave half, you can never eat it all. This situation could pose a problem because you would end up depreciating a million dollar piece of equipment at pennies a year, and never fully depreciate it. 1-2-3 takes care of this problem for both variable-declining balance and double-declining balance by switching into straight-line depreciation once the salvage value of an asset falls below the equation (book value * ((1−(rate/life))^life)).

Example

Figure 6.8 shows the variable-declining balance rate using a rate of 150% (1.5). Since these assets are the same as those used in the double-declining balance and straight-line methods of depreciation, you may find it useful to compare the results of the different methods. In this example, you can see the "acceleration" of depreciation for the newer assets, but not for the older assets.

Figure 6.8 Variable declining balance depreciation of assets

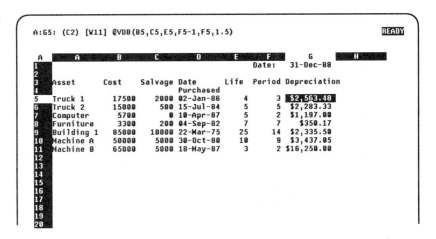

```
A:G5:  (C2) [W11] @VDB(B5,C5,E5,F5-1,F5,1.5)                    READY

 A        A         B        C      D           E    F      G          H
 1                                              Date:  31-Dec-88
 2
 3      Asset      Cost    Salvage Date         Life Period Depreciation
 4                                Purchased
 5      Truck 1    17500    2000 02-Jan-86       4     3   $2,563.48
 6      Truck 2    15000     500 15-Jul-84       5     5   $2,283.33
 7      Computer    5700       0 10-Apr-87       5     2   $1,197.00
 8      Furniture   3300     200 04-Sep-82       7     7     $350.17
 9      Building 1 85000   10000 22-Mar-75      25    14   $2,335.50
10      Machine A  50000    5000 30-Oct-80      10     9   $3,437.05
11      Machine B  65000    5000 18-May-87       3     2  $16,250.00
12
13
14
15
16
17
18
19
20
```

TIME VALUE OF MONEY CALCULATIONS

1-2-3 has eight functions that perform calculations relating to the time value of money. All of these functions have as their basis that a dollar today is worth more than a dollar received at some future point. Thus, if you delay the receipt of money to a future time, you will expect to receive more than the original amount. If you do not receive more, the transactions will not be equivalent. The reason for the difference is that the dollar received today can earn interest from today until a later point in time. The amount you are willing to accept at the later time should be at least equal to the original amount plus the interest it would have earned.

@CTERM

The @CTERM function computes the number of time periods it takes to reach a future value from a present value given a fixed interest rate. This function is only available in Release 2.0 or higher.

The format of the function is @CTERM(int,fv,pv). The **int** is the interest rate per period. If you provide a yearly interest rate, the function returns the number of years required to equal the future value given the fixed rate of interest provided. The **fv** is the future value that you are trying to reach. The **pv** is the amount that you have now. Each of these arguments is a number, formula range name, or cell reference.

Example

You can use @CTERM to determine the length of time needed to generate your desired retirement savings. In Figure 6.9, @CTERM computes the number of months required for a present value in the first column to earn the future value at the fixed rate of interest. For the first set of values, it takes 168.74 months for $5,000 to become $25,000 at 11.5 percent yearly interest. Since the interest rate is the annual rate, divide it by 12 to obtain the monthly rate. The Years Required to Reach Goal column divides the number of months by 12 to show how many years each of the savings plans requires. Note that interest compounded yearly instead of monthly yields different numbers. With monthly compounding, interest is computed and added to the principal at the end of each month, and consequently earns more interest than does yearly compounding. Figure 6.10 shows the computation for yearly compounding. The difference between column D and column F illustrates the dramatic difference between the two.

Figure 6.9 Using @CTERM for present value computations

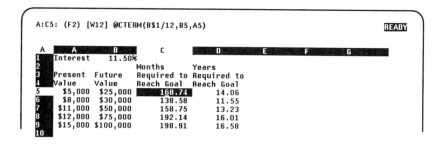

```
A:C5: (F2) [W12] @CTERM(B$1/12,B5,A5)                        READY

 A       A          B          C           D          E       F       G
1     Interest    11.50%
2                             Months      Years
3     Present    Future    Required to  Required to
4     Value      Value     Reach Goal   Reach Goal
5      $5,000    $25,000      168.74       14.06
6      $8,000    $30,000      138.58       11.55
7     $11,000    $50,000      158.75       13.23
8     $12,000    $75,000      192.14       16.01
9     $15,000   $100,000      198.91       16.58
10
```

Figure 6.10
Compounding of
interest rates

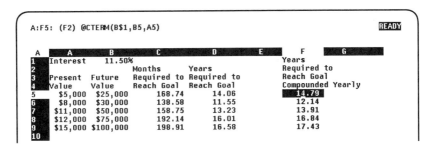

```
A:F5: (F2) @CTERM(B$1,B5,A5)                                    READY

A       A         B          C          D         E      F        G
1    Interest   11.50%                                   Years
2                          Months     Years            Required to
3    Present    Future   Required to Required to       Reach Goal
4    Value      Value    Reach Goal  Reach Goal        Compounded Yearly
5     $5,000    $25,000     168.74      14.06             14.79
6     $8,000    $30,000     138.58      11.55             12.14
7    $11,000    $50,000     158.75      13.23             13.91
8    $12,000    $75,000     192.14      16.01             16.84
9    $15,000  $100,000     198.91      16.58             17.43
10
```

@FV

The @FV function computes the future value of a series of equal cash flows at a given interest rate. This function assumes that the investment is an ordinary annuity, which is an investment where you invest a fixed amount at the end of every period. When the annuity reaches maturity, you receive the amount that you have deposited plus the interest earned on the investment.

The format of the @FV function is @FV(pmt,int,term). The **pmt** represents a fixed payment that is made every period. The **int** represents the interest rate per period. The **term** represents the number of periods that the investment covers. Each of these arguments is a number, formula, range name, or cell reference. The function assumes that interest is compounded at the end of each period within the term.

Example

Many banks have Christmas clubs to encourage you to save for Christmas shopping. With these clubs, you save a fixed amount, such as five dollars every week. With the $5 club, by Christmas, you have the $260 deposited plus the interest earned on those savings.

Figure 6.11 provides an example of a Christmas club plan. In this example, the worksheet displays the amount that you receive at Christmas for depositing different amounts at different interest rates. The formula takes the annual interest rate in column B and divides it by 52 to get the weekly interest rate. Then the formula uses fifty-two periods for the fifty-two weeks of the year. This analysis can help you decide how much you want to put aside for Christmas spending.

Figure 6.11 Deposit
rate variations

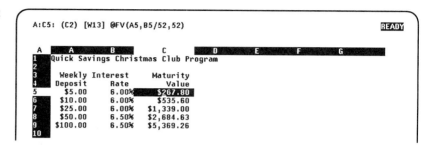

Other Applications

@FV is a useful tool for projecting the future value of a steady stream of cash payments over a fixed period of time. Companies can use this tool to project the future total cost of interest payments over the life of a bond. Other uses include projecting the cost of annuities and the proceeds that will be available in a sinking fund. Parents may use @FV to find the future value for different cash payments and interest rates in planning a college fund for their children. @FV can also be used to find the future value of IRA accounts.

@NPV

The @NPV function computes the present value of a stream of future cash flows.

The format of the function is @NPV(int,range). The **int** represents the interest rate for the period, **range** represents the range of cash flows. The @NPV function assumes that the cash flows are in the order of their occurrence and that every period has cash flows unless the cell for that period is blank. The function also assumes the cash flows occur at the end of the period. Both of the arguments are a number, formula, or cell reference to either.

Example

You can use the @NPV to compute the net present value of investment opportunities. In Figure 6.12, the projected cash flows are stored in the range B3..B7. The formula in B9 takes the interest rate in cell B1 and discounts the cash flow for the each year. By setting the range to B3..B7, this function assumes that the cash flow in B3 is one period away from the current time. The cash flow in B4 is two periods away from the current time and so on.

Figure 6.12
Projected cash
flows

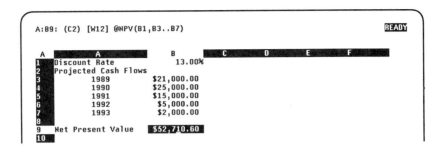

If a portion of the cash flows is generated at the beginning, you cannot include it in the @NPV function. For example, if you are initially paying $47,000 for the investment opportunity, you need to modify the worksheet to match Figure 6.13 In this formula, the up-front payment reduces the net present value computation. The interest rate does not affect the up-front payments.

Figure 6.13 Present
value modifications

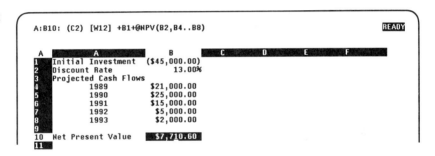

@IRR

The @IRR function computes the internal rate of return for a series of cash flows. The internal rate of return is the rate of interest the cash flows must earn to have a net present value of 0. This internal rate of return is the minimum interest rate a project or asset should earn to be worthwhile.

The format of the function is @IRR(guess,range). The **guess** represents your best estimate of what you think the internal rate of return is. When some cash flows are positive and some are negative, the cash flows have more than one internal rate of return. In a series of cash flows, there is another potential internal rate of return for every alternation between positive and negative numbers. Some of the internal rates of return are not reasonable. Your guess shows 1–2–3 which one of the potential internal rates of return it should use.

The **range** represents the range of cash flows. @IRR assumes that the cash flows are in the order of their occurrence and that every period has cash flows unless the cell for that period is blank. @IRR assumes positive numbers are cash inflows and negative numbers are cash outflows. Unlike @NPV, @IRR assumes the first number in the range is the initial cash outflow for the investment opportunity. Both of these arguments are a number, formula, or cell reference to either.

1-2-3 uses iterative calculations to compute the @IRR. If it cannot approximate the result within 0.0000001 after 20 attempts, the function returns an error message.

Example

Management uses the internal rate of return to evaluate an investment opportunity's discount rate. The discount rate can determine if the company should proceed with the investment opportunity. Also, management uses the internal rate of return to compare it to the minimum that it expects its investment opportunities to earn. Figure 6.14 is an example of the @IRR function used to evaluate an investment opportunity. In the figure, the cash flows are in the range B2..B6. By making a reasonable guess, you reduce the number of iterations 1-2-3 performs and select which internal rate of return the function returns if there is more than one potential result. In this example, you would pursue this investment opportunity if you require your investment opportunities to have an internal rate of return of 14.18 percent.

Figure 6.14 Using @IRR for internal rate of return

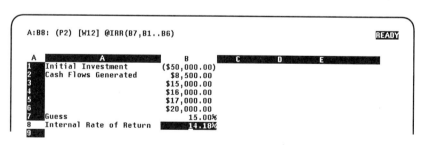

@PMT

The @PMT function computes a loan payment based on the principal, an interest rate, and a number of periods. You can use @PMT to compute mortgage payment amounts or the payments for a car loan.

The format of the @PMT function is @PMT(prin,int,term). **Prin** is the principal of the loan, **int** is the interest rate you are paying on the loan, and **term** is the number of periods for the loan. Each of these arguments is a number, formula, or cell reference to either.

Example

Figure 6.15 shows several loan options. To determine if you can afford one of the loans, you need to know the loan principal, the interest rate, and the term. In this example, the term numbers are in years. The goal is to calculate the monthly payments for each of the loans. Therefore, @PMT in column D converts the annual interest rate into a monthly rate by dividing it by 12. (The function can also converts the term from years to months by multiplying the term by 12.)

Figure 6.15 Loan schedules

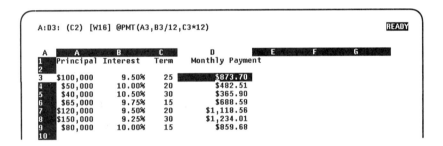

Other Applications

This function can also determine the amount of an annuity payment. Simply put the principal into an investment opportunity at a specified rate of interest. You can then withdraw a fixed amount every period for a set number of periods, and thereby deplete the investment amount at the end of the term. An example of this type of an annuity is a trust designed to provide income for an individual. At the beginning of a trust, you invest money at a specific rate of interest. During the term of the trust, you withdraw a fixed sum of money every period. At the end of the trust, you have depleted both the money initially put in the trust and the interest earned on these investments.

@PV

The @PV function computes the present value of an annuity, or series of equal cash flows, invested at a specific interest rate for a number of periods. You can use this function to determine what you are willing to pay for an investment that will generate this stream of future cash flows.

The format of the @PV function is @PV(pmt,int,term). The **pmt** represents the amount of a fixed payment that you will make every period. The **int** represents the interest rate per period. The **term** represents the number of periods that the investment covers. These arguments can be a number, formula, or cell reference to either. The function compounds interest at the end of each period within the term.

Example

One method of providing income for later years is buying an annuity. By paying a fixed sum now, you can acquire an annuity that pays you a fixed amount for a number of years. Figure 6.16 shows a computation of the present value of an annuity that pays you $10,000 each year for the next 15 years. Since this is a yearly payment, both the term and the rate of an alternative investment are expressed in yearly terms. In this example, @PV determines that an annuity that pays $10,000 for the next 15 years earning 11.5% interest is worth $69,967 now. If the price of the actual annuity is less than $69,967, you should consider purchasing it.

Figure 6.16 Present value of an annuity

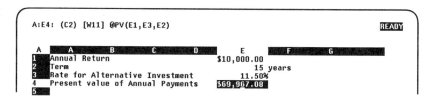

@RATE

The @RATE function returns the interest rate required for a present value invested over time to equal a future amount. This function differs from @IRR since the basis is one cash flow rather than a series of cash flows. @RATE is available only in Release 2.0 or higher.

The format of the function is @RATE(fv,pv,term). The **fv** represents the future value you want to have. The **pv** represents the amount that you have available for investment now. The **term** represents the number of periods for the investment. These arguments can be a number, formula, range name, or cell reference to either.

Example

When you invest in stocks, many choices are possible, depending upon your preference for the rate of return, risk, and long-term or short-term holdings. You can determine the required rate of return with the @RATE function if you know the future value that you expect at a specific point in time. In Figure 6.17, you start with $10,000 and want to end up with $25,000 in 10 years. Using @RATE in cell D4 determines that your required rate of return must be at least 9.6%. Once you have your required rate of return, you must decide how much risk to accept when evaluating stocks.

Figure 6.17
Determining the
required rate of
return using @RATE

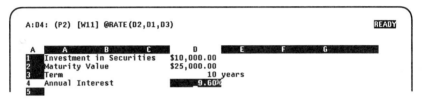

@TERM

The @TERM function determines the number of periods for an investment given a payment, interest, and future value. This function is only available in Release 2.0 or higher.

The format of the function is @TERM(pmt,int,fv). The **pmt** represents a fixed periodic payment that will be made. The **int** represents the interest of the investment opportunity. The **fv** represents the future value you want to have. These arguments can be a number, formula, range name, or cell reference to either.

Example

When a company needs to invest in equipment, it has can either borrow money from a bank or it can save the required funds from its profits. Figure 6.18 shows an example of a company using the second method of financing. In this example, the first row shows the equipment to be obtained. The formulas in column B compute the number of months required to save for the equipment. As shown in the worksheet, the amount that you must save decreases as the monthly savings decrease and the amount of time increases. The option that you chose depends upon how quickly you need the equipment and the amount that you can save.

Figure 6.18 Time period using @TERM

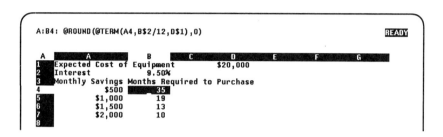

7

String Functions

A string is a group of characters that 1–2–3 does not recognize as either a number or a formula. Strings include text and numbers preceded by a label prefix. Note that a number without a label prefix is not a string. Such numbers must be converted to strings before you can use them in the string function.

Strings serve different needs than non-string entries. For example, strings record text data and provide descriptive information not used in arithmetic calculations. String functions can also correct errors in string data.

MANIPULATING STRINGS WITH FUNCTIONS

1–2–3 cannot perform mathematical calculations on a string. Even if the string contains only numbers, you must convert it to a value before using it in calculations. Neither does 1–2–3 understand expressions that include both characters and arithmetic operators. For example, if you enter ''RCA''+''Victor'' in a worksheet cell, 1–2–3 returns an error message. This type of situation requires that an approach joins the contents of two cells containing string entries. 1–2–3 provides the ampersand character (&) for joining two strings, as well as a number of special operations invoked with string functions.

Mathematical operators also will not allow you to remove part of a string. You need a new method for eliminating part of a string since subtraction returns ERR.

Because string functions were not available with the first release of 1–2–3, you could not manipulate text string entries. However, with Release 2.0's string functions, you can manipulate strings in many different ways. For example, you can dissect a string to access a portion of it, change the case of string entries to create a sorted list in alphabetical sequence, and correct entry errors in a series of string entries with string functions.

NEW OPTIONS WITH STRING FUNCTION CAPABILITIES

String functions allow you to combine, reverse, separate, and in other ways change character string entries on the worksheet. You can convert string entries into uppercase, lowercase, or propercase characters. The case change options allow you to present character entries in a consistent case. You can also search for a sequence of characters in a string and supply a replacement for those characters. In addition, you can extract parts of a string and choose the parts of the string you want to retain.

The string manipulation features also allow you to incorporate cell values into text. This feature lets you create more readable worksheets. When you reference text already on the worksheet you do not have to duplicate existing entries to place them in the heading.

Before text strings were introduced, retyping was needed to change the presentation format. Thus, if you had entered names as First Name, Last Name, sorting the data was not possible. String functions allow you to restructure these name entries to Last Name, First Name without retyping.

ERROR CORRECTION POTENTIAL

String functions are useful for error detection and correction. For example, the @EXACT function compares strings to test whether they are exactly alike. You can take appropriate action if the strings are not the exact match you expect. Another example is the @LENGTH function which determines the length of a string entry. For an entry such as a social security number, you can display an error message if the length is different from the necessary eleven characters (nine digits and two hyphens).

Counting the Position Numbers in 1–2–3's Strings

Several of the string functions reference a position within the string. It is important to understand how 1–2–3 computes position numbers within strings because the computation method is probably different from yours.

1–2–3 counts string characters from left to right and regards the first character in a string as position zero. Think of 1–2–3's position numbers as the offset from the first character in the string. This position number indicates the number of characters you must move to the right of the first character. 1–2–3 does not count the label-alignment prefix at the beginning of a cell as a position. Thus, the hyphen is in position five in the string "House-boat".

Arguments for String Functions

You can use any of 1–2–3's three valid label prefixes when storing string data. In a string function, the reference to a cell containing string data can be either a cell address or a range name.

You can also enter string arguments directly within the function. If you choose this approach, the string is always encased in quotation marks as in @UPPER("mary smith"). Note that you do not enter a label prefix.

The maximum length for a string entry prior to Release 3 was 240 characters. With Release 3, the length limit is 512 characters. Since 240 or 512 characters are the maximum lengths for a cell entry, placing a string within a function limits the length of a string argument to something less than the length limit because the keyword for the string and other characters and arguments will use a portion of the particular character limit.

Functions That Alter the Case of String Entries

1–2–3 provides three functions that alter the case of string entries. These functions give you a choice of uppercase, lowercase, or proper-case letters for a string entry. When combined with the /Range Value then the /Move command, these functions replace existing entries with entries in the selected case.

@UPPER

The @UPPER function converts a string to uppercase letters. @UPPER expects a string or a reference to a string as an argument.

The format for the function is @UPPER(string). The **string** can be a string enclosed in parentheses or a cell reference to the cell containing the string. 1–2–3 does not alter numeric digits within the string when it performs the case conversion.

Example

When you enter data, 1–2–3 does not check that you are entering data in a consistent manner. For example, when you are entering data in an employee database table, 1–2–3 does not check that all of the names use the same capitalization. The names you enter might look like the ones in Figure 7.1. When you print the data in a report, the changing capitalization style looks unprofessional. You can use @UPPER to convert all of the entries to uppercase. Using @UPPER(A3) in cell F3 converts the entry DONALD Tripp to uppercase. When you copy this formula for all names, the display matches Figure 7.2.

Figure 7.1 Report for names and salaries

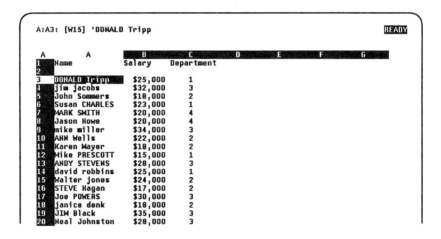

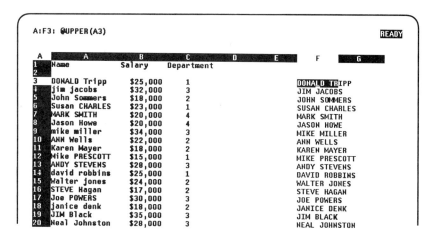

Figure 7.2 Using @UPPER to convert the names to uppercase

To conserve space and make this worksheet more readable, replace original names with the uppercase names. Before moving these entries, you need to freeze the entries at their current value. With the cell pointer on F3, enter /Range Value. This command invokes a special copy process to make the change. The cells that you want to copy from are the entries in column F. The cells that you want to copy to contain the original entries, but you can copy the converted entries to column F first.

If you copy the frozen entries over the original names column, the @UPPER functions will return an error message the next time 1–2–3 recalculates the worksheet. This is not a problem since you want to delete this column anyway. However, the safer approach is to copy the frozen values over the @UPPER entries. This approach retains the original entries in case you are not satisfied with the result. To complete the conversion, specify the entries in column F as the from range and F3 as the to range. Next, use the /Copy with a from range that includes all the entries in column F and a to range of A3. Finally, use the /Range Erase command to erase the entries in column F.

Other Applications

Case conversions such as @UPPER are frequently needed after a new user has worked with a 1–2–3 database because the new entries may not match the case of earlier entries. You can convert either all of the entries to achieve consistency or only the records requiring conversion.

Each field in the record that requires a case change needs a separate formula. Once converted, one /Range Value command will freeze all the entries if they are in adjacent columns.

@LOWER

The @LOWER function converts a string to lowercase. @LOWER expects a string or a reference to a string as an argument.

The format for the function is @LOWER(string). The **string** is either the string enclosed in quotation marks or a reference to a cell containing a string.

Example

The model in Figure 7.3 displays department entries with different capitalization styles. A consistent capitalization style makes the model easier to use.

Figure 7.3 Using @LOWER to convert departments into lowercase

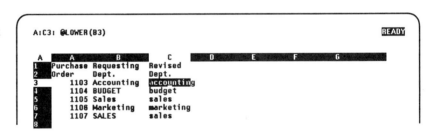

Placing the formula @LOWER(B3) in C3 converts the first department entry to lowercase. After copying this formula for all departments, the display matches Figure 7.3. If you use column C as the primary key in a sort operation, 1-2-3 produces an alphabetical list by department.

You can replace the original department entries with the converted entries. First, use the /Range Value command to freeze the converted entries. Next, use /Copy to replace the original entries with the converted entries. Finally, /Range Erase to remove the extra entries. The description for @UPPER contains a complete explanation.

@PROPER

The @PROPER function converts a string to propercase. In propercase, the first letter in each word of the string is an uppercase letter and the other letters are in lowercase. Numbers within the string are not affected by the conversion.

The format for the function is @PROPER(string). The **string** is a set of characters enclosed in quotation marks or a reference to a cell that contains the string. As with @UPPER, you may want to replace the original strings with the converted entries.

Example

You can use @PROPER to convert names to propercase. Type the formula **@PROPER(A3)** in F3 of Figure 7.4 to convert DONALD Tripp to Donald Tripp. F3 displays the proper entry. After copying this formula for all names, all the names are propercase. You can sort the worksheet to produce an alphabetical list of names. Unfortunately, the alphabetical sequence will be by first name since the first name is first in each of the cells. Later in the chapter, you will use other string functions to reverse the order of string entries.

Figure 7.4 Using @PROPER to convert names into initial uppercase

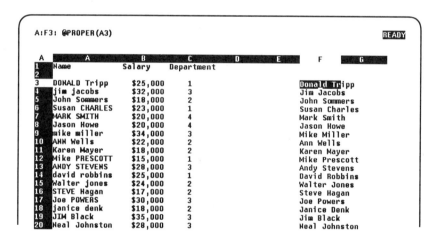

EXTRACTING A PORTION OF A STRING ENTRY

1–2–3 provides several functions that allow you to extract part of a string. You can choose to extract characters from the right, left, or middle of the string. These functions let you extract a warehouse location from a part number that contains the warehouse information, a last name from a full name entry, or the type of customer from the account number.

@RIGHT

The @RIGHT function extracts a specified number of characters from the right of a string. 1–2–3 returns the extracted characters as the result of the function. If the extracted characters are numeric digits, 1–2–3 stores them as a label. @RIGHT expects a string or a reference to a string as an argument.

The format for the function is @RIGHT(string,n). The **string** is a string enclosed in parentheses or a reference to the cell containing a string. The **n** is the number of characters that 1–2–3 extracts from the string.

Example

The model in Figure 7.5 uses @RIGHT to extract the building code from course number entries. In this example, the course entries consist of a course number, time, and description. The course numbers contain the department, number of the course within the department, room number, and building code. This information is combined in one cell. The combination entry makes it difficult to identify the building.

Figure 7.5
Course listing

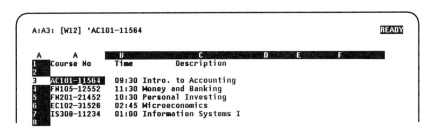

You can separate the building from the course number and place the building code in column D. To extract the building, type @RIGHT(A3,2) in D3. This formula extracts the first two characters from the right of A3 and places them in D3. After copying the formula for all courses, the display matches Figure 7.6. The worksheet shows the building location for each course in a separate cell.

Figure 7.6 Using
@RIGHT to list
building of courses

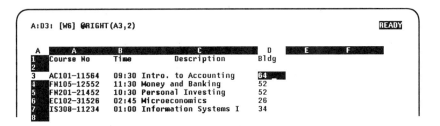

Other Applications

If you are willing to invest some time, you can combine string functions to produce some sophisticated operations with the string functions. If you have a worksheet that contains name entries listed in the order of first name, middle initial, and last name and need to change these to last name first to sort them, the string functions can handle the task.

Be prepared for a little trial-and-error since it is easy to specify the combination of functions incorrectly. Following the example will help you get the major steps correct. When you add a little fine-tuning, your conversions will work smoothly.

Using the name entries in column A of Figure 7.7, you can enter this formula to convert the entries to the new format shown in column B. One method for obtaining the last name is the first part of the formula:

@RIGHT(A2,@LENGTH(A2)−@FIND(" ",A2,0)−4)

The entry &", " appends a comma (,) and a space to the last name. You can append the first name and middle initial with the remaining entry:

&@LEFT(A2,@FIND(" ",A2,0)+3)

All of the required functions are covered in detail within this chapter.

Figure 7.7
Combining string functions to reverse names

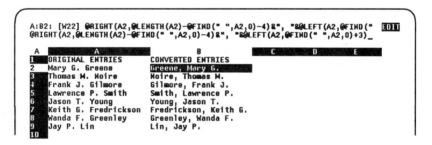

As your function formulas become more complex, it can be difficult to remember all the logic behind your entries. You can annotate any formula, however, if you have Release 3. After the last character in the formula, enter a semicolon (;). Next, type your explanation or comments. You can use as many characters as you need as long as the total cell entry (including the formula) does not exceed 512 characters. Another option available with Release 3 is the addition of notes to range names. After naming any cell or range, use /Range Name Note Create and enter your note. You can also use /Range Name Note Table to view all the notes attached to ranges in your worksheet.

@LEFT

The @LEFT function extracts a specified number of characters from the left side of a string. 1-2-3 stores the extracted characters in a cell. @LEFT expects a string or a reference to a string as an argument.

The format for the function is @LEFT(string,n). The **string** is a string enclosed in parentheses or a reference to a cell containing a string. The **n** is the number of characters that 1-2-3 extracts from the string.

Example

The model in Figure 7.8 uses the @LEFT function to extract the department number from the course number. The entries for each course are the course number, description, time, and location. To extract the department from the course number, type the formula @LEFT(A3,4) into E3. This formula extracts the first four characters from the left side of the string. 1-2-3 places these characters in E3. After copying this formula for all courses, the display matches Figure 7.9.

Figure 7.8
Different course
listing

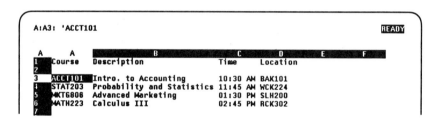

Figure 7.9
Using @LEFT to
list department
offering course

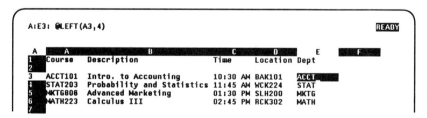

Other Applications

Once you extract part of a string with the @LEFT function, you can combine the output with other functions. For example, once you extract the department, you can use the @VLOOKUP function described in Chapter 8 to supply the department chairman for each department. Figure 7.10 shows the result of the @VLOOKUP function. Each chairperson entry is created with @VLOOKUP.

Figure 7.10
Combining
@VLOOKUP and
@LEFT to list
department
chairmen for
courses

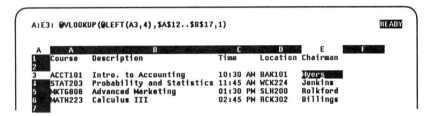

The entries in A12..B17 contain department numbers in the first column and the chairperson's name in the second column. Since @LEFT returns a string, the department numbers must be entered in the table as labels. This offers another advantage since @VLOOKUP finds exact matches with string entries. All the string entries can be in random order in column A, whereas value entries would require an ascending order since the match is not an exact one. A few entries in A12..B17 might be

| MKTG | Rolkford |
| STAT | Horne |

@MID

The @MID function extracts a specified number of characters from the middle of a string. You can specify the starting position and the number of characters needed. 1–2–3 returns extracted characters as the function result. @MID expects a string or a reference to a string as an argument.

The format for the function is @MID(string,start number,n). The **string** is a string enclosed in quotation marks or a reference to a cell containing a string. The **start number** is the position in the string where 1–2–3 begins the extraction. Since the zero- base method discussed earlier in the chapter is used for the start number, the first position in the string is in position zero. The **n** is the number of characters that 1–2–3 will extract from the string.

Example

Earlier examples showed the use of @RIGHT to extract the building from the course number. You cannot extract the room number with this method. @RIGHT and @LEFT cannot handle the task since the room number is not at the left or right side of the string. Figure 7.11 shows the use of the @MID function to extract the room number from the string. To separate the room number from the course number and place it in column E, type **@MID(A3,6,3)** in E3. This formula begins the extraction with the sixth character and extracts three characters. After copying this formula for all courses, the display matches Figure 7.11.

Figure 7.11 Using @MID to list room numbers for courses

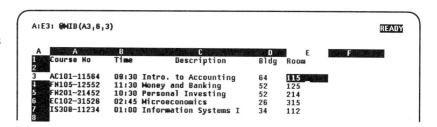

When you extract from entries that vary in length, you need variable starting positions for the @MID function. For example, there can be either three or four characters between the department and the hyphen. This means that the starting point for the @MID function is position 5 or 6. If the building and room numbers are always the last five digits, you can create an @MID function that adjusts for the varying lengths of course numbers. In Figure 7.12, the @MID function adjusts for varying length course numbers. The starting point is dependent on the length of the course number. Since 5 is subtracted from the length, the starting position is the fifth place from the end. The @MID function extracts the characters in the fifth, fourth, and third position from the end of the course number.

Figure 7.12 Using @MID to list room numbers for courses when course number length fluctuates

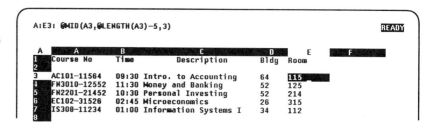

You can create an @MID function that accommodates varying length extract strings and a varying number of characters to extract. The last example showed how to create a @MID function that supported a different number of digits between the department and the hyphen. In each instance, the same number of digits represented the room and the building. If you remove the assumption that the room number is always three digits, you must change the @MID function. The new entry accommodates a varying room number length. In Figure 7.13, the @MID function relies upon the hyphen as a reference point. Since the hyphen always precedes the room number, the formula for its location relies on the assumption that the building number is always two digits. The starting location is one position to the left of the hyphen.

Figure 7.13 Using @MID to list room numbers for courses when course number and room number lengths fluctuate

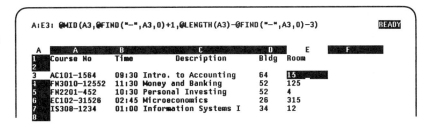

The @FIND function, which is discussed later in the chapter, determines the position of the hyphen. Adding 1 to the hyphen position determines the starting position for the room number. The number of characters extracted from the string is the length of the string less the number of characters from the start of the string to the hyphen less 3. This formula provides for the two-character building code and the position of the hyphen. By combining these functions, you create an @MID function that can adjust for varying string lengths and varying length room numbers.

Determining the Location of a Character

Many of 1-2-3's string functions are more useful when you use variables for their arguments. For example, the last figure and example for the @MID function handled varying length strings and the extraction of a varying number of characters. Many of the situations where an argument's value fluctuates are dependent on the position of a character within the string. The @FIND function provides the position number of a character within a string. @REPLACE is a related function that replaces characters in a string. This function replaces part of an original string with a new string. These two functions can be used alone, together, or in combination with any of 1–2–3's other functions.

@FIND

The @FIND function returns the position number of a specified character in a string. You can use this function alone or in combination with other functions.

The format of the @FIND function is @FIND(search string, string, start number). The **search string** is the character or characters that 1–2–3 attempts to find. If the search string is a single character, 1–2–3 looks for the character within the string. If the search string contains several characters, 1–2–3 attempts to find the group. The search string is a string enclosed in quotes or a reference to the cell containing a string.

The **string** is the string you wish to search, enclosed in quotes, or a reference to a cell which contains the string. The **start number** is the position number within the string where the search begins. Like all 1–2–3 position numbers, you begin the count with zero. If the start number is set to zero, the search starts at the beginning of the string. If you set the start number to something other than zero, 1–2–3 starts at that position. 1–2–3 counts the position number that the function returns from the beginning of the string. Any of these function arguments can be another function such as @LENGTH or another @FIND.

Example

You can use @FIND to check for errors in a column of entries. For example, in Figure 7.14, column D shows the column position of the hyphens in the part numbers in column A. The formula in column D adds 1 to the result of the function. A 3 appears in the appropriate row in column D if the hyphen is in the correct location. After completing this step, you can combine the result with the @IF function discussed in Chapter 3. Figure 7.15 displays the combination formula where a message or a blank replaces the numbers.

Figure 7.14 Using @FIND to list position of hyphen to check for part-number errors

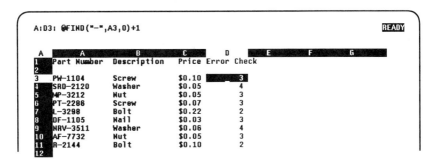

Figure 7.15 Combining @FIND and @IF to display error messages for incorrect part numbers

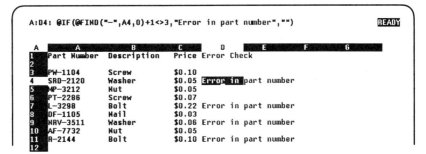

@IF displays an error message if the hyphen is not in position three of the string. The parts with correct entries produce a blank result in column D. The error message resulting from the @IF function draws attention to the part numbers that need attention.

Other Applications

Figure 7.16 displays employee data. Although you can sort this data by first name, you will probably want to sort by last name. To display the names with the last name first, type the last name, comma, and the first name.

Figure 7.16
Combining several
functions to
rearrange names

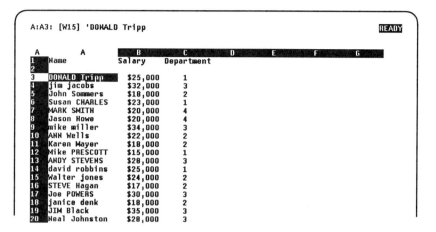

Several steps are required to rearrange the names. First, use @FIND to locate the space that separates the first and last names. Next, use @LENGTH to determine where to split the two parts of the name.

The results of these combined functions are shown in Figure 7.17. @RIGHT extracts the last name. The number of spaces is determined by the length minus the number of spaces before the hyphen and the hyphen itself. The ampersand (&) combines the result from @RIGHT with a comma and a space. Another ampersand joins the first name which @LEFT extracts with the other entries. @LEFT extracts all the characters before the space. After this formula is created, you can copy it for all of the names. You can use the /Range Value command to freeze the function values.

Figure 7.17
Employee data

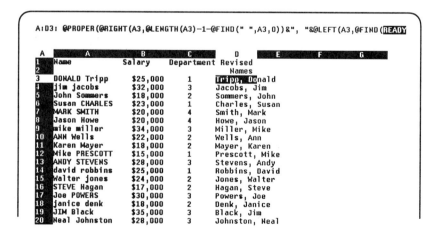

You can nest an @FIND function within an @FIND. You can also use nested @FIND functions to find a second or third occurrence of a character. For example, to find the second hyphen in a string, use the formula shown in Figure 7.18.

Figure 7.18
Finding the second hyphen in a string

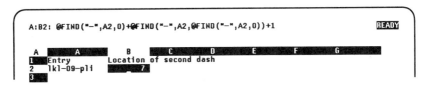

@REPLACE

The @REPLACE function eliminates a portion of the original string and replaces it with a new string. The characters in the replacement string can be a different length than the characters in the original string.

The format of the @REPLACE function is @REPLACE(original string, start number,n,new string). The **original string** is the string that the function operates on enclosed in quotes or a reference to a cell containing a string. The **start number** is the position number which is the beginning position in the original string. The **position number** is an actual number or a function such as @FIND, which produces a position number. 1-2-3 begins counting from the left with zero. The **n** is the number of characters that you want removed from the original string. If n equals zero, 1-2-3 does not remove characters. 1-2-3 inserts the replacement string at the start number. The **new string** is the string 1-2-3 inserts at the start number. You can use the @FIND function with the @REPLACE function to determine the position of the text to be replaced.

Example

You can use @REPLACE to replace or insert characters in a string. The form generated in Figure 7.19 uses @REPLACE to replace part of a string. Simply enter the relevant information next to each request. For example, you might enter $1,000,000 next to the year's gross sales in D92. Once you enter this information, 1-2-3 converts it into an income statement.

Figure 7.19 Using
@REPLACE to create
a customized
income statement

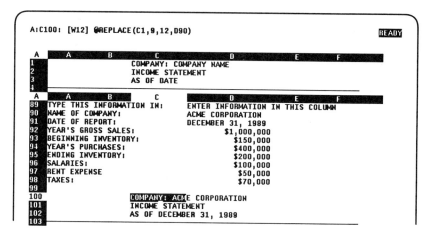

You can also use the @REPLACE function for the company name and date. For the company name, @REPLACE begins at position 9 in the string in C1, removes the next twelve characters, and replaces them with the company name that you type in D90. For the date, @REPLACE begins at position 6 in the string in C3, removes four characters, and inserts the string in D91. This worksheet is set up so that you can protect the formulas; you need only enter the data that the income statement requires.

Other Applications

You can use @REPLACE to insert characters without removing any characters. For example, if you set n (the number of characters to be removed) to zero, @REPLACE acts as an insert function. Figure 7.20 shows part numbers entered in the improper format. Since all of the part numbers need a hyphen between the letters and the numbers, @REPLACE placed in cell B3 uses the entry in A3 and inserts a hyphen without removing characters. If you copy this formula for all part numbers, you will change all the part numbers.

Figure 7.20
Incorrect part-
number format

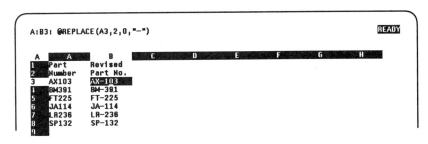

@LENGTH

The @LENGTH function provides the length of a character string. Although you can use this function by itself, its greatest utility is in combination with other functions, such as @MID.

The format of the @LENGTH function is @LENGTH(string). The **string** is either a string enclosed in quotes or a reference to a string.

Example

You can use @LENGTH to determine the number of parts ordered if you have a listing of those parts. Column A in Figure 7.21 lists the parts ordered with each part entry consisting of a single letter. Column B contains @LENGTH, which determines the number of parts ordered and the length of each string. Once you determine the length of the string, you can divide by two to remove the effect of the comma. Since the item count is one greater than the number of commas, the result ends in a .5. You can calculate the number of parts ordered by rounding the result or adding one to the resulting number and using the integer portion.

Figure 7.21
Using @LENGTH to
determine number
of items ordered

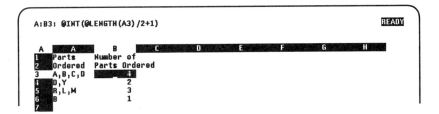

Other Applications

You can use @LENGTH as an argument for other functions. For example, knowing the length of a string can help you determine how many characters to extract in combination functions.

@REPEAT

The @REPEAT function creates a string of characters from an initial string and repeats the initial string a number of times. Unlike the backslash, which only makes a string as wide as the column, @REPEAT can exceed the column width and borrow display space from adjacent cells. This function is often used for creating lines within a worksheet. The string this function creates can be used with other string functions and the ampersand to build longer strings.

The format of the @REPEAT function is @REPEAT(string,n). The **string** is a string enclosed in quotation marks or a reference to a cell that contains a string. The **n** is the number of times that you want 1-2-3 to repeat the string.

Example

Figure 7.22 displays an example of a line created with @REPEAT. In this example, 1-2-3 repeats the dash eighty times.

Figure 7.22 Using @REPEAT to create lines in the worksheet

```
A:A3: [W15] @REPEAT("-",80)                                    READY

A          A              B                C            D         E           F
1    Employee            Date of          SS#        Dept Anniversary
2                        Hire                                   Month
3
4    Jim Jacobs          01-Dec-84    234-43-3747    BUDG        12
5    Ann Howell          12-Apr-78    176-68-9092    ACCT         4
6    Susan Beyer         28-Feb-80    276-96-4548    ACCT         2
7    Mark Horvath        10-Nov-87    275-50-3824    BUDG        11
8    Dennis Carver       21-Sep-76    186-45-2143    PROD         9
9    Janice Sauer        03-Jan-84    145-38-9361    ENGR         1
10   David Townsend      14-Dec-82    225-84-2120    ENGR        12
11   Thomas Werner       22-Jun-84    190-83-9897    ACCT         6
12
```

Other Applications

You can use @REPEAT for tasks that a backslash cannot handle. For example, to insert twenty asterisks into the text, type

"YOUR TEXT"&@REPEAT(*,20)&"SECOND PART OF YOUR TEXT"

You can use @REPEAT to repeat a word across the worksheet. For example, to have "CALL BACK" appear eight times in your worksheet, type @REPEAT("CALL BACK ",8) The entire entry is stored in one worksheet cell, but the long string entry borrows space from empty cells to the right.

@EXACT

1–2–3 provides several comparison functions. As discussed in Chapter 3, @IF can combine two numbers or strings to determine if they are equal. If you are working with characters, you can use @EXACT to compare two strings. @EXACT returns a 1 if the strings are exactly alike and returns a 0 if the strings are not exactly alike.

Because the @EXACT function is case-sensitive, the entry @EXACT ("JOHN","john") returns a 0. The @EXACT function can be combined with @UPPER and @LOWER if you want to compare two strings and disregard case differences. If you do not want the comparison to be case-sensitive, you can also use @IF because @IF("ABC"="abc", "EQUAL","NOT EQUAL") returns EQUAL since @IF ignores case differences. Comparison features are useful for error checking. The @EXACT function flags minute differences that you could overlook easily with a visual examination.

The format for the function is @EXACT(string1,string2). Both **string1** and **string2** are strings enclosed in quotes or references to cells containing strings.

Example

Figure 7.23 uses @EXACT to compare the item ordered with the item received. In rows 3 and 5, the two strings do not match. In the first case, the first entry is missing a space between the 0 and the 3. In the second case, B5 has a V after the J and C5 has a X after the J. You can enhance this example by putting @EXACT inside an @IF function.

Figure 7.23 Using @EXACT to compare items ordered and items received

```
A:D2: [W11] @EXACT(B2,C2)                                    READY

  A         A          B            C          D        E      F
1  P.O. Number  Item Ordered  Item Received  Same Item
2  T1903        AZ 192 37     AZ 192 37              1
3  R1705        BA 19037      BA 190 37              0
4  T1904        TR 170 52     TR 170 52              1
5  R1704        JV 142 99     JX 142 99              0
6  T1902        RY 111 98     RY 111 98              1
7  Z1194        ZB 094 51     ZB 094 51              1
8
```

In Figure 7.24, the error-checking formula is different. In this example, an error message is displayed for numbers that do not match. This is an example of the use of the @EXACT function in combination with @IF for error checking.

Figure 7.24
Combining @EXACT
and @IF to display
error messages for
different parts
ordered and
received

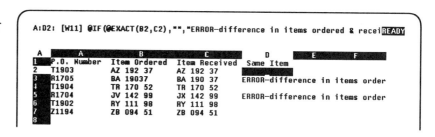

Removing Unwanted Characters

The @CLEAN and the @TRIM functions remove unwanted characters. @CLEAN removes unprintable ASCII/LICS characters from a string in Releases 2.0 and 2.01; @TRIM removes the leading and trailing blanks from a string in Release 2.0 and later releases.

@CLEAN

Cells sometimes contain non-printable ASCII codes. This often occurs when you import the data from another source. Some of these codes disrupt the printing of your worksheet. The @CLEAN function strips away all non-printable characters from a cell. This function is primarily for Release 2 to remove characters that Release 2 cannot print.

The format of this function is @CLEAN(string). The **string** is either a string enclosed in quotes or a reference to a cell containing a string.

Example

Figure 7.25 shows a Release 2.01 screen that contains some cells with unprintable characters. Even though you do not see them, the characters are there and take up space. For example, cell B2 contains the ASCII characters 10, 20, and 30 preceding the ABC. In this example, the first three characters affect the operation of the printer when you print this data. When you use @CLEAN in cell B4, 1–2–3 removes the first three characters. By replacing the range value of B1 with B4, the unprintable characters are eliminated.

Figure 7.25 Using
@CLEAN to remove
unprintable ASCII
characters

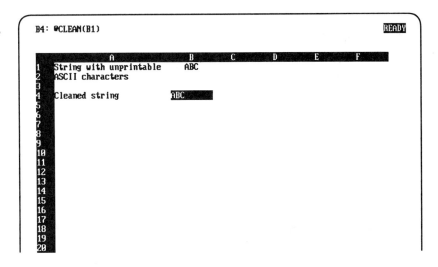

@TRIM

The @TRIM function removes the leading and trailing blanks from a string. @TRIM also removes the extra spaces from within a string.

The format of the @TRIM function is @TRIM(string). The **string** is a character string in quotes or a reference to a cell containing a string.

Example

Figure 7.26 contains a worksheet using @TRIM. In this example, the first names and the last names are in different columns with both sets of entries containing extra spaces. Column C combines the two entries using the ampersand (&). @TRIM eliminates the excess spaces at the beginning and the end of the first and last names.

Figure 7.26 Using
@TRIM to remove
leading and trailing
blanks

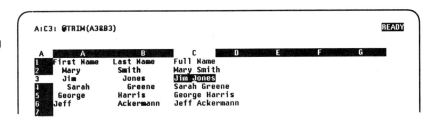

Avoiding Errors

An error may result if you reference a cell that contains a different type of entry than 1–2–3 expects. For example, attempting to use a value in place of a label or the reverse causes a problem for 1–2–3. Labels cannot be used in arithmetic computations and values cannot be joined with an ampersand or be used in string functions. 1–2–3 provides two special string functions that can help prevent these problems.

@S

The @S function lets you display the same text in more than one location. One use of this function could be displaying the top item in a sorted list in another location. @S will return the value in the upper-left corner of a range. @S is useful for error prevention because it prevents errors that would otherwise result from the use of the wrong type of data.

The format of this function is @S(range). The **range** is a range address or a range name. Although you can use this function with one cell, the cell reference must be in a range format in Release 2. To reference D3, type **D3..D3** rather than D3. Another way to specify one cell as the beginning and ending of the range is to use an exclamation point before the cell reference as in !A1. Releases 2.01, 2.2, and 3 automatically convert single cell references to range addresses. If the upper-left corner of the range contains a numeric value or is blank, @S returns a blank string. The null string is another name for this blank string.

Example

You can use @S to pick out the first value in a sorted range. You might want to sort a worksheet containing listings of sales personnel. If you sort by total sales, your list will show the top salesperson first, as in Figure 7.27. To emphasize the sales generated by the best salesperson, add several lines and use the @S function to display the best salesperson. The @S function in cell D13 refers to the entire range of the sales personnel and their sales. Because @S returns the first cell in the range, it displays the top salesperson in D13.

Figure 7.27 Using @S to display top salesperson

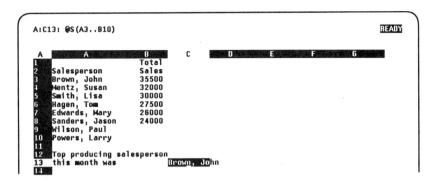

Other Applications

You can use this function to prevent calculations returning an error message. @S converts cells that contain numeric values to blank strings. If you process this data further, the problem of incorrect data type is eliminated before you use string manipulation functions.

@N

You may need to retrieve a value from your worksheet while in the middle of a macro or another function. The @N function retrieves the numeric value from the upper-left corner of a range. This function prevents errors from occurring in calculations by changing strings to zeros.

The format of this function is @N(range). The **range** is a range address or a range name. This function works on one cell but requires you to express the single cell reference as a range in Release 2 or 2.01. (In Release 2.2 or 3, 1-2-3 automatically converts a single cell address to a range address.) Therefore, to reference only one cell, use that cell as the beginning and ending of the range. Only the upper-left cell will be used if you reference a group of cells.

Example

You can use @N to select the first value in a sorted range, such as a worksheet containing the names of sales personnel, their sales, and commissions. After sorting by commission, the sales person earning the highest commission is listed first as shown in Figure 7.28. To emphasize the commission earned by the best salesperson, you can add the Highest Commission Earned line at the bottom and use @N to display the highest commission. @N in cell D12 uses the entire range of commissions. The function displays the top commission in the range since it references the upper left cell in the range.

Figure 7.28 Using
@N to display top
commission earned

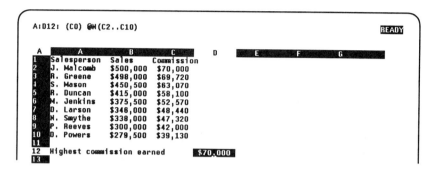

Other Applications

@N can prevent your formulas from returning an error message. You can also use @N to avoid referencing cells in an arithmetic formula that contain a string. @N converts cell references that contain a string to a zero.

Converting Data

1-2-3 lets you change values and strings. (Strings and values are not interchangeable.) Use @STRING to change a value into a string. Use @VALUE to convert a number stored as a string to a value.

@STRING

The @STRING function converts a value entry into a string. Once the value is converted, you can combine it with text. You can also use @STRING with the ampersand (&) to join values and labels.

The format of the @STRING function is @STRING(x,n). The **x** is a value or a cell reference to a value. The **n** is the number of digits that you want to display after the decimal point.

Example

Figure 7.29 provides an example of the @STRING function. In this figure, a formula combines the warehouse number and the bin number to create a part number. Since the column A entries are strings and the column B entries are labels, +A3&B3 would produce an error. The entries in column B must be converted to strings. The use of 0 as the second argument in the @STRING function eliminates decimal digits in the converted entry.

Figure 7.29
Using @STRING to combine text and a value

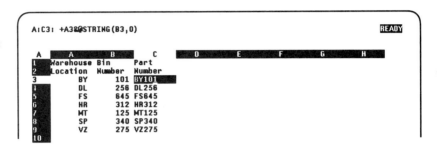

@VALUE

The @VALUE function converts a label entry containing numeric characters to a value. Once you convert the data, you can perform mathematical calculations with the result. You can use this function with other functions such as @LEFT and @RIGHT to convert numbers extracted from strings to values.

The format of the @VALUE function is @VALUE(string). The **string** is either a string encased in quotation marks or a reference to a cell containing a string. The string must contain numeric characters stored as a label. This means that @VALUE(''ABC'') is invalid. @VALUE (''123'') is valid and returns 123.

Example

If you enter numbers as labels in your worksheet and want to change them to values, @VALUE solves the problem. If you press the Space Bar before typing a number, the number is entered as a label. If you type numbers as labels to use the alignment features of labels, your entry is a label. Figure 7.30 shows an example of the latter type of entry. In this example, a caret (^) precedes the quantity to center the entry. However, to compute the total cost, you need to multiply the unit price times the quantity. The formula in cell D3 of Figure 7.30 shows the value of B3 multiplied by the converted value of the string in C3. You can compute the total price after copying this formula for all items.

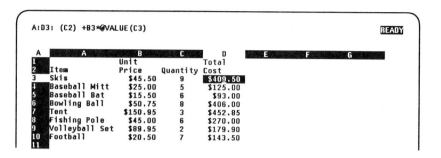

Figure 7.30 Using @VALUE to convert a number before calculating the final cost

Working with the LICS/LMBCS Codes

1-2-3 lets you use special characters beyond those shown on the keyboard. These symbols include foreign language characters, graphic symbols, and mathematics symbols. With Release 2, you can use any of the symbols in the Lotus International Character Set (LICS). With Release 3, Lotus still recognizes special characters but uses the LMBCS codes. Both sets of codes are found in Appendix B. For characters with LICS or LMBCS numbers less than 128, the numbers are the same as the ASCII character set.

The LICS/LMBCS codes use different numbers for some characters than the ASCII set. ASCII numbers greater than 127 will vary in appearance from printer to printer. The LICS/LMBCS codes print the way they appear on the screen. You can create the LICS/LMBCS characters by pressing Alt-F1 and then typing the two letter combinations that will create the character that you want. The character sequences that you need to create these characters are in Appendix B.

@CHAR

While you can create a LICS/LMBCS character from anywhere in your worksheet, a macro does not have an equivalent for Alt-F1. To create a LICS/LMBCS character within a macro, use the @CHAR function.

The format of this function is @CHAR(x). The **x** represents the number of the character that you want. You can determine the number of the character by looking at the table in Appendix B.

Example

Figure 7.31 shows the different LICS characters for code entries. The formula in B1 shows the @CHAR function, which creates the LICS/LMBCS character with the value of 145. You can create the rest of the characters in the figure with different code numbers.

Figure 7.31 Using @CHAR to display the ASCII/LICS characters for different numbers

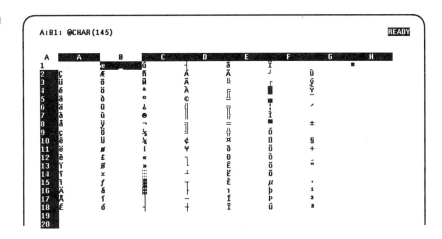

@CODE

The @CODE function provides the ASCII/LICS/LMBCS code for the first letter in a string. The format for the @CODE function is @CODE (string). The **string** is a string enclosed in quotes or a cell reference to a string. This function will accept numbers only when they are enclosed in double quotes or when the function refers to a cell containing a number stored as a label.

Example

Figure 7.32 shows the ASCII/LICS/LMBCS codes for many characters. The formula in each cell has an @CODE function that contains a character within quotes for an argument.

Figure 7.32 Using @CODE to display the ASCII/LICS codes for different characters

```
A:A1: @CODE("@")                                                    READY
```

A	A	B	C	D	E	F	G	H
1	64	56	70	45	102	32		
2	33	57	71	61	103	135		
3	35	81	72	113	104	150		
4	36	87	74	119	106	136		
5	94	69	75	101	107	163		
6	38	82	76	114	108	144		
7	42	84	58	116	59	155		
8	40	89	90	121	39	159		
9	41	85	88	117	122	156		
10	95	73	67	105	120	190		
11	43	79	86	111	99	383		
12	49	80	66	112	118	143		
13	50	123	78	91	98			
14	51	125	77	93	110			
15	52	124	60	92	109			
16	53	65	62	97	44			
17	54	83	63	115	46			
18	55	68	70	100	47			
19								
20								

8

Special Functions

1-2-3's special functions provide some of the most sophisticated function capabilities in the package. There are four distinct groups of functions within this category: table lookup features, cell and range data, error trapping features, and system information.

APPLICATIONS FOR THE SPECIAL FUNCTIONS

The special functions provide even more flexibility than a two-option IF function, creating formulas that look up values in tables. Four different functions provide a variety of options for accessing table data.

Another group of functions within this category adds error trapping capabilities to your models so that you can place special values like ERR and NA in cells to inform you of errors or missing data.

The largest group of special functions provides cell and range information. You can use this group of functions in macros to assist with decisionmaking in other macro commands. These functions are also used for adding logic to your models by creating steps in formulas or macros that let current values determine the next step or value used.

The last type of function is single purpose. It provides information about the current system settings and is available only to Release 3 users. Although only one function, the many possible variations make it seem like many more.

Functions That Provide Cell and Range Information

As noted above, this is the largest group of special functions. Although you will find frequent use for these functions in macros, you can use them to examine a large worksheet or to add flexibility to your models. Two new functions, the @COORD and @SHEETS functions, were added to this group for Release 3.

@@   The @@ function provides the value of a cell referred to by the function's argument. The @@ function uses indirect addressing. Thus, rather than referring to the value of the function's argument, the @@ function assumes that the argument is a cell address containing another cell address the value of which the @@ function returns. This function is normally used as an argument for another function.

The format of the @@ function is @@(cell address). The **cell address** is either a cell address preceded by a label prefix, a range name assigned to a cell, or a string formula that produces a cell address or name. An example of the first one is ^A1. An example of the second type of cell address is START, where start has been predefined to refer to cell A1. An example of the last type of cell address is +''A''&''1''.

Example

Figure 8.1 shows an example of the @@ function. In this example, the @@ function is an argument to the @PMT function described in Chapter 6. The @@ function uses the value of the cell referred to in cell A12. It is the value of cell B10, which is 10 percent. You can use the @@ function instead of typing the 10 percent directly into the formula. This approach allows you to change the percentage used in the @PMT computation. To make the change, you can alter the cell address in A12. For example, to change the percentage used in the @PMT function to 12 percent, move the highlight to A12 and type D10. All of the formulas change to use 12 percent as the new percentage in computing the yearly payment.

Figure 8.1 @@
used with @PMT

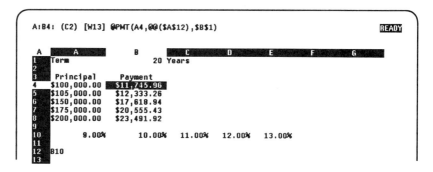

Other Applications

You can use the @@ function to generate a cash flow analysis. Figure 8.2 shows an example of the @@ function used for this purpose. In the highlighted cell, the @@ function's argument is a string formula that joins B12 with a 2. The @@ function uses the value of the cell address generated by the string formula. Each of the cells in the cash formula analysis combines the letter of the assumption with the proper row number to generate the value for that line of the cash analysis. To change the entire series of assumptions, change the letter in cell B12. To create additional assumptions, type in the appropriate numbers in another column, such as F, and change the value of B12 to your new column of assumptions. You can use the @@ function whenever you want to change the numbers on which your formulas are based.

Figure 8.2 @@
used in a cash flow
analysis

```
A:B15: (,0)  -@@($B$12&"2")                                          READY

A              A                    B         C         D         E
1   Four Assumptions                B         C         D         E
2   Building Price               25000     30000     26000     30000
3   Interest                     9.00%     11.00%    10.50%    10.00%
4   Years of Loan Payments           4         5       3.5         7
5   Years the Building is Used      10        11         7        12
6   Yearly Payment                7717      8117      9256      6162
7   Yearly Depreciation           5000      6000      5200      6000
8   Tax Rate                       40%       40%       40%       40%
9   Yearly Cash Inflows        $20,000   $16,000   $22,000   $25,000
10
11  Cash flow analysis
12  Assumption Used                  B
13  Year                             1         2         3         4
14
15  Building Price             (25,000)
16  Depreciation tax shield      5,000     4,000     3,200     2,560
17  Yearly Cash Inflows         20,000    20,000    20,000    20,000
18  Loan Payments               (7,717)   (7,717)   (7,717)   (7,717)
19  Total                       (7,717)   16,283    15,483    14,843
20  Total Present value         29,097
```

Looking at Various Cell Attributes

Two of 1–2–3's functions that look at cell information allow you to provide specific instructions concerning the information you want to examine. An attribute argument is provided to these functions to inform 1–2–3 of your information needs.

Although both functions use the same attribute arguments, there is a distinct difference in the two functions. With the @CELLPOINTER function, the referenced cell is always the current cell, which is the cell the highlight is on. With the @CELL function, a second argument lets you to specify a cell address. The attributes that you can check are found in Table 8.1. The table entries discuss the value that the function returns to you for each of the attribute options.

TABLE 8.1: ATTRIBUTE ARGUMENTS FOR THE @CELL AND @CELLPOINTER FUNCTIONS

Address	Provides the absolute cell address for the referenced cell. The cell row and column are preceded by dollar signs.
Col	Provides the column number of the referenced cell. The column is designated by numbers rather than letters, with the numbers 1 through 26 representing the letters A through Z, the numbers 27 through 52 representing the letters AA through AZ, and so forth.
Contents	Returns the referenced cell's contents.
Coord	In Release 3, returns the full address with the worksheet letter, a colon, column letter, and row number.
Filename	In Releases 2.2 and 3, returns the name of the file that contains the cell.
Format	Returns letters or numbers to represent how the referenced cell is formatted. The symbols used for showing different formats are:
	F0 to F15 if the format is fixed with the number representing the number of decimal places.

(Continued)

TABLE 8.1: Continued

S0 to S15 if the format is scientific with the number representing the number of decimal places.

C0 to C15 if the format is currency with the number representing the number of decimal places.

,0 to ,15 if the format is comma with the number representing the number of decimal places.

G if the format is general, or if the cell is blank or contains a label.

P0 to P15 if the format is percent with the number representing the number of decimal places.

+ if the format is set to +/− for horizontal bar graph format.

D1 if the referenced cell is a date set to the DD-MMM-YY format.

D2 if the referenced cell is a date set to the DD-MMM format.

D3 if the referenced cell is a date set to the MMM-YY format.

D4 if the referenced cell is a date set to the MM/DD/YY, DD/MM/YY, DD.MM.YY or YY-MM-DD format.

D5 if the referenced cell is a date set to the MM/DD, DD/MM, DD.MM or MM-DD format.

D6 if the referenced cell is a time set to the HH:MM:SS AM/PM format.

D7 if the referenced cell is set to the HH:MM AM/PM format.

D8 if the referenced cell is a time set to the HH:MM:SS 24hr, HH.MM.SS 24hr, HH,MM,SS 24hr, or HHhMMmSSs format.

(Continued)

TABLE 8.1: Continued

	D9 if the referenced cell is a time set to the HH:MM 24hr, HH.MM 24hr, HH,MM 24hr, or HHhMMm format.
	T if the referenced cell is in the text format.
	H if the referenced cell is in the hidden format.
	L if the referenced cell is in the label format in Release 3.
	A if the referenced cell is in the automatic format in Release 3.
	( ) if the referenced cell is formatted for parentheses in Release 3.
	− if the referenced cell is formatted for color in Release 3.
Prefix	Returns an apostrophe (') if the referenced cell has a left-aligned label; a double quote ('') if the referenced cell contains a right-aligned label; a caret (^) if the referenced cell contains a centered label; a number, a formula, and a \ if the cell contains a repeating label; a | if the cell contains a non-printing label; or a blank if the referenced cell is blank or contains a number or a formula.
Protect	Returns 1 if the referenced cell is protected and 0 if it is not.
Row	Provides the row number of the referenced cell.
Sheet	In Release 3, returns the worksheet letter as a value. Worksheet A is a 1 and worksheet IV returns 256.
Type	Returns a b if the referenced cell is blank, a v if the referenced cell contains a value, or an l if the referenced cell contains a label.
Width	Returns the width of the referenced cell's column.

@CELLPOINTER   The @CELLPOINTER function returns a value representing a specified attribute of the current cell. (The current cell is the cell where the highlight appears.)

The format of the @CELLPOINTER function is @CELLPOINTER ("attribute"). The **attribute** is one of the words like Format and Prefix described in Table 8.1 and must be enclosed in quotation marks or in a cell referenced by the function. You can use either uppercase or lowercase for the attributes.

You can use @CELLPOINTER as part of a macro to check a current cell's attributes. You can store an attribute to be used later in the macro.

Example

Figure 8.3 shows an example of the @CELLPOINTER function that obtains the format of the current cell each time you press F9 (Calc). For example, if you move the highlight to B7 which displays 1,200, and press F9, the value in E10 changes to ,0. This tells you that the format used for cell B7 is comma with zero decimal places. If you move the highlight to the 10.50% in cell B5 and press F9, E10 displays P2. The result indicates that the format of the current cell is percent with two digits after the decimal point.

Figure 8.3
@CELLPOINTER
used to display the
current cell format

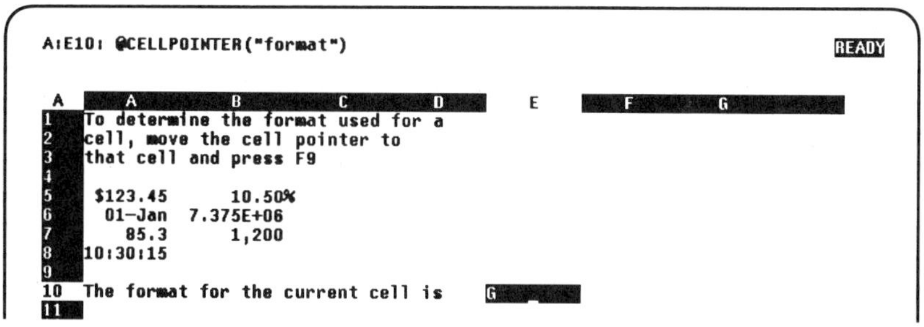

Other Applications

@CELLPOINTER is primarily used in macros. It can be combined with @IF to test for conditions. For example, you might want to check if the current cell is blank. You can then use this information to determine which of two steps to perform. The combined function entry is

@IF(@CELLPOINTER("TYPE") = "b",STEP1,STEP2)

In this example, **STEP1** represents the condition for the cell if the current cell is blank. **STEP2** represents the condition that is used when the current cell is not blank.

@CELL

The @CELL function returns a value representing a specified attribute of a cell. The format of the @CELL function is @CELL("attribute", range). The **attribute** is one of the words like Format and Prefix in Table 8.1. You can use any of the attribute values that work with @CELLPOINTER. The attribute must be enclosed in quotation marks or in a cell referenced by the function. The range is a single-cell or multi-cell range. If it is a multi-cell range, the @CELL function determines the specified attribute of the cell in the upper-left corner. In Releases 2 and 2.01, a single cell must be expressed as a range address rather than a cell address. (Releases 2.2 and 3 automatically convert a single cell address to a range address.) You can make this change by specifying the single cell with the same beginning and ending points for the range as in A1..A1. Another option is putting an exclamation point before the single cell address as in !A1.

The @CELL function is often used in macros to check a cell's attributes or to store an attribute to be used later in the macro.

Example

Figure 8.4 shows an example of the @CELL function in several cells. These functions display different attributes of the specified cell. The entries in column B show the different attribute values, and the entries in column D show the formulas used in column B.

Figure 8.4 @CELL
used to look at
several attributes
of a specific cell

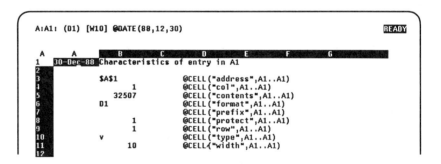

Other Applications

@CELL is primarily used in macros and other functions. For example, you can combine it with the @IF to test for conditions. To check if a cell is blank and establish one of two values depending on the result, type

@IF(@CELL("TYPE",A3) = "b",STEP1,STEP2)

Since @CELL("TYPE",A3) is equal to b if A3 is blank, **STEP1** represents the formula computed if A3 is blank, and **STEP2** represents the formula that is computed when A3 is not blank. The function is also used in worksheets as part of the header or footer in a Release 2.2 or 3.0 worksheet, or as part of the print range. To include the filename, enter a formula like this in a cell:

+"Filename: "&@CELL("Filename",A1..A1)

The range the function references is irrelevant as long as it does not include the cell with the formula. When a worksheet range is printed that includes this formula in the range or in the header or footer, it will include the worksheet filename on the printed output.

Other Cell and Range Functions

1-2-3 provides additional functions that work with cell and range attributes. The @ROWS and @COLS functions are available in Release 2 and above. Release 3 includes the @SHEETS and @COORD functions.

The @ROWS, @COLS, and @SHEETS functions are especially useful with range names. 1-2-3's ranges names are used within commands and formulas to describe areas of your worksheet. Naming ranges makes it easier to understand the effect of commands and formulas. The use of range names provides a logical connection between the command or formula and the area of the worksheet affected. Although names can be easier to remember than a range address, you cannot tell by the range name how many rows, column, or worksheets are included.

@ROWS

The @ROWS function determines the number of rows in a range. @ROWS is available only in Release 2.0 or higher.

The format of the @ROWS function is @ROWS(range). The **range** is a range or range name that the function uses to count the number of rows.

Example

@ROWS counts the number of items in a range if each item is on a separate line. In Figure 8.5, the deliveries are kept in the range DELIVERY__INFO. To determine the total number of deliveries, cell C13 uses @ROWS to count the number of rows in the DELIVERY__INFO range. As more items are added to the range, the @ROWS function keeps track of the number of deliveries.

Figure 8.5 @ROWS used to obtain the total deliveries

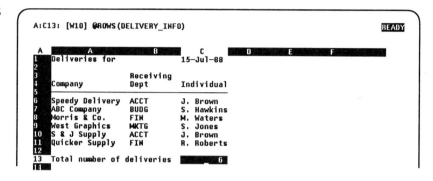

A:C13: [W10] @ROWS(DELIVERY_INFO)   READY

```
     A          A            B          C          D      E       F
1       Deliveries for                 15-Jul-88
2
3                           Receiving
4       Company             Dept       Individual
5
6       Speedy Delivery     ACCT       J. Brown
7       ABC Company         BUDG       S. Hawkins
8       Morris & Co.        FIN        M. Waters
9       West Graphics       MKTG       S. Jones
10      S & J Supply        ACCT       J. Brown
11      Quicker Supply      FIN        R. Roberts
12
13      Total number of deliveries            6
14
```

Other Applications

@ROWS is also used in macros. For example, if your macro performs several steps on the data in a row before moving to the next row, you can use the @ROWS function as a counter to perform the steps for an entire group of lines.

@COLS

The @COLS function determines the number of columns in a range. It is available only in Release 2.0 or higher.

The format of the @COLS function is @COLS(range). The **range** is a range or range name that the function uses to count the number of columns.

Example

@COLS counts the number of items in a range if each item is in a separate column. In Figure 8.6, the product line sales are in different columns by product line. To determine the total number of products, cell C15 uses @COLS to count the number of columns used for the different product lines. As more products are added to the range, @COLS keeps track of the number of product lines.

Figure 8.6 @COLS
calculating the
total number of
products

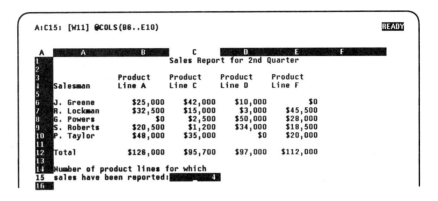

Other Applications

@COLS is also used in macros. For example, if your macro performs several steps a column at a time, you can use @COLS as a counter to perform the steps for an entire group of columns.

@SHEETS

The @SHEETS function determines the number of worksheets in a range. Since only one worksheet is available prior to Release 3, @SHEETS is only available for this release.

The format of the function is @SHEETS(range). The **range** is a range address or name. The function returns the number of sheets in the range.

Example

@SHEETS can tell you how many sheets you have used if you have a range name assigned to these sheets. First look at Figure 8.7 where 1-2-3 is assigning the name ALL to A:A1..C:D4. The /Range Name Create command handles the task. After creating the name, you can determine how many sheets are included with @SHEETS by typing @SHEETS(ALL) in F2. 1-2-3 returns a 3.

Figure 8.7
Assigning a range
name

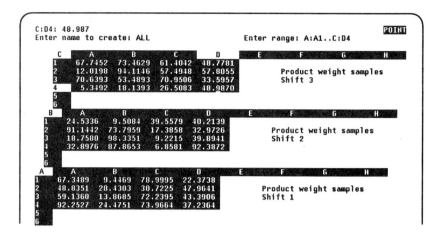

Other Applications

You can use @SHEETS within a macro. For example, you might use it to control the iterations for a specific task. If you use five sheets, you might need to perform a particular task five times.

@COORD

The @COORD function constructs an address from three separate components. The address that you create can be relative, absolute, or mixed. The format of the @COORD function is @COORD(worksheet,column, row,absolute).

The **worksheet** is a value, a range name, or a cell address that refers to a value. Although worksheets are assigned letters from A to IV, the worksheet argument uses the numbers 1 to 256. The number 1 corresponds to worksheet level A, and the number 256 corresponds to worksheet level IV. The **column** is a value, range name, or cell address that reference a value. Like worksheet, any number between 1 and 256 can be used. A 1 represents column A and 256 represents column IV. The **row** is a value, range name, or cell address that references a value. Any number between 1 and 8192 is a valid entry. **Absolute** determines the type of address that is created. It is a value between 1 and 8 or a range name or address that references this value. Table 8.2 shows the effect of absolute on each component of an address.

TABLE 8.2: VALUES FOR THE ABSOLUTE ARGUMENT IN @COORD

Value	Possible Address	Worksheet Address Type	Column Address Type	Row Address Type
1	$B:$A$3	Absolute	Absolute	Absolute
2	$A:F$4	Absolute	Relative	Absolute
3	$C:$F4	Absolute	Absolute	Relative
4	$A:F5	Absolute	Relative	Relative
5	C:$Z$2	Relative	Absolute	Absolute
6	B:G$4	Relative	Relative	Absolute
7	D:$A1	Relative	Absolute	Relative
8	A:A1	Relative	Relative	Relative

Example

You can use @COORD to create an address for the @@ function. Figure 8.8 contains an example that builds a cell address with @COORD. @COORD contains the two @VLOOKUP functions to obtain the correct cell address for the purchase discount. Displaying the result of @COORD allows you to see the cell address of the discount. The @@ function is used to obtain the discount percentage stored in the cell.

Figure 8.8
@COORD used to
create a cell address
for use with @@

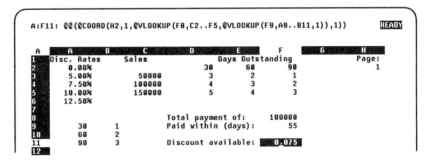

Other Applications

To determine the address based on a condition test, you can use the @IF function to determine which of two worksheets will be used. This determination might be made based on a customer type in F4. You might use a formula that looks like

@COORD(@IF(F4=1,B,A),@VLOOKUP(F6,A9..B13,1),
@VLOOKUP (F5,A16..B20,1),4)

Functions That Work with Tabular Data

Data can be organized into tables so that you can easily find the data you need. Tables come in all sizes; you can have a table that contains entries in a single row or column, or you can also have tables that consist of many rows and columns. In all cases, the entries that comprise tables are in contiguous worksheet cells. It is not possible to have a table that consists of entries in column A and column D with columns B and C unused. If you have entries in columns A and D with no intervening entries, you have two separate tabular arrangements of data, not one.

1–2–3 lets you create tables for various purposes. One purpose for creating a table is to create a lookup table, which lets you look up a value based on one or two criteria. 1–2–3 provides two functions that use lookup tables within formulas and macros.

The other two table functions work differently. Rather than matching worksheet entries, they allow you to specify the location of the data you want to use. You can use @CHOOSE to select a value from a list built into the function, and you can use @INDEX if you prefer to specify a row and column offset to retrieve a value from a table.

Preliminary Work

To use either of the two table lookup functions or the index function, you must first create a table. Creating a table is as simple as finding an area of a worksheet that you are not using and entering the table data. Simply enter the data in columns and rows, using the same arrangement that you would use if you wrote the table on paper.

When you work with @VLOOKUP and @HLOOKUP, you must create either a vertical or a horizontal table. The difference between the two is whether you store the values that 1-2-3 attempts to match across a row (horizontal table) or down a column (vertical table).

The lower half of Figure 8.9 shows a vertical table. The lower half of Figure 8.10 shows a horizontal table. In a vertical table, the @VLOOKUP function checks a code against the entries on the left side of the table. The second argument specifies the table, and the third argument allows you to specify the column of values to use once you find the matching row.

Figure 8.9 Vertical
table for use with
@VLOOKUP

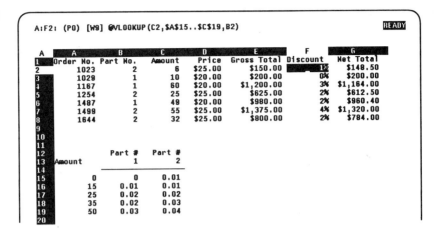

Figure 8.10
Horizontal table
for use with
@HLOOKUP

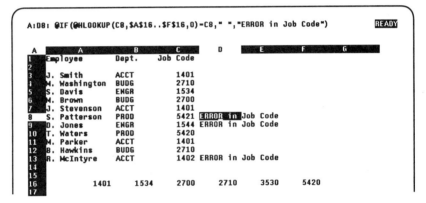

In a horizontal table, @HLOOKUP compares a code in your data against
the top row of the table. A second argument specifies the table location, and a third argument allows you to specify which row from the
column with the matching entry you want to use.

Since the lookup command stops when it reaches a higher value than
the one you are looking for, you must put the first criteria values in
order. With strings in Version 2.0 or higher, the entries do not have
to be in any order as @VLOOKUP and @HLOOKUP commands perform an exact match. Version 1.A can look up numbers, but not strings.

@VLOOKUP

The @VLOOKUP function allows you to create macros and formulas
that look up a value in a table on your worksheet. You can base the
lookup on one or two criteria.

The format of the function is @VLOOKUP(x,range,column number). The **x** is the first criterion. When you use the @VLOOKUP function, the formula looks for the value of x in the table. @VLOOKUP starts from the left column of the table (the index column) and looks for the value of x. If x is a number and it finds a larger number before it finds the value of x, it takes the highest value that is less than x. The x can be a number, string, or cell reference to a number or string. If x is a string or a cell reference to a string, 1-2-3 looks for an exact match between the value of x and the strings in the index column.

You must define **range** as the address where the table is located. The range must include the index column, the column used for the values, and all columns in between. Range is either the range or a range name. The **column number** is the number of columns to the right of the index column from which @VLOOKUP gets the value. Column number must be an integer 0 or greater. If the column number is zero, the function returns the value of x. If it does not find x and x is a number, it returns the next largest number. If it does not find x and x is a string, or if the column number is negative or exceeds the range of the table in the function, the function returns an error message.

Example

Figure 8.9 shows @VLOOKUP used to determine the discount available for a purchase to determine the net purchase amount. The value of x is determined by the amount sold and the column number is determined by the part number. The dollar signs in the range address keep the range address correct as the formula is copied through column F. This application can be expanded to accommodate additional parts by adding more columns at the right side of the lookup table.

Other Applications

Like the example for @HLOOKUP which uses the function with the @IF function to determine if Job Codes are correct, @VLOOKUP can also be used for error detection. @VLOOKUP can be used with strings as well as numbers. For example, if each salesman has a different commission percentage, a vertical table can be created to include the salesmen's names and their commission percentage. In this example, @VLOOKUP would look up each salesman's name in the table and use the appropriate sales percentage. This example can be further expanded by having different commission percentages for each salesman and product line.

@HLOOKUP

The @HLOOKUP function allows you to create macros and formulas that look up a value in a table on your worksheet. You can base the lookup on one or two criteria. The difference between the @HLOOKUP and @VLOOKUP functions is the orientation of the table of information. Version 2.0 and higher handles searching for strings; version 1.A cannot.

The format of the function is @HLOOKUP(x,range,row number). The **x** is the first criterion. When you use the @HLOOKUP function, the formula looks for the value of x in the table. @HLOOKUP starts from the left corner of the table and looks for the value of x along the top row of the table, the index row. If x is a number and the function finds a larger number before it finds the value of x, it takes the highest value not larger than x. Note that x does not have to be a number; x may be a string or a cell reference to a string. In the latter case, 1–2–3 looks for an exact match between the value of x and the strings in the index column.

The **range** is the range where the table is located. It must include the index row, the rows containing the values and all columns in between. It is either a range address or a range name.

The **row number** is the number of rows below the index row where @HLOOKUP obtains the return value. Row number must be an integer 0 or greater. If the row number is zero, the function returns the value of x. If it does not find x and x is a number, it returns the next largest number. If it does not find x and x is a string, or if the column number is negative or exceeds the range of the table in the function, the function returns an error message.

Example

Figure 8.10 shows the @HLOOKUP function used to check for proper error codes. In the table located in row 16, the valid Job Codes are listed in ascending order. The @HLOOKUP function looks for the Job Code in row 16. Since the row number is 0, it returns a value equal to the Job Code or the highest number of the group of numbers lower than x. When the Job Code is incorrect, the returned number does not match the Job Code in column C. When the Job Code differs the returned number, @IF puts an error message in column D. In the function, note that the range is referenced by its absolute address rather than relative address. This allows you to copy the formula in D3 to D4 and D13 and keep the range for the table correct. You can expand this application to accommodate all Job Codes by putting the rest of the Job Codes to the right of the current ones and expanding the range argument in @HLOOKUP.

Other Applications

You can use any @VLOOKUP applications with @HLOOKUP if you change the orientation of the table entries. The /Range Trans command in Releases 2.2 and 3 can change a horizontal table into a vertical table and vice versa since it copies values instead of formulas. Figure 8.11 shows an example very similar to the example used for @VLOOKUP. In this example, @VLOOKUP looks at the table for the amount of sales divided by $1,000. The product line determines the number of rows from which the function will retrieve a value. You can also use @HLOOKUP with strings as well as numbers. For example, you may have a situation where each salesman has a different commission percentage. For this case, you can create a horizontal table to include the salesmen's names and their commission percentage. In this example, @HLOOKUP looks up each salesman's name in the table and uses the appropriate sales percentage. This example can be further expanded by having different commission percentages for each product lines. The offset could indicate the product line.

Figure 8.11 @VLOOKUP using sales

A:E4: (C0) [W10] @HLOOKUP(D4/1000,$A$13..$H$15,C4)*D4 READY

A	A	B	C	D	E	F	G
1	Sales		Product				
2	Person	Region	Line	Amount	Commission		
3							
4	J. Smith	East	1	$5,000	$150		
5	M. Davis	West	2	$17,000	$1,360		
6	S. Jones	South	2	$8,000	$560		
7	D. Lyon	South	1	$41,000	$3,690		
8	B. Park	North	2	$4,500	$135		
9	M. Clark	West	1	$23,000	$1,840		
10							
11							
12				LOOKUP TABLE			
13	1	5	7	10	15	20	25
14	0.01	0.03	0.03	0.05	0.08	0.08	0.085
15	0.03	0.05	0.07	0.08	0.08	0.09	0.1
16							

@CHOOSE   The @CHOOSE function returns one argument from a list of choices, based your specification. The @CHOOSE function has the same capabilities as a @VLOOKUP or @HLOOKUP function with one row or column in the table. This is because you use only one criterion to determine the value of the @CHOOSE function.

The format of the function is @CHOOSE(x,v0,v1,...,vn). The **x** is the number of the choice that the function returns from its list of options. It is a number, formula, or a range name or cell reference to a number or formula. If it is not a whole number, the value is truncated to a whole number. If it exceeds the number of choices available or is a negative value, the function returns an error message. If it is blank or a string, the @CHOOSE function assumes the value of 0 for x.

The **v0, v1, ..., vn** represents the different choices that @CHOOSE has available. The first value is value 0. To select the second choice, x must be 1. While the number of choices are unlimited, you must limit the entire formula to 240 characters in Release 2 or 512 characters in Release 3.

Each choice may be a number, string, formula, range name, or cell reference. The different choices need not be in the same format. Hence, you can return a string from one choice and a number or formula from another. To omit one of the choices, do not put anything in between the two commas on either side of the argument. For example, you could type

    @CHOOSE(F1,42,"Smith",,A1,F2 + G3)

1-2-3 evaluates F1. If F1 equals 0 or is blank, the cell containing this function equals 42. If F1 equals 1, the cell containing this function equals Smith. If F1 equals 2, the cell containing the function equals a blank cell. If F1 equals 3, the cell containing the function equals the value of cell A1. If F1 equals 4, the cell containing the function equals the value of F2 added to the value of G3.

Example

Figure 8.12 shows an example of @CHOOSE used to determine the cost per pound of shipping packages. The cost depends on the zone. In this example, the zone is in column B. Since the zone numbers start with 1 rather than 0, you must subtract 1 from the zone to choose the correct cost per pound for each zone. Each value in the @CHOOSE function represents the cost for shipping to a different zone.

Figure 8.12 Using @CHOOSE to compute shipping costs

```
A:C3: (C2) [W17] @CHOOSE(B3-1,0.6,0.7,0.9,1.25,1.5)                    READY

     A           A        B          C           D        E       F       G
                Order #   Zone    Cost per Pound  Weight   Cost
  1
  2
  3             7514      3           $0.90        5      $4.50
  4             7515      2           $0.70        8      $5.60
  5             7516      1           $0.60       10      $6.00
  6             7517      4           $1.25       12     $15.00
  7             7518      5           $1.50        3      $4.50
  8
```

In the first order, reduce the zone of 3 to 2 when you enter it in the @CHOOSE function before the first comma. 1-2-3 selects the third value, which is value 2 with 1-2-3's zero-base counting system.

This example can be further expanded by combining the @CHOOSE and @VLOOKUP or @HLOOKUP to make determining the zone and cost easier. Thus, rather than typing in the zone, you can type in the state the order is being sent to and use @VLOOKUP to find the appropriate zone for the state as in Figure 8.13. The formula in column C takes the string in column B and looks it up in the vertical table below. Once it finds the string, it uses the value one column to its right. This is the zone for the state. At this point the zone is reduced by 1. That value determines which choice is made from the available choices in the @CHOOSE function. The results are the same as in Figure 8.12. Note that you do not have to know the zone that you are sending the order to since the formula looks for it for you.

Figure 8.13 Finding the zone for a state

```
A:C3: (C2) [W17] @CHOOSE(@VLOOKUP(B3,$A$11..$B$20,1)-1,0.6,0.7,0.9,1.25,1.5 READY

     A           A        B          C           D        E       F       G
                Order #   State   Cost per Pound  Weight   Cost
  1
  2
  3             7514      CA          $0.90        5      $4.50
  4             7515      NY          $0.70        8      $5.60
  5             7516      OH          $0.60       10      $6.00
  6             7517      FL          $1.25       12     $15.00
  7             7518      AK          $1.50        3      $4.50
  8
  9      Look Up Table
 10      State      Zone
 11      FL           4
 12      AZ           3
 13      CA           3
 14      MA           2
 15      AK           5
 16      OR           4
 17      NY           2
 18      OH           1
 19      IL           2
 20      TX           4
```

There are other advantages to storing the state to zone conversion in a table and the zone to cost per pound in a formula. This approach lets you change the zone a state is in or the cost per pound of a zone more quickly than if you combined everything into a formula.

Other Applications

@CHOOSE provides a good solution whenever you have a limited set of selections where options are numbered sequentially. You could use this function successfully with four different types of sales discounts: cash and carry, cash and delivery, credit and carry, credit and delivery. If the numbers 0 through 3 are assigned to the purchase types, @CHOOSE can provide the correct discount percentage.

@INDEX

The @INDEX function returns a value from a table of information given the row and column from which you want to select the information. This function is only available in Release 2.0 and higher. A new option in Release 3 can use data from tables that span multiple worksheets. It differs from @HLOOKUP and @VLOOKUP since you must give the @INDEX function the row and column. @INDEX does not find the correct row and column automatically like @VLOOKUP function and @HLOOKUP.

The format of this function is @INDEX(range,column,row,worksheet). The **range** is the range or range name of the location of the table. In Release 3 worksheet files, it can include more than one worksheet in the range. The **column** is the column from which you want to select a value. It is provided as the number of columns away from the left-most column of the table rather than a column letter. For example, if column is 0, the function will take the value from one of the rows in the left-most column of the table. If column is 3, the function takes the value from one of the rows in the column that is three columns away from the left-most column in the table. This is the fourth column of the table.

The **row** is the row from which you want to select a value. It is the number of rows away from the top row of the table. As with the column argument, the top row is row 0 and the fourth row of the table is row three.

The **worksheet** is an optional argument in Release 3 that selects which worksheet in the range to return a value to. Like the column and row argument, it is the offset from the first worksheet. For example, the third worksheet in the range has an offset of 2. If the optional argument is omitted, this function uses the first worksheet. @INDEX returns the value at the intersection of the row, column, and worksheet of the table.

Column, row, and worksheet arguments are a number, formula, range name, or cell reference. If the value is not a whole number, 1-2-3 truncates the value. If the value refers to a column, row, or worksheet that you have not included in the range, the function returns an error message. The function will also return an error message if an argument is negative. If it is a string or blank, the value is treated as 0.

Example

Figure 8.14 shows how @INDEX determines the shipping charge for various items. In the formula in column E, @INDEX takes the value from the Shipping Cost Per Pound table at the bottom of the figure. You can determine the row and column values of @INDEX by the positions for shipping location and packing code. The formula subtracts 1 from both the shipping location and the packing code to determine the row and column where the @INDEX function obtains data.

Figure 8.14
@INDEX computing
shipping costs

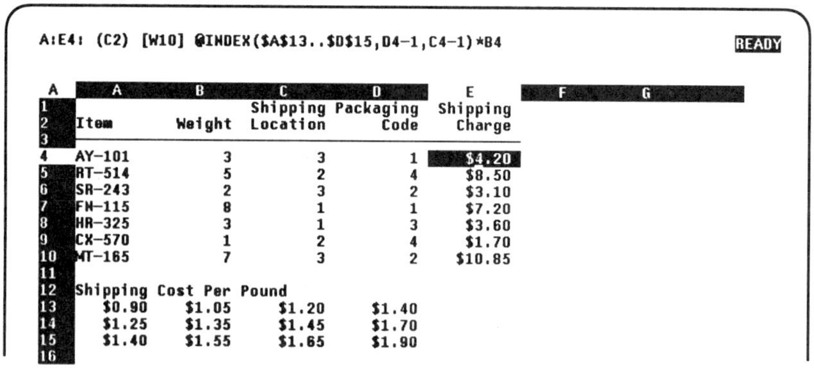

```
A:E4: (C2) [W10] @INDEX($A$13..$D$15,D4-1,C4-1)*B4                      READY

  A       A          B          C          D          E        F       G
1                              Shipping  Packaging  Shipping
2          Item      Weight    Location   Code       Charge
3
4          AY-101       3          3          1       $4.20
5          RT-514       5          2          4       $8.50
6          SR-243       2          3          2       $3.10
7          FW-115       8          1          1       $7.20
8          HR-325       3          1          3       $3.60
9          CX-570       1          2          4       $1.70
10         MT-165       7          3          2      $10.85
11
12         Shipping Cost Per Pound
13           $0.90     $1.05      $1.20      $1.40
14           $1.25     $1.35      $1.45      $1.70
15           $1.40     $1.55      $1.65      $1.90
16
```

You should define the table in the @INDEX function by its absolute address. This is advantageous because it maintains the proper table address when you copy the formula for the rest of the items. Once the proper shipping cost per pound is obtained, 1-2-3 multiplies that value by the weight to obtain the shipping charge.

Other Applications

Since @INDEX can obtain data from tables of information based on a row, column, and worksheet offset, you can use the @INDEX function for quoting insurance rates, shipping charges and commission percentages.

Making Special Cell Entries for Error Trapping

1-2-3 has two special values that look like functions. You can use the first one, @NA, meaning Not Available, for missing data. You can use the second, @ERR, to return a value of ERR. Both of these are used for flagging errors and missing information. These functions are often used with other functions.

@NA returns the value NA to the cell where it is recorded. Cells that subsequently reference the NA value return the value NA. This can have a ripple effect throughout the worksheet since the missing value may affect all of the formulas on a worksheet.

The format of the function is @NA, and it has no arguments. You can combine this function with @ISNA to check for the value of @NA. (Note that the @NA function is not the same as typing NA into a cell. If you type NA into a cell, 1-2-3 treats it as a label.)

Example

Figure 8.15 shows an example where you can use the @NA for missing values. Instead of values, type @NA in cells C3, D6, and B9. The ripple effect causes the salesperson's totals to have a value of @NA. Thus, any computations on the entire group of salesperson totals will also have a value of @NA. @NA prevents further analysis of the group of numbers until you include the three missing sales numbers.

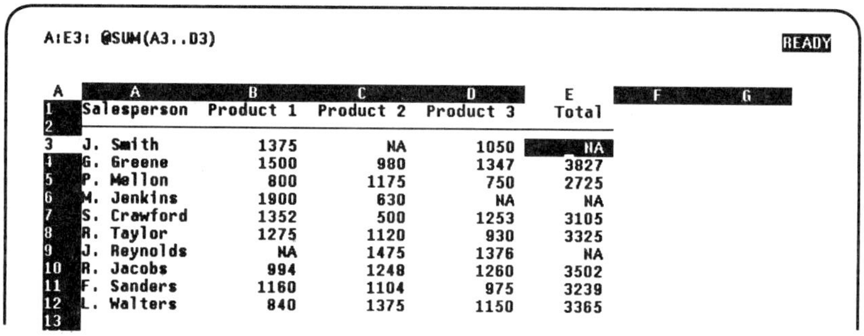

Figure 8.15 @NA
substituted for
unavailable data

```
AiE3i @SUM(A3..D3)                                                    READY

A        A           B           C           D         E      F      G
 1  Salesperson  Product 1   Product 2   Product 3   Total
 2
 3  J. Smith        1375          NA         1050       NA
 4  G. Greene       1500         980         1347       3827
 5  P. Mellon        800        1175          750       2725
 6  M. Jenkins      1900         630           NA        NA
 7  S. Crawford     1352         500         1253       3105
 8  R. Taylor       1275        1120          930       3325
 9  J. Reynolds       NA        1475         1376        NA
10  R. Jacobs        994        1248         1260       3502
11  F. Sanders      1160        1104          975       3239
12  L. Walters       840        1375         1150       3365
13
```

Other Applications

You can also use @NA in other formulas. For example, if you are dividing A1 into A2, you may want to combine the division formula with the @IF function and the @NA function such as in @IF(A2< >0,A1/A2,@NA). In this example, 1-2-3 divides the two numbers if A2 does not equal zero. If A2 equals 0, the cell will have a value of @NA. Because the ripple-through effect can cause more formulas to equal @NA than intended, you may want to use the value of 0 instead of @NA for some computations. Using an @IF to check for @NA values allows you to modify formulas to change the @NA value to something else.

You can also use @NA in checking values. For example, a formula comparing a value to a number that it should not exceed can use @NA if it in fact exceeds the specified maximum. In this case it serves as a flag that a correction is necessary.

@ERR

The @ERR function returns the value ERR to the cell where you enter it. Cells that reference the ERR value return the ERR value; this is referred to as a ripple effect. The value produced with the @ERR function is identical to the ERR displayed when a formula contains an error.

The format of the function is @ERR, and it has no arguments. You can combine this function with @ISERR to check for the value of @ERR. When a worksheet contains both NA and ERR values, a formula that reference both returns ERR.

Example

Figure 8.16 shows an example where @ERR has been used for incorrect values. In cells D4 and D7, @ERR was entered instead of a value. The ripple effect causes some total cost figures to have a value of @ERR. Any computations on the entire group of invoice totals will also have a value of @ERR. @ERR prevents further analysis of the group of numbers until you correct the two errors.

Figure 8.16 @ERR used to indicate an error condition

```
A:D4: (C2) @ERR                                           READY

   A       A          B        C        D        E        F       G       H
   1    Invoice     Part                        Total
   2    Number      Number   Quantity   Price    Cost
   3      1102      MT-101       4     $42.00   $168.00
   4      1103      FR-402       6       ERR      ERR
   5      1104      SP-234       1     $14.50    $14.50
   6      1105      NL-212       3     $32.00    $96.00
   7      1106      LH-306       1      ERR       ERR
   8      1107      TS-195       4     $9.50     $38.00
   9      1108      EX-241       2     $58.00   $116.00
   10
```

Other Applications

You can also use @ERR in other formulas. For example, you can perform validation checks on your data by combining the @IF function and the @ERR function such as in @IF(A2 < 451,A2,@ERR). In this case, if A2 is less than 451, the formula uses A2. If A2 is 451 or more, the formula uses @ERR. This flags any value that is too large. Before 1-2-3 performs further computations, you can correct the problem. For some computations, you may want to use the value of 0 instead of @ERR. Using an @IF to check for @ERR values allows you to use one formula if a cell equals @ERR and another formula if it equals something else.

Obtaining System Information

Release 3 includes a new function that allows you to obtain information on the current session. You can use this information in combination with @IF statements to warn a user when available memory is low or to take an action based on some other condition.

@INFO

The @INFO function looks at the current mode indicator displayed in the upper-right corner of the screen as well as many other attributes that are not visible on your screen. You can display these attributes in a cell to provide a clear picture of attributes affecting the current session.

The format of the function is @INFO(attribute). The **attribute** is a character string enclosed in quotes or a reference to a cell containing a character string. Table 8.3 contains a list of all the valid attribute values.

TABLE 8.3: ATTRIBUTE ARGUMENTS FOR @INFO

Attribute	Return Value
directory	The current directory
memavail	The amount of available memory
mode	The mode indicator expressed as a value using the following numbers:
	0 WAIT
	1 READY
	2 LABEL
	3 MENU
	4 VALUE
	5 POINT
	6 EDIT
	7 ERROR
	8 FIND
	9 FILES
	10 HELP
	11 STAT
	13 NAMES
	99 All others
numfile	Number of active files
origin	Cell address of the first cell in the current window
osreturncode	Value returned by the most recent /System or {SYSTEM} command
osversion	Operating system version in use
recalc	The recalculation mode returned as the character string automatic or manual.

(Continued)

TABLE 8.3: Continued	
Attribute	Return Value
release	Release version in use. Three components are returned: major release, upgrade level, and revision.
system	Name of the operating system
totmem	Total available memory (used + unused)

Example

You can create a screen that contains many attribute values and refer to it when you want to monitor available memory or some other 1-2-3 attribute. Figure 8.17 provides a look at a screen that contains many @INFO functions. Each function is used with a label that lets you see at a glance what the data returned represents.

Figure 8.17 @INFO to look at current session information

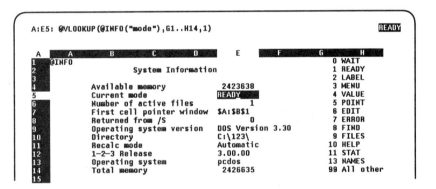

Other Applications

You can use @INFO in a macro in combination with the IF statement. If you check available memory and find that there is little left, you can ask the user to delete information that is no longer needed. You can then check the current path name or the recalculation mode and take an action to change it. Based on the result of the last system operation, you might want to call an error processing routine. As you can see, @INFO gives you the ability to add sophistication to macros that was previously not possible.

9

Using Functions in the Data Management Environment

1-2-3 has a special set of functions that are designed to support computations in the data management environment. One group of these functions lets you selectively compute statistical calculations on the worksheet data. If you have never worked with a 1-2-3 database before, you will want to look at the database concepts in the next section to learn about the new terms used for these features.

The second group of database functions works with an external database. These functions are able to access data and functions in an external database. They are only available for Release 3.

FUNCTION ARGUMENTS FOR STATISTICAL FUNCTIONS

Database statistical functions perform the same statistical functions on a field in a database as the regular statistical functions perform on a list. The database statistical functions, however, perform only the functions on rows of information that meet specific criteria.

A database in a worksheet is similar to a table that lists the types of information in the first row and the actual data below. The columns of a database are referred to as fields. Fields can contain information such as name, social security number, and location if the data concerns employees. An inventory file might have entries such as quantity on hand, supplier, and price.

Except for the field names, the rows of the database are referred to as records. A record contains all the information about any one item in the database.

The database statistical functions have a D as the first letter of the function and the statistical function after the D. The database statistical functions operate the same way on a database as the regular statistical functions operate on lists of data. Hence, 1-2-3 selects records from the database for use in the computation based upon entries in a criteria area that lists the field name and the desired entries for that field.

1-2-3 allows you to use the same criteria area to compute different statistics on one group of records. It also allows you to use different criteria for each computation.

ARGUMENTS IN DATABASE STATISTICAL FUNCTIONS

All database statistical functions have the same format. The format of database statistical functions is @FUNCTION(input,field,criteria). **FUNCTION** represents the database statistical function you are using, such as DSUM, DAVG, or DSTD. The **input** represents the location of the database and includes the field names and the database records. You can refer to a section of the database; however, you must make sure that you include the field names in the input range. The input argument must be a range, such as A1..Z200, or a range name. Note that input can refer to more than one range. 1-2-3 determines whether you are referring to one or more ranges by assigning function arguments from the back of the function. With Release 3, you can reference an external database as an input range.

The **field** represents the location of the field on which you are performing statistical functions. You specify the location as number of the columns from the left edge of the database table. If you want to work with entries in the first column of the table, you specify 0 to represent the left edge. Field must be a number, a formula that produces a number, a range name, or a cell reference. With Release 3, you can specify the field name enclosed in quotes instead of using the column offset. If the input range is a external database or contains multiple ranges, you must use a field name instead of a column offset.

The **criteria** is the range or range name of the criteria you use in selecting records. The field names for the criteria must be in the first line of the criteria area. These entries must match field names above the database. In Release 2, a blank line in the criteria range matches all database records. In Release 3, you can include blank lines in the criteria range without including all records.

Effects of Labels on Database Statistical Functions

The result of your database statistical functions may vary when your database has numbers and labels within the same column. Labels have a value of 0 for many mathematical functions, and this affects the results of some functions. For example, you may want to count the number of records that meet certain criteria. @DCOUNT counts the number of values or labels in the offset column. Therefore, if you have a cell that says Not Available in a column of numbers and the record matches your criteria, it is counted as if you had typed in a 0 and increments the count for @DCOUNT. However, you may affect @DMIN and @DMAX if 0 is the smallest or largest number in the records used. The other functions treat strings as if the cell contains 0.

Effect of @ERR and @NA

1-2-3's two special values, @ERR and @NA, can be used with the database statistical functions. @ERR and @NA cause the database statistical function to return @ERR or @NA only if the record with the @ERR or @NA matches the function's criteria. For example, if a record with @NA does not match the criteria, the database statistical function will be unaffected by it. However, if the record with @NA in the offset column matches the criteria, the value of the database statistical function is @NA regardless of the values in the other records.

Criteria

Criteria refers to the small tables in your worksheet that tell 1-2-3 which records to use in the database statistical functions. The criteria you enter determine the records that are used for other Query operations like Find and Extract as well. Although there is no fixed location in the database, the tables should be in a location that does not interfere with the database's expansion or an area of the worksheet used as the Output area for an Extract operation.

The first line of a criteria must contain the field names, unless the criteria is a formula. Below the field name is the value that a database record must meet. The database statistical function only includes those records that meet those values. For example, if your criteria look like

Item
Paper
Pens

1-2-3 matches any database record where the Item field equals Paper or Pens. By having the values on different lines, 1-2-3 uses an OR connector. In order for the database statistical function to include a record, the record must meet one of the criteria.

1-2-3 also uses an AND connector between criteria. By having two criteria on the same line, a record must meet both criteria to be included in the database statistical function, as in

Item   Vendor
Paper   High Price Supplies

In this example, the database statistical function would only include a record that has its item field equal to Paper and the vendor equal to High Price Supplies. To look for two different values in the same field, you must express the criteria as a formula. Usually this type of condition is not used with exact matches since a field cannot have two values at once. For example, the Item field cannot contain both Paper and Pens at the same time. However, if you are looking for entries within a range of the alphabet or numeric entries within a range, you will have to check one field for two conditions and will need to use the logical formula capability (covered later in the chapter).

Finally, 1-2-3 also has a NOT operator. By putting a tilde (~) in front of a criteria value, the criteria match all records that do not equal the criteria value, as in

Item
~Paper

In this example, the criteria match all records that do not have their item field equal to paper.

Criteria can use the two wildcard characters—the question mark and the asterisk. The question mark matches any single character. For example, if the criteria might be

Name
Jo?n

In this case, the ? takes the place of any single character. The criteria match records that have John, Joan or Join in the name field.

The other wildcard character is the asterisk. This special character matches any group of characters at the end of an entry. Unlike the ?, the * cannot be used throughout the entry or at the beginning of an entry. You might have criteria of

Name
Al*

In this example, the criteria match Albert, Alice, Allison and Alex among others. As you can see, these wildcard characters expand the matching capabilities for criteria entries.

Criteria are not case-sensitive. For example, you can illustrate many of the functions with a listing of invoices that include item, cost, vendor, and department. If your criterion is looking for invoices for Pens, it will also find PENS and pens.

Besides using labels as a criterion for your database statistical functions, you can also use numbers or logical formulas. Numbers follow the same entry rules as labels except they do not support wildcard entries and do not require a label indicator when you enter them in the criteria area. Formulas work well when comparing values to a range of acceptable entries, and Release 2.0 and higher allows you to use string formulas in your criteria.

Since a formula is evaluated as a logical statement, it returns either a true or false value. Formulas do not need to have the field name they reference as the first line of the criteria range. However, including the field name makes the criteria easier to understand.

To create a formula in the criteria range, type the cell formula as if you were referencing the first record of your database. It is important to reference the first field value rather than the field name. It does not matter whether the first database record matches the criteria or not. For example, to include only the records with a cost greater than $100, which is located in column B, your formula looks like +B2>100. Even though your formula only references B2, the criteria applies to all records. If your formula contains a cell reference, use the cell's absolute address. For example, to include all records with a cost greater than the value in cell F1 in your database statistical function, the formula looks like +B2>$F$1. The absolute address anchors the cell reference as the record checked moves farther down the database.

With Release 3, criteria formulas are even easier. You can enter them as labels as in '<100 to locate records, where the value in the field indicated in the cell above the criteria entry is less than 100.

Formulas also use the #AND#, #OR#, and #NOT# logical connectors to connect different parts of a formula in the same cell. Since formulas are criteria, formulas are also bound by the same AND, OR, and NOT connectors determined by their position within the criteria area.

@DSUM

To add all of the values in a database that fit a certain criterion, you can look for the cell locations and add the cell locations together. However, the process of finding, remembering, and adding these cells is time-consuming and error prone. The specific cell references in formulas would not work if the cell addresses of the data were changed by sorting or the insertion of new records. For example, records meeting your criteria might have required a formula like +B6+B9+B11 before the sort and +B2+B21+B35 after the sort. It is much easier to tell 1-2-3 to add a range of numbers that match a criterion with the @DSUM function.

Example

@DSUM adds entries from a column of numbers only when the record matches a criteria entry. For example, in Figure 9.1, @DSUM adds only the item costs when the vendor is High Price Supplies. The range specified, A1..D10, covers all the database's records and the field names in the first row. You could choose the field Cost by having the offset column as 1. This adds the specified values in the field one column from the left-most one. You specify the criterion as the range A12 to A13, which matches all records whose vendor is High Price Supplies.

Figure 9.1 Using @DSUM to add a column of numbers with one criteria entry

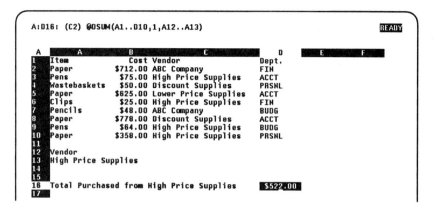

You can also use @DSUM with multiple criteria. Figure 9.2 shows the same worksheet as Figure 9.1 with another criterion added. With the addition of the second criterion, only pens purchased from High Price Supplies will be totaled.

Figure 9.2 Using @DSUM to add a column of numbers with multiple criteria

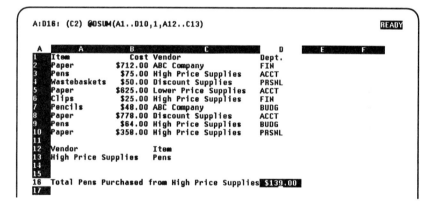

Other Applications

You can use the @DSUM for management reports since it can scan and summarize large databases. You can provide a total of sales for each location, for each product line, or any other grouping available in your data. Each function entry references a different criterion entry.

@DCOUNT

The @DCOUNT function counts the number of records that meet certain criteria. The @DCOUNT function counts both labels and values but it does not count the field names.

Example

You might count the number of records when you need the number of paper purchases. If you are considering changing to one supplier for your company's paper needs, you need to know how much paper you use to apply for a volume discount. If you set up your database as in Figure 9.3, the @DCOUNT function used in cell D16 counts the number of paper purchases. Although the offset appears unnecessary, it specifies the column to check for an entry. For example, if the paper purchase from the ABC Company is missing the cost, @DCOUNT only counts three paper purchases. The criteria set in A12..A13 find the records where the Item equals paper. Like the other database statistical functions, the criterion area may have multiple criteria entries.

Figure 9.3 Using @DCOUNT to count the number of items purchased

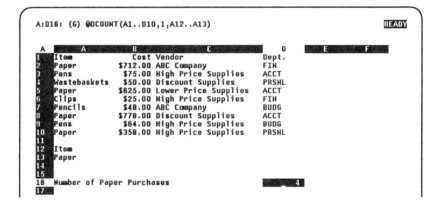

Other Applications

You can use @DCOUNT to check for missing data in certain columns. You can perform several @DCOUNT operations for a specific set of data to ensure that all the fields in these records contain data. Counts returned that are lower for some fields are missing data values for some of the records.

@DAVG

The @DAVG function selects records that meet your criteria and computes the average for a specific field in these records. @DAVG is equivalent to @DSUM divided by @DCOUNT. If any of the included records have a label in the field that you are averaging, the label is treated as a zero.

Example

You can use @DAVG to compute the average purchases for the accounting department. In Figure 9.4, 1-2-3 computed the average purchase as the sum of all accounting department purchases divided by the number of accounting purchases. Although @DSUM and @DCOUNT perform the same function, @DAVG is quicker.

Figure 9.4 Using @DAVG to calculate the average price of the items purchased

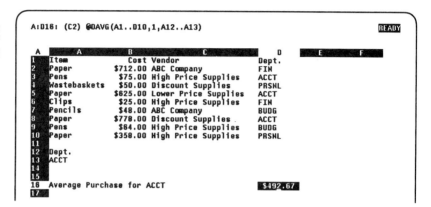

```
A:D16: (C2) @DAVG(A1..D10,1,A12..A13)                              READY

A        A            B              C              D        E        F
1   Item            Cost Vendor                     Dept.
2   Paper         $712.00 ABC Company               FIN
3   Pens           $75.00 High Price Supplies       ACCT
4   Wastebaskets   $50.00 Discount Supplies         PRSNL
5   Paper         $625.00 Lower Price Supplies      ACCT
6   Clips          $25.00 High Price Supplies       FIN
7   Pencils        $48.00 ABC Company               BUDG
8   Paper         $778.00 Discount Supplies .       ACCT
9   Pens           $64.00 High Price Supplies       BUDG
10  Paper         $358.00 High Price Supplies       PRSNL
11
12  Dept.
13  ACCT
14
15
16  Average Purchase for ACCT                  $492.67
17
```

Other Applications

You can create a management summary report displaying the average sales for each of your product lines in five different sales regions. If you have six different product lines in your database records, thirty different criterion areas are required to create the report of summary statistics. The first time you need this report, you must invest some time to create the required criterion areas. Month after month, 1-2-3 continues to produce your management summary without making any entries.

@DMIN

The @DMIN function locates the lowest number in a field. You might use this number in another formula to display the lowest cost in a group of expenses. Or, if the numbers in the group are negative, you can use @DMIN to check that a particular column is wide enough. Any string in the field used as the offset has the value of 0.

Example

Knowing the lowest number in a range is necessary for determining the lowest purchase amount. In Figure 9.5, @DMIN calculates the lowest value of the different items purchased. You can use the information to verify accuracy. For example, if the result of @DMIN is negative, someone in the purchasing department must confirm that the number is correct. In this situation, the person would most likely find an error and correct it.

Figure 9.5 Using @DMIN to determine the lowest value

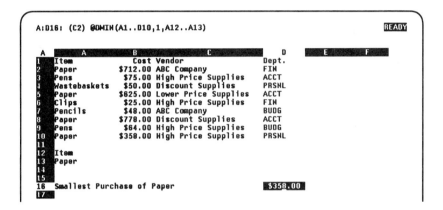

You can also use this information to determine the least expensive place to purchase office supplies. Like @DCOUNT, the criterion for this function is that Item must equal paper. If Item equals paper, @DMIN checks to determine if the record has the minimum cost.

Other Applications

Different applications often use @DMIN. For a sales report that separates sales by salesperson, displaying the lowest sales from any salesperson can be useful as a motivational and performance evaluation tool. When you are printing a lengthy worksheet, this function is combined with @DMAX, to help you judge how wide or narrow you can make a column of numbers. For a professor who uses 1-2-3 to keep track of a class's grades, the professor can use the lowest score for a graded assignment to assess whether the class requires additional time on the topic.

@DMAX

You often need to know the highest number in a group. You might be using this number in another formula, perhaps to display the highest cost in a group of expenses or to check that a column is wide enough. The @DMAX function determines the largest number of the records that meet the function's criteria.

Example

Knowing the highest number in a range is necessary for determining the highest purchase amount. In Figure 9.6, @DMAX returns the highest value of the different items purchased. In this example, you can use the information for verifying accuracy. If the result of @DMAX is above a predetermined amount, someone in the purchasing department must confirm that the number is correct.

Figure 9.6 Using @DMAX to determine the highest value

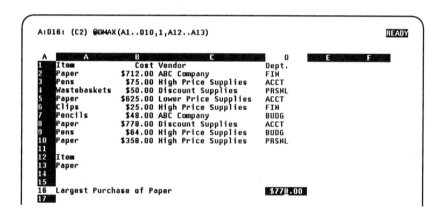

```
A:D16: (C2) @DMAX(A1..D10,1,A12..A13)                          READY

    A         A            B            C              D      E      F
1    Item            Cost  Vendor               Dept.
2    Paper          $712.00  ABC Company        FIN
3    Pens            $75.00  High Price Supplies ACCT
4    Wastebaskets    $50.00  Discount Supplies  PRSNL
5    Paper          $625.00  Lower Price Supplies ACCT
6    Clips           $25.00  High Price Supplies FIN
7    Pencils         $48.00  ABC Company        BUDG
8    Paper          $778.00  Discount Supplies  ACCT
9    Pens            $64.00  High Price Supplies BUDG
10   Paper          $358.00  High Price Supplies PRSNL
11
12   Item
13   Paper
14
15
16   Largest Purchase of Paper                  $778.00
17
```

This can be a useful review procedure since it may indicate an error or a departmental purchase of a capital good as an office supply. The function result might also indicate where the company should not buy paper. The criteria set in A12..A13 forces @DMAX to only look at the cost for paper items.

Other Applications

You can use @DMAX for a sales report that separates sales by salesperson. For example, @DMAX can display the highest sales by any salesperson and thus be a motivational and performance evaluation tool.

@DMAX may be helpful when you print a lengthy worksheet. When combined with @DMIN, @DMAX helps you judge how wide or narrow a column of numbers is before asterisks replace the values.

For a teacher who uses 1–2–3 to keep track of a class's grades, @DMAX provides the highest score for a graded assignment. The result helps the teacher evaluate student progress.

Measuring Dispersion

The last four functions described in this chapter handle the dispersion of data. Two of these functions, @DSTD and @DVAR, expect your database to contain the complete population of data. The other two, @DVARS and @DSTDS, are new to Release 3 and work with a population sample.

You may want to review the concept of dispersion in Chapter 2 before beginning to use the @DSTD, @DVAR, @DSTDS, and @DVARS functions. Once you understand the concept of dispersion, you can apply the concepts used in the @DSTD, @DVAR, @DSTDS, and @DVARS functions to aid you in computing the data dispersion.

Applications

You can use dispersion of data in many fields such as marketing and accounting. Often, an audit test or a release of a product relies upon tests of a trial-sized sample. For example, an accountant bases his assessment of the number of invoices that he must check on the dispersion of the trial sample. A company uses market research data to find out how effective its marketing strategy is and uses the information about its product to determine what features are most effective in selling the product.

@DVAR

One measurement of the dispersion of data is the variance, which is a measure of the degree to which the individual values in a group of data vary from the average of that group. The lower the variance, the less individual values vary from the average and the more reliable the average is as a representative value of the data. If you are not familiar with how the variance is computed, Chapter 2 contains a step-by-step example. The @DVAR function calculates the variance for records in a database that meet the function's criteria.

Example

There are two types of variances: One is for a sample and another is for an entire group. @DVAR uses the n method (biased) to calculate variance for an entire population. You would use this formula to find the variances for all packages made, as done in Figure 9.7.

Figure 9.7 Using @DVAR to compute the variance for an entire group

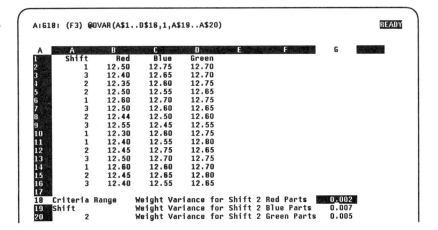

```
A:G18:  (F3)  @DVAR(A$1..D$16,1,A$19..A$20)                              READY

 A      A         B         C         D         E         F         G
1       Shift     Red       Blue      Green
2         1       12.50     12.75     12.70
3         3       12.40     12.65     12.70
4         2       12.35     12.60     12.75
5         2       12.50     12.55     12.65
6         1       12.60     12.70     12.75
7         3       12.50     12.60     12.65
8         2       12.44     12.50     12.60
9         3       12.55     12.45     12.55
10        1       12.30     12.60     12.75
11        1       12.40     12.55     12.80
12        2       12.45     12.75     12.65
13        3       12.50     12.70     12.75
14        1       12.60     12.60     12.70
15        2       12.45     12.65     12.80
16        3       12.40     12.55     12.65
17
18      Criteria Range      Weight Variance for Shift 2 Red Parts    0.002
19      Shift               Weight Variance for Shift 2 Blue Parts   0.007
20          2               Weight Variance for Shift 2 Green Parts  0.005
```

In this particular example, you can check the weight for every package in the production run because the run is quite small. However, some data contain too many individual values to include every member of the group. In such a case, you can take a random sample of the group to approximate the results of the entire population.

If you are working with Release 2 and want to calculate the variance for a sample of the population, you should use the n–1 method (unbiased). You can modify the variance formula to work for a sample. The variance formula for a sample is

@DCOUNT(LIST)/(@DCOUNT(LIST)–1)*@DVAR(LIST)

This formula compensates for the bias in the @DVAR function. An example of this formula in use would be Figure 9.8. This is the same example as Figure 9.7, except the formula computes the variance of a sample for the red, blue, and green parts.

Figure 9.8 Using
@DVAR to compute
the variance for a
sample

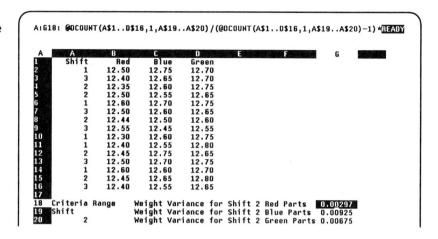

The @DVARS function provides a special function to compute the variance for a population sample. The function should be used whenever you need to calculate the variance for a sample.

Example

Figure 9.9 displays a model that measures the variance of the population sample shown in column D. It only computes the variance in the diameter for a sample of chocolate chip and macadamia nut cookies. You would use a sample test when the population number is too large to test every unit. In such a case, a random sample of the group approximates the results of the entire population. As the number of data values included in the variance calculation increases, the value returned with the @DVARS function is almost the same as the result with the @DVAR function.

Figure 9.9 Using
@DVARS to compute
the variance for a
sample

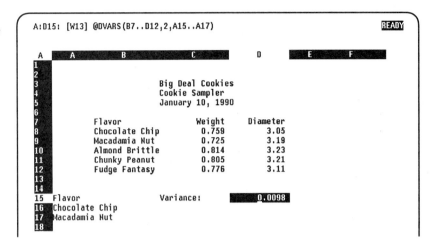

@DSTD

Another measurement of data dispersion is the standard deviation, which measures the degree to which the individual values in a group of data vary from the average of that group. The standard deviation is the square of the variance. The lower the standard deviation, the less individual values vary from the average and the more reliable the average is as a representative value of the data. @DSTD calculates the standard deviation for records meeting specified criteria.

Example

There are two types of standard deviations; one is for a sample and one is for an entire group. @DSTD calculates standard deviation for an entire population. This standard deviation uses the n method (biased). For example, Figure 9.10 shows the standard deviations of income for all respondents that answered Y to question 2. The result indicates that most of the respondents' income are within $12,000 of the average.

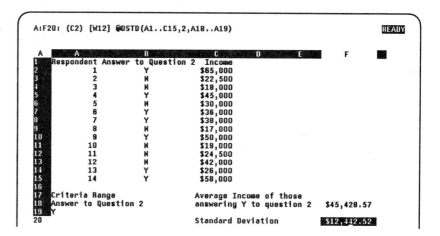

Figure 9.10 Using @DSTD to compute the variance for an entire group

Since the date shown in the above example is probably a sample of a larger group, this computation should have used the n–1 method (unbiased) of a standard deviation. The standard deviation formula for a sample is

@SQRT(@DCOUNT(LIST)/(@DCOUNT(LIST)–1))*@DSTD(LIST)

This formula compensates for the bias in @DSTD. An example of this formula used for the same data is in Figure 9.11. The different standard deviation is caused by the assumption that the data represents a sample rather than the entire group.

Figure 9.11 Using @DSTD to compute the standard deviation of a sample

```
A:F20: (C2) [W12] @SQRT(@DCOUNT(A1..C15,2,A18..A19)/(@DCOUNT(A1..C15,2,A18.  EDIT
@SQRT(@DCOUNT(A1..C15,2,A18..A19)/(@DCOUNT(A1..C15,2,A18..A19)-1))*@DSTD(A1..C15
,2,A18..A19)
```

	A	B	C	D	E	F	
7	6	Y	$36,000				
8	7	Y	$38,000				
9	8	N	$17,000				
10	9	Y	$50,000				
11	10	N	$19,000				
12	11	N	$24,500				
13	12	N	$42,000				
14	13	Y	$26,000				
15	14	Y	$58,000				
16							
17	Criteria Range		Average Income of those				
18	Answer to Question 2		answering Y to question 2	$45,428.57			
19	Y						
20			Standard Deviation	$13,439.46			

@DSTDS
(Release 3 only)

The @DSTDS computes the standard deviation for records that represent part of a population. 1-2-3 compensates for the fact that you are not working with the entire population sample when you use this function. It provides the same results as using the modified version of @DSTD.

Example

Figure 9.12 displays a model that measures the diameter's standard deviation of the population sample shown in column D. The function includes only the database table records for a sample of chocolate chip and macadamia nut cookies. You would use a sample test when the population number is too large to test every unit. In such a case, a random sample of the group approximates the results of the entire population. As the number of data values included in the variance calculation increases, the values returned with the @DSTDS and the @DSTD functions become closer.

Figure 9.12 Using @DSTDS to compute the standard deviation of a sample

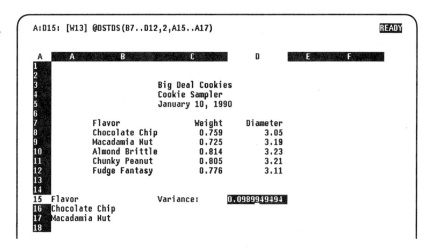

This function is also used in place of the lengthy sample formula that modifies the @DSTD function's result. If you substituted @DSTDS (A1..C15,2,A18..A19) for the lengthy formula in F20 in Figure 9.11, 1-2-3 returns the same results.

Using Database Statistical Functions with /Data Table

You can combine the database statistical functions with the /Data Table command to provide summary statistics quickly. For example, to get a count of the different supplies that each department purchases, you can combine @DCOUNT with the /Data Table command to create the table shown in Figure 9.13. This table uses the data shown in Figure 9.14. To create this table, an entry for each department is placed in column F with the /Data Query Unique command. For the /Data Query Unique command, the input range was column D, the criterion was F1..F2 after Dept. was typed in F1, and the output range was F4. The same command was used with the Item entries where the input was A1..A10, the criterion was G1..G2, and the output range was G4. Once the items were listed, they were moved to a row with the /Range Transpose command with the input range of G4..G8 and the output range of G3. Next this formula was put in F3:

@DCOUNT(A3..D12,1,F1..G2)

An offset of 1 was chosen so that items with no cost would not be counted. Then, this cell was hidden with the /Range Format Hidden command. Finally, the /Data Table command was executed. A two-way table was selected and the range F3..K7 was chosen for the table's range. The final output looks like Figure 9.13. This is an example of how the database statistical functions can be combined with the /Data Table functions to quickly create summary tables.

Figure 9.13 Using database statistical function with /Data Table

A:F3: (H) @DCOUNT(A2..D12,1,F1..G2)						READY

A	F	G	H	I	J	K	L
1	Dept.	Item					
2							
3		Paper	Pens	Wastebaskets	Clips	Pencils	
4	FIN	1	0	0	1	0	
5	ACCT	2	1	0	0	0	
6	PRSNL	1	0	1	0	0	
7	BUDG	1	1	0	0	1	
8							

Figure 9.14 The completed data table

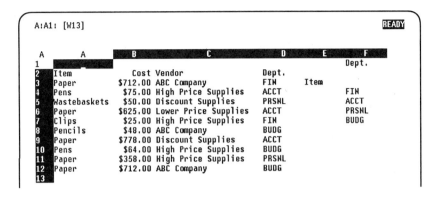

```
A:A1: [W13]                                                          READY

  A         A            B              C              D      E      F
  1                                                                  Dept.
  2   Item             Cost Vendor                   Dept.
  3   Paper          $712.00 ABC Company             FIN      Item
  4   Pens            $75.00 High Price Supplies     ACCT            FIN
  5   Wastebaskets    $50.00 Discount Supplies       PRSNL           ACCT
  6   Paper          $625.00 Lower Price Supplies    ACCT            PRSNL
  7   Clips           $25.00 High Price Supplies     FIN             BUDG
  8   Pencils         $48.00 ABC Company             BUDG
  9   Paper          $778.00 Discount Supplies       ACCT
 10   Pens            $64.00 High Price Supplies     BUDG
 11   Paper          $358.00 High Price Supplies     PRSNL
 12   Paper          $712.00 ABC Company             BUDG
 13
```

Database Functions That Extract Data Values and Perform Computations

Release 3 offers two new database functions that work differently than the database statistical functions. One of these functions returns a data value from an existing database, and the other performs a function from an external database.

@DGET

The @DGET function follows the same syntax as the database statistical functions but does not require any computations. @DGET returns a value from a database field for a record matching your criteria. If more than one record matches your specifications, @DGET returns an error message.

Example

You can use @DGET to obtain the cost of items from different suppliers if you have a database of items, suppliers, and costs. In this example, since the database has only one cost for pencils from Yellow Rule Supply, @DGET provides a good solution.

Figure 9.15 shows the function and the return value. @DGET returns the cost of pencils from Yellow Rule Supply. The function uses the field name in quotes instead of a column offset so it is easier to understand. A series of these functions, each using a different criterion area, can create a quick management summary report. However, if you specified your criteria as A15..A16 or B15..B16, an error message would be returned since more than one record would match the criteria.

Figure 9.15 Using
@DGET

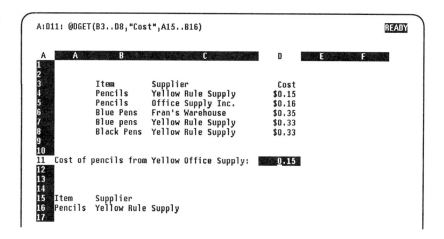

@DQUERY
The @DQUERY function sends a command to an external database management program. This function is often used in the criteria area. It uses a different syntax than the other database statistical functions.

The syntax of @DQUERY is @DQUERY(function,ext-arguments). The **function** is the name of the external command or function that @DQUERY performs in the database. The **ext-arguments** are the arguments that the external database management program command or function uses. They are determined by the external database management program and are strings enclosed in quotes or cell references to cells that contain the function or external arguments. 1-2-3 calculates @DQUERY when you perform the /Data Query Delete, /Data Query Extract, /Data Query Modify Extract, or /Data Query Unique commands.

Example

You can use @DQUERY in the criteria to list the paid invoices in a dBASE III database called INVOICES. Figure 9.16 shows an example of this. The connection to the external database is established with the /Data External Use command. The /Data External List Fields command generates the field names. The /Range Transpose command copies the field names to A5 and A8 for the criteria area and output range. The @DQUERY function in F6 uses the 1 or 0 typed in D2 to select the inclusion of paid or unpaid invoices. Paid invoices that have a T in the PAID field have a 1 value to 1-2-3. Paid invoices which have an F in the PAID field have a 0 value to 1-2-3. To perform the query, the /Data Query Input command selects INVOICES as the input range. You then select Criteria and A5..F6 for the criteria area. For the output area, select Output and A8..F8. Select Extract to extract the records. Figure 9.16 shows the final result.

Figure 9.16 Using @DQUERY

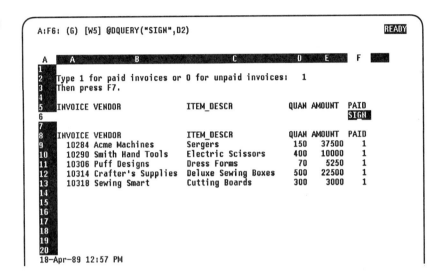

```
A:F6: (G) [W5] @DQUERY("SIGN",D2)                                    READY

  A     A              B                C              D    E   F
  1
  2    Type 1 for paid invoices or 0 for unpaid invoices:   1
  3    Then press F7.
  4
  5    INVOICE VENDOR                  ITEM_DESCR           QUAN AMOUNT PAID
  6                                                                    SIGN
  7
  8    INVOICE VENDOR                  ITEM_DESCR           QUAN AMOUNT PAID
  9      10284 Acme Machines          Sergers              150  37500   1
  10     10290 Smith Hand Tools       Electric Scissors    400  10000   1
  11     10306 Puff Designs           Dress Forms           70   5250   1
  12     10314 Crafter's Supplies     Deluxe Sewing Boxes  500  22500   1
  13     10318 Sewing Smart           Cutting Boards       300   3000   1
  14
  15
  16
  17
  18
  19
  20
  18-Apr-89 12:57 PM
```

RELEASE DIFFERENCES

Release 3 supports all of the functions of the other releases and offers some new options. When working with databases, you can store the database, criteria, and output on different sheets. This allows you to expand the database without having to move either of the other areas. The /Data Fill feature supports the entry of all types of functions for either the start value or the increment. In addition, new increment options for dates and times make it easy to generate monthly or quarterly reporting dates, payment schedules, or time scheduling increments. The new /Data Table features can be used with @functions just as the existing /Data Table 1 and 2 can.

/Data Fill

The /Data Fill feature allows you to generate a series of evenly spaced values on the worksheet. Although you can specify numbers as the start value for the series and the series increment, you can also supply functions. Release 3 expands the practical application of this concept by supplying new date and time increments.

To use the new date features, type **/Data Fill** and highlight the range you wish to fill. Next, type the date in one of 1–2–3's acceptable date formats. Use a fixed number of days as an increment or any of the new options such as 1w for a week, 1q for a calendar quarter, 1m for a month, or 1y for one year. After finalizing the increment, the stop value is increased since it must be higher than the highest value you plan to generate. The series of values is then generated when you press Enter. Since dates are stored as date serial numbers, they do not look like dates until after formatting. Figure 9.17 shows a series of dates generated with the new quarterly increment. It also shows the entries for /Data Fill that are used to generate this series.

Figure 9.17 Using /Data Fill with the new increment of 1q for quarterly date entries

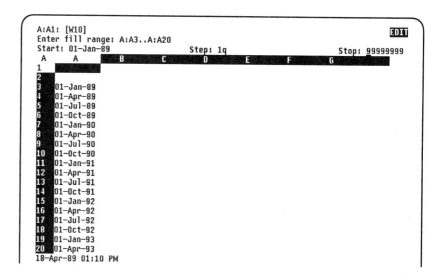

To use the new time features, type **/Data Fill** and highlight the range you wish to fill. Next, type the time using an acceptable time format. Use a fixed number for an increment or any of the new options like 1s for a second, 1min for a minute, or 1h for 1 hour. The stop value usually does not have to be changed since time serial numbers are often lower than the current stop value. When you press Enter, the series of time serial numbers is generated. These time serial numbers do not look like times until after formatting. Figure 9.18 shows a series of times generated with a 15min increment value. It also shows the entries for /Data Fill that are used to generate this series.

Figure 9.18 Using /Data Fill with the new increment of 15min for 15 minute increment time entries

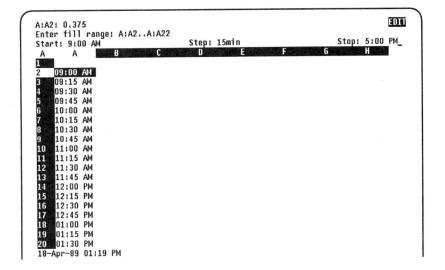

/Data Table 3

Just like the /Data Table 1 and 2 commands, you can combine the database statistical functions with the /Data Table 3 command to create three-way tables that span several worksheets. For example, to count the number of customer assistance requests your department must handle, combine @DCOUNT with the /Data Table 3 command to count the types of problems each person handles each hour. For this table, you need to determine the type of problem, who handled the problem, and when the problem was reported. Figure 9.19 shows a database that contains this information, stored in a data table in the first worksheet.

Figure 9.19
Database for
customer service
department

```
A:A1: [W6]                                                              READY

   A    A                         B                          C      D
1         Customer Service Department
2
3      Hour  Problem                                       Person  Time Compl.
4      15:00 Customer overcharged                          Mark           5
5      09:00 Package in box does not match description Ellen           14
6      17:00 Unhappy with color                           Sharon         8
7      13:00 Does not fit                                 Ellen          6
8      09:00 Clothing Torn                                Tracey         15
9      17:00 Missing Accessory                            Mark           2
10     13:00 Warranty card missing                        Steve          5
11     14:00 Changed their mind                           Mark          21
12     09:00 Does not fit                                 Tracey        14
13     11:00 Wrong color                                  Steve          8
14     13:00 Missing Accessory                            Mark          24
15     10:00 Does not work                                Ellen         21
16     17:00 Complaint about an employee                  Tracey        35
17     15:00 Left shoe different size than right          Steve         16
18     15:00 Unhappy with color                           Mark          11
19     14:00 Pick up rebate slip                          Steve         19
20     11:00 Customer overcharged                         Tracey        23
    18-Apr-89 02:08 PM
```

The additional worksheets in the file look like the one in Figure 9.20. Every worksheet contains the same information in the same format: the problem is in the first table row, the hour the problem was reported is in the top table row, and the name of the person who handled the problem is in the upper left cell. To create the list of problems, place an entry for each problem in column A with the /Data Query Unique command. For the /Data Query Unique command, the input range is column D, the criterion is F1..F2 after typing **Dept.** in F1, and the output range is F4. Add the hours with the /Data Fill command. The data fill range is B2..B10, the start value is 9:00:00, and the increment is 1h. Once the problems and hours are entered on the first sheet, they can be copied to the other sheets to complete the table entries.

Figure 9.20
Worksheets
prepared for /Data
Table 3 command

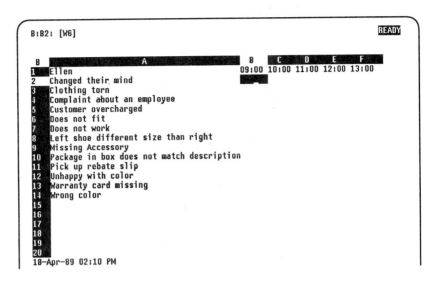

```
B:B2: [W6]                                                              READY

B                      A              B    C    D    E    F
1    Ellen                          09:00 10:00 11:00 12:00 13:00
2    Changed their mind
3    Clothing torn
4    Complaint about an employee
5    Customer overcharged
6    Does not fit
7    Does not work
8    Left shoe different size than right
9    Missing Accessory
10   Package in box does not match description
11   Pick up rebate slip
12   Unhappy with color
13   Warranty card missing
14   Wrong color
15
16
17
18
19
20
18-Apr-89 02:10 PM
```

After you create the input values for the three-way table, you can create the formulas and the input cells for the input values. Then put this formula in A:F1: @DCOUNT(A:A3..A:D12,0,A:F3..A:I4).

Choose an offset of 0 since any field in the column can be counted. Then copy the field names from A3..D3 to F3. You can use three of the cells below the field name for input cells. Finally, execute the /Data Table command. Select a three-way table and choose the range B:A1..G:J10 for the table's range. Select F1 for the formula the table uses. When 1–2–3 prompts for the first input cell (input values in the first column), select G4. When 1–2–3 prompts for the second input cell (input values in the top row), select F4. When 1–2–3 prompts for the third input cell (input values in the upper left corner), select H4.

The first three tables of the worksheet are shown in Figure 9.21, which has the first column in the five worksheets set to a width of 18 so you can see the data in the other columns. By following this sequence, you can combine the database statistical functions with the /Data Table functions to quickly create summary tables.

Figure 9.21 Results
of /Data Table 3
command

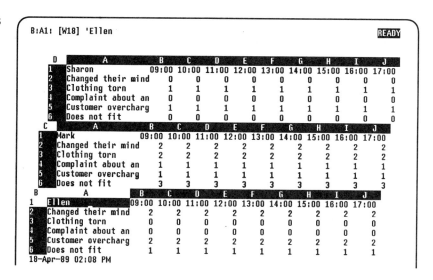

Data Table Labeled

With the one-, two- and three-way data tables, 1–2–3 places several restrictions on where you can put your data. 1–2–3's labeled tables bypass many of these restrictions. Labeled tables eliminate some of the restrictions that exist with the other data tables including the location of formulas, two- and three-way tables that evaluate more than one formula, and text insertion in the data table without affecting the table's results.

Using the previous example for three-way tables, suppose you want different types of information about the data. For example, you may want to calculate the number of different problems each person handles, the average time each person takes for a different type of problem, the maximum time it takes to handle one type of problem, and the breakdown by time for handling customers. You may also want to group the problems and compute summary statistics on each group.

Figure 9.22 shows a modified data table sheet for one of the customer representatives. The table contains text at the top that 1–2–3 uses as formula names. When a column has a formula name in this formula name range, it computes values for all of the cells included in the data table. 1–2–3 skips columns in the worksheet that do not have formula names and skips rows that do not have row values. In the example in Figure

9.22, 1–2–3 skips rows 3, 4, 10, 11, 13, and 14 since they do not have a value in the column with the row input values (column B). Also notice that the worksheet input value is in a different location. Labeled tables can have worksheet input values anywhere in the worksheet as long as the worksheet input values are in the same column and row in each worksheet included in the data table.

Figure 9.22 Data table shell for labeled table

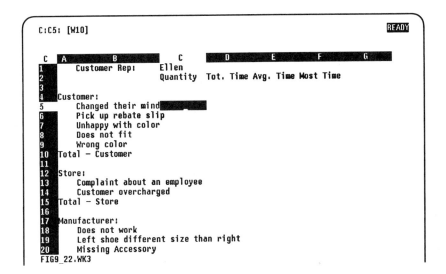

```
C:C5: [W10]                                                    READY

C   A        B          C        D        E        F       G
1       Customer Rep:   Ellen
2                       Quantity Tot. Time Avg. Time Most Time
3
4   Customer:
5       Changed their mind
6       Pick up rebate slip
7       Unhappy with color
8       Does not fit
9       Wrong color
10  Total — Customer
11
12  Store:
13      Complaint about an employee
14      Customer overcharged
15  Total — Store
16
17  Manufacturer:
18      Does not work
19      Left shoe different size than right
20      Missing Accessory
FIG9_22.WK3
```

When a column, row, or worksheet is not included in the data table, you can put in other information and the /Data Table Labeled command will not overwrite it. For example, C10 and D10 include @SUM(C5..C9) and @SUM(D5..C9) formulas. Like the data table shell for the three-way table, this shell is copied to the other worksheet for the other customer representatives. However, you can insert blank columns and rows in the other worksheets. Adding rows and columns do not affect the table results if the worksheet input values and the first row and column input values remain in the same row and column positions.

Once the data table shell is created, you can create the formulas and the input cells for the input values, as shown in Figure 9.23. The format of the formulas is text. As required of labeled tables, the formula names in the formula range must exactly match the formula names in the data table shell. Execute the /Data Table Labeled command to create the table. Select Formulas and choose B:A2..B:D3 as the formula range, including the formula names and formulas. Then select C3..F3 as the formula name range. For the row input variables, select Down, and select C:C5..C:C23 for the input range. Press Enter to confirm the range and select B7 as the input range. Select Sheets for the sheet input variables and C:C1..G:C1 for the input range. Press Enter to confirm the range and select C7 as the input range. Finally, select Go. The resulting table for Ellen is shown in Figure 9.24.

Figure 9.23
Worksheet
containing
formulas and
criteria range

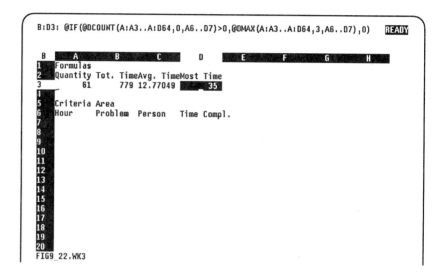

```
B:D3: @IF(@DCOUNT(A:A3..A:D64,0,A6..D7)>0,@DMAX(A:A3..A:D64,3,A6..D7),0)   READY

  B    A         B        C        D       E       F        G        H
 1 Formulas
 2 Quantity Tot. TimeAvg. TimeMost Time
 3       61       779 12.77049          35
 4
 5 Criteria Area
 6 Hour      Problem  Person   Time Compl.
 7
 8
 9
10
11
12
13
14
15
16
17
18
19
20
FIG9_22.WK3
```

Figure 9.24
Results of /Data
Table Labeled
command

```
C:C5: [W10] 2                                                            READY

  C    A           B            C       D           E          F        G
 1      Customer Rep:        Ellen
 2                           Quantity Tot. Time Avg. Time Most Time
 3
 4 Customer:
 5      Changed their mind         2        19        9.5       12
 6      Pick up rebate sli         2        23       11.5       12
 7      Unhappy with color         2        24         12       16
 8      Does not fit               1         6          6        6
 9      Wrong color                1        20         20       20
10 Total - Customer
11
12 Store:
13      Complaint about an         0         0          0        0
14      Customer overcharg         2        36         18       18
15 Total - Store
16
17 Manufacturer:
18      Does not work              2        22         11       21
19      Left shoe differen         1        17         17       17
20      Missing Accessory          0         0          0        0
FIG9_22.WK3
```

10

Using Built-in Functions with HAL (Releases 1A, 2, and 2.01 Only)

Lotus introduced HAL to provide an intelligent interface to 1–2–3 Release 2. HAL supports many of 1–2–3's tasks without the need for memorizing commands in 1–2–3's menu structure. You can use English commands to request HAL to perform tasks like printing and formatting. Thus, a simple request like **graph this** produces a graph.

HAL also supports the work of some of 1–2–3's @functions without the syntax requirements of an @function. Instead of entering @SUM(F2..F14), you can ask HAL to **total sales**. This chapter will focus on the HAL features that support the work of @functions.

ADVANTAGES OF USING HAL FOR SUPPORTED FUNCTIONS

HAL has several advantages over 1–2–3 when handling function tasks. First, HAL allows novice 1–2–3 users easier access commands. Second, HAL provides several options unavailable to 1–2–3. Third, HAL provides several shortcuts to 1–2–3.

This chapter focuses on using HAL with the 1–2–3 built-in functions. After reviewing HAL basics, you will learn how to perform calculations covered earlier in the 1–2–3 function chapters. Finally, you will learn how to use HAL to create powerful reports that extend 1–2–3's data management functions.

HAL Basics

Working with HAL is similar to telling someone what to do with your worksheet. When you talk to someone about your worksheet, you convey your request as sentences with each sentence describing one step in the process. As when you provide directions to an individual, you make a number of assumptions about that person's understanding of the topic. You work with HAL in a similar fashion. Using sentences, you tell HAL what to do. HAL then makes assumptions about the tasks you want it to accomplish unless you provide specific instructions to override these assumptions.

Since the requests you make of HAL are commands, these sentences do not have a subject. HAL expects that the commands start with a verb, such as add, average, or graph, that defines the basic task HAL should perform. In some instances, these verbs correspond to a 1-2-3 command such as Print or Format.

HAL requests have three optional components after the verb. These components tell HAL more about the action you want HAL to perform. A *location* after the verb tells HAL what area of the worksheet the action will affect. You can provide a specific location such as **A10** in **format A10 as percent**. A *qualifier* limits the scope of the action and makes the request more specific. The words **as fixed** in the request **format this as fixed** qualify the format request. The *destination* tells HAL where to put the results of the request. In the request **copy this to F1**, F1 is the destination.

For some actions, one or more qualifiers are needed. For other actions, you use only the components to change how HAL performs the action.

Using HAL's Special Location Options

1-2-3 supports cell addresses, range names, and range addresses as locations in its commands and functions. The location component of HAL requests need not be in the form that 1-2-3 uses.

HAL divides up your worksheet into *tables*, which are areas of your worksheet containing data of any type. At least two blank rows and two columns separate a table from other information. You can refer to the current table in a HAL request by using the word **this** in your request. You might enter **copy this to F1**. HAL then copies the current table to a location beginning at F1. The current table is defined by the location of the cell pointer and the boundary from other data created by two blank rows and columns.

Another special location designation is the word **it**, which always refers to the cell or range reference used in the last command. For example, if your first request is **format A1..H10 as currency** and your second request is **print it**, HAL prints A1..H10 when the second request is executed.

Your HAL requests can also refer to your worksheet by column letter or row number, as in **total column C**. As in 1-2-3, you can also refer to a location by the cell address, range name, or range address. Unlike 1-2-3, you can also refer to columns of rows by using Next and Previous. HAL defines a column or row name as the name at the beginning of the row or the top of the column within the table. For example, in Figure 10.1, Sales refers to row 5 and 1988 refers to column C.

Figure 10.1 HAL table with row and column labels

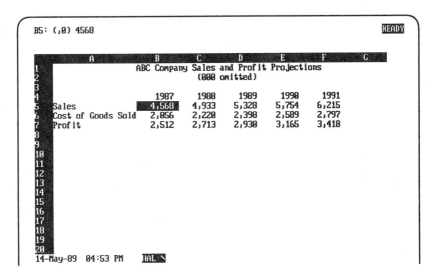

Entering HAL Requests

To enter a HAL request, you must have a request box like that in Figure 10.2. You can activate HAL's request box by typing a backslash (\) anytime 1-2-3 is in READY mode. After bringing the request box to the screen, you can have it stay on the screen by entering request **stay**. When you are finished entering HAL commands, you can tell HAL to **go away** to remove the request box from the screen.

Figure 10.2 HAL
request box

Editing HAL Requests

If you notice a mistake as you are typing, HAL lets you edit your request. Simply use the Left and Right Arrow keys to move to the area of your mistake and correct it. If you decide to start over, press the escape key to eliminate the entire request.

Pressing the Home and End keys has the same effect in a HAL request box as in 1-2-3's edit line. They move you to the beginning and end of the request. Ctrl + Right Arrow and Ctrl + Left Arrow move a word to the right or left within the request box.

Reexecuting a HAL Request

HAL remembers up to five hundred characters of request entries. You can use special keys to redisplay and execute these previous requests. The F3 key moves you backward through the requests that HAL has saved. One request at a time is displayed in the request box. After moving backward in the list, you can use the F4 key to move forward again. To reexecute any of the requests, press Enter with the request in the request box. This feature saves significant time if you repeat a series of similar requests because you can edit the request to create the new request.

Handling Problems

If HAL does not understand what you type, it either displays your request and prompts you to make changes, or it provides another dialog box and lets you insert the text that it does not understand into the current cell.

HAL has an undo feature that lets you undo your last request (but no others). Thus, if you make a request then change your mind, you can undo that particular request unless you have changed HAL's defaults or performed an action that affects an external device like a disk or printer. If you accidentally sort your data, add statistical functions with the report feature, or erase your worksheet, pressing Backspace undoes the action if there are no intervening requests. Release 2.2 and Release 3 users also have access to this Undo feature even though they do not work with HAL.

HAL's Vocabulary

Hal's vocabulary includes hundreds of words, many of which are synonyms for other words in that list. For example, you can use the word **sum** to request that HAL total a group of values. You can also use **add** or **total** to perform the same task. The description of each @function HAL supports includes a full list of allowed synonyms.

You can add your own synonyms to HAL. These synonyms can equate to an existing HAL word, a phrase composed of HAL words, or a 1–2–3 command. You can add your entries to one of the two synonym files supplied with HAL: SYN__US.PRN or SYN__UK.PRN. If you decide to add a new file, it must begin with SYN and have a filename extension of .PRN.

You can also import an existing synonym file into 1–2–3 to make changes. If you prefer, you can use your word processor. If you use 1–2–3, you must print the updated file to disk. Figure 10.3 provides a glimpse of some of the sample entries of the synonym file SYN__US.PRN.

Figure 10.3 A look at the entries in one of HAL's synonym files

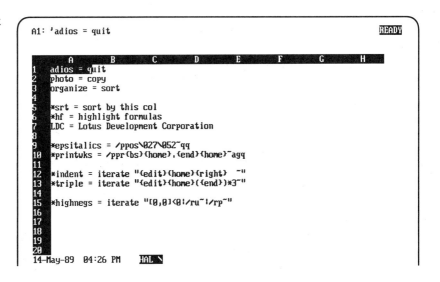

Abbreviating Entries

HAL lets you abbreviate many words in your sentences. Most of the words HAL uses can be typed as the first three letters of the word. For example, **format column A as general with 2 places** can be typed as **for col A as gen with 2 pla**. You will use these shortcuts as you become more comfortable working with HAL. The commands used in the remainder of this chapter will not be abbreviated, although you can enter them in abbreviated form if you prefer.

HAL does not let you abbreviate column and row labels, range names, and any synonyms that you add to HAL's word list. Note that several words have different abbreviations than the first three letters. Some of these words are first (1st), average (avg), standard (std) and percent (%).

STATISTICAL FUNCTIONS

HAL translates your requests for statistical computations into 1-2-3's statistical functions. Because you can use all of HAL's options for indicating the data that you want to use in the computation, the function is easy to enter. Since the end result is the same function you would have entered with 1-2-3, copying the entry is an easy task. This section discusses how you can use HAL to perform the same statistical functions you mastered in Chapter 2 for 1-2-3.

Using the Functions Across Rows or Down Columns

Many of HAL's requests operate on groups of columns or rows. By using a group of rows or columns to specify your needs, you save significant time. (With 1-2-3, you need to enter the formula in one cell and copy it to other locations as a separate step.) HAL accepts requests like **add all rows** or **add all columns**. HAL places the formula in the last row or column of a table. You can tell HAL to perform an action on a group of columns or rows such as **total columns D to G** or **add rows 10 to 20**.

Computing a Total

The verb **sum** tells HAL to compute the sum of a group of worksheet entries. When HAL executes your request, it records @SUM in a worksheet cell and references a list of worksheet entries. **Add** and **total** are two additional words that HAL recognizes as synonymous with sum.

You must specify a location for a sum request. Your location can be a range address, range name, column or row name, or a group of rows or columns. The sum request supports a destination if you want to tell HAL where to put the result of the computation. If you tell HAL to **total column A**, HAL will use a default destination for the total. If you tell HAL to **total column A in A100**, the result is placed in A100.

Figure 10.4 part one shows a worksheet just before HAL sums each row in the table. After this request is entered, the worksheet looks like Figure 10.3 part two. HAL has automatically determined the range for each of the @SUM functions in column H. When using HAL, you do not need to determine the range for the @SUM function or copy the formula from one cell to another.

Figure 10.4 (part one) Using HAL to compute the sums of each row

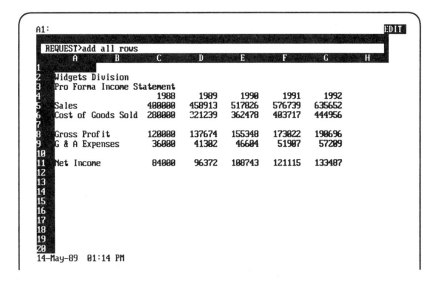

Figure 10.4
(part two)

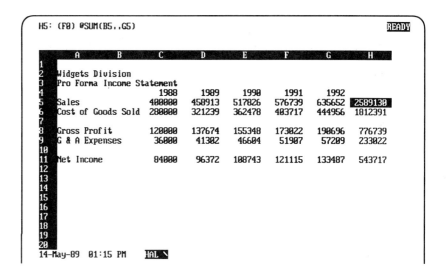

```
H5: (F0) @SUM(B5..G5)                                              READY

          A     B        C        D        E        F        G        H
1
2   Widgets Division
3   Pro Forma Income Statement
4                         1988     1989     1990     1991     1992
5   Sales               400000   458913   517826   576739   635652  2589130
6   Cost of Goods Sold  280000   321239   362478   403717   444956  1812391
7
8   Gross Profit        120000   137674   155348   173022   190696   776739
9   G & A Expenses       36000    41302    46604    51907    57209   233022
10
11  Net Income           84000    96372   108743   121115   133487   543717
12
13
14
15
16
17
18
19
20
    14-May-89  01:15 PM       HAL ⑤
```

Averaging

The verb average tells HAL to compute the average for a group of worksheet entries. When HAL executes your request, it records @AVG in
a worksheet cell and references a list of worksheet entries. **Avg** and
mean are two additional words that HAL recognizes as synonymous
with average.

You must specify a location for an average request. Your location can
be a range address, range name, column or row name, or a group of
rows or columns. The average request supports a destination if you
want to tell HAL where to put the result of the computation. If you
tell HAL to **average column A**, HAL uses a default destination for
the total. If you tell HAL to **average column A in A100**, the result
is placed in A100.

Figure 10.5 shows a worksheet just before HAL computes the average
for each column in the table. The request is entered as **average all
columns**. After HAL computes the average, the worksheet looks like
Figure 10.6. HAL automatically determines the range for each of the
@AVG functions in row 20. By using HAL, you do not need to copy
the formula from one cell to another. HAL also automatically puts a
row of hyphens between the table and the averages of the columns.

Figure 10.5
Worksheet before
HAL computes the
average

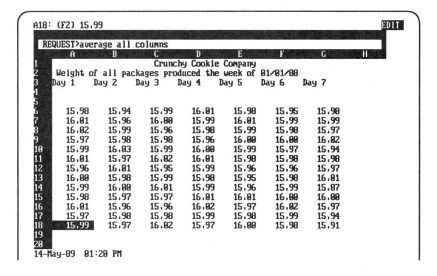

Figure 10.6
Worksheet after
HAL computes the
average

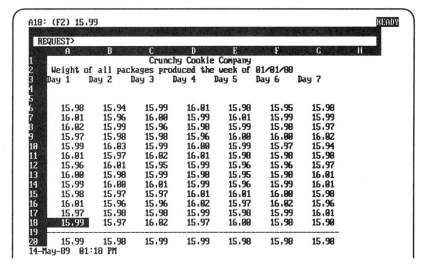

Determining the Highest or Lowest Value

HAL contains verbs that duplicate the function of the @MIN and @MAX
functions. To find the maximum value, use the verb **max** or **maximize**.
To find the minimum value, use the verb **min** or **minimize**.

Like the other verbs that duplicate statistical functions, **minimize** and **maximize** require a location in the request. You can use an optional destination if you want to store the result in a specific cell. Without a destination, HAL uses its assumptions to control the placement of the result.

HAL computes the minimum or maximum value in a table either by row or column or for the entire table. For example, if your table looks like Figure 10.7, asking HAL to determine the minimum value of each column produces a display like Figure 10.8. Row 21 contains the minimum value for each column. Adding the request shown at the top of Figure 10.9 computes the maximum value of the columns and places the value for each column in row 22. Since the minimize and maximize requests have specified where the output should go, HAL does not automatically create a line of hyphens to separate the table from the minimization or maximization functions. If the two requests did not have the destination specified, the second request would have replaced the first one.

Figure 10.7
Worksheet before
HAL determines
the minimum of
each column

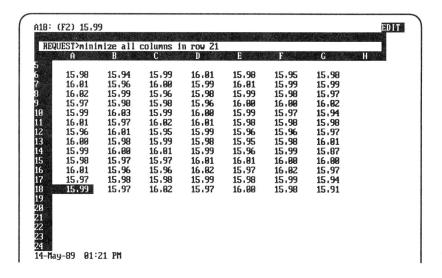

Figure 10.8
Worksheet after
HAL determines
the minimum of
each column

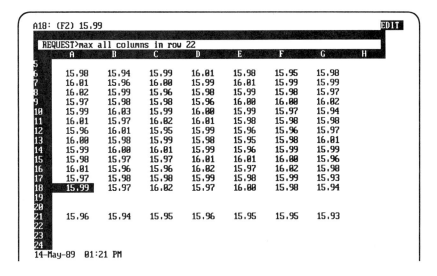

Figure 10.9
Worksheet after
HAL determines
the maximum of
each column

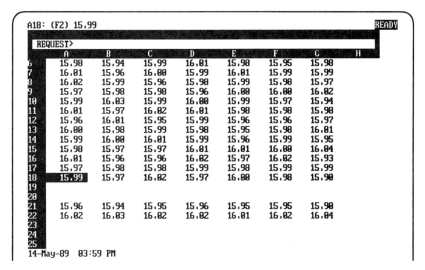

Determining the Variation in Data

HAL can easily compute variations and standard deviations in data. 1-2-3's variance function is invoked with **var** or **variance** in a HAL request. The standard deviation is represented by **std** or **standard deviation**. If you have not used these two measures of data dispersion in 1–2–3, read the descriptive material for the corresponding 1–2–3 functions in Chapter 2.

If your data looks like Figure 10.10, computing the variance is as simple as telling HAL **variance all columns**. The resulting display is Figure 10.11. The standard deviation for this data is computed the same way by telling HAL **std all columns**, which creates Figure 10.12.

Figure 10.10
Worksheet before computing each column's variances

```
A18: (F4) [W14] 15.99                                                    EDIT
 REQUEST>variance all columns
          A               B               C               D               E
5
6      15.9800         15.9400         15.9900         16.0100         15.9800
7      16.0100         15.9600         16.0000         15.9900         16.0100
8      16.0200         15.9900         15.9600         15.9800         15.9900
9      15.9700         15.9800         15.9800         15.9600         16.0000
10     15.9900         16.0300         15.9900         16.0000         15.9900
11     16.0100         15.9700         16.0200         16.0100         15.9800
12     15.9600         16.0100         15.9500         15.9900         15.9600
13     16.0000         15.9800         15.9900         15.9800         15.9500
14     15.9900         16.0000         16.0100         15.9900         15.9600
15     15.9800         15.9700         15.9700         16.0100         16.0100
16     16.0100         15.9600         15.9600         16.0200         15.9700
17     15.9700         15.9800         15.9800         15.9900         15.9800
18     15.9900         15.9700         16.0200         15.9700         16.0000
19
20
21
22
23
24
14-May-89  03:20 PM
```

Figure 10.11
Worksheet after HAL computed each column's variances

```
A18: (F4) [W14] 15.99                                                    READY
 REQUEST>
          A               B               C               D               E
5
6      15.9800         15.9400         15.9900         16.0100         15.9800
7      16.0100         15.9600         16.0000         15.9900         16.0100
8      16.0200         15.9900         15.9600         15.9800         15.9900
9      15.9700         15.9800         15.9800         15.9600         16.0000
10     15.9900         16.0300         15.9900         16.0000         15.9900
11     16.0100         15.9700         16.0200         16.0100         15.9800
12     15.9600         16.0100         15.9500         15.9900         15.9600
13     16.0000         15.9800         15.9900         15.9800         15.9500
14     15.9900         16.0000         16.0100         15.9900         15.9600
15     15.9800         15.9700         15.9700         16.0100         16.0100
16     16.0100         15.9600         15.9600         16.0200         15.9700
17     15.9700         15.9800         15.9800         15.9900         15.9800
18     15.9900         15.9700         16.0200         15.9700         16.0000
19 ------------------------------------------------------------------------------
20      0.0003          0.0005          0.0005          0.0003          0.0003
21
22
23
24
14-May-89  03:20 PM
```

Figure 10.12
Worksheet after
HAL computed
each column's
standard deviation

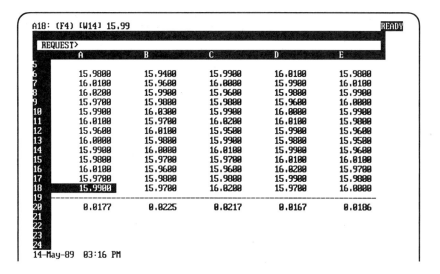

USING HAL FOR STRING FUNCTIONS

HAL supports some 1–2–3 string functions. You can create requests
that parallel @UPPER, @LOWER, and @PROPER functions in 1–2–3.
There are also verbs that correlate to @STRING and @VALUE. These
two functions convert 1–2–3 data entries between labels and values.
The final string function supported is @LEFT, which serves to abbreviate worksheet entries at a specific number of characters.

Converting Data

Converting data from values to labels or from labels to values is a cum-
bersome process that normally requires several steps. Ordinarily, you
enter the conversion function @STRING or @VALUE for one cell. Next,
you copy it to the other cells that you want to convert. Then, you use
/Range Value to freeze the results and copy them back over the original
entries.

Performing the same steps with HAL is easier since you simply tell
it to **convert column C to labels**. HAL then determines the formula,
enters it, copies it, and replaces the old entries with the new ones.

The verb **convert** is used to begin the HAL request whether you are converting labels to values or values to labels. You must include the qualifier **to labels** in your request to convert values to labels.

If you use the verb **convert** without a location, it converts the current cell. You can use any of the other valid HAL entries for location. Some valid requests might be **convert col G to labels**, **convert codes**, **convert this row to labels**. If you tell HAL to **convert this**, HAL converts the entire table.

Figure 10.13 shows a column of quantities entered as centered labels. When the request **convert Quantity** is entered, Hal converts the labels to values as shown in Figure 10.14.

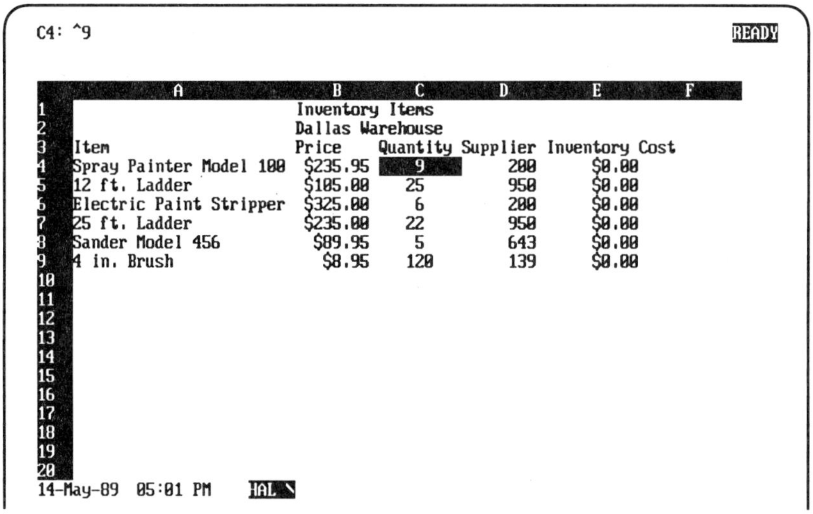

Figure 10.13 Label data requiring conversion to values

```
C4: ^9                                                          READY

         A              B        C        D        E        F
1                 Inventory Items
2                 Dallas Warehouse
3  Item           Price    Quantity Supplier Inventory Cost
4  Spray Painter Model 100 $235.95     9       200     $0.00
5  12 ft. Ladder          $105.00    25       950     $0.00
6  Electric Paint Stripper $325.00     6       200     $0.00
7  25 ft. Ladder          $235.00    22       950     $0.00
8  Sander Model 456        $89.95     5       643     $0.00
9  4 in. Brush             $8.95    120       139     $0.00
10
11
12
13
14
15
16
17
18
19
20
14-May-89  05:01 PM    HAL
```

Figure 10.14
Converted data
stored as values

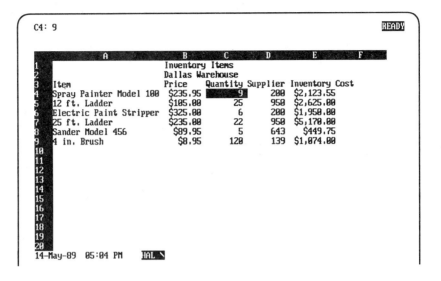

```
C4: 9                                                           READY

              A              B       C        D        E        F
1                     Inventory Items
2                     Dallas Warehouse
3      Item           Price    Quantity Supplier Inventory Cost
4      Spray Painter Model 100 $235.95      9      200  $2,123.55
5      12 ft. Ladder          $105.00     25      950  $2,625.00
6      Electric Paint Stripper $325.00      6      200  $1,950.00
7      25 ft. Ladder          $235.00     22      950  $5,170.00
8      Sander Model 456        $89.95      5      643    $449.75
9      4 in. Brush              $8.95    120      139  $1,074.00
10
11
12
13
14
15
16
17
18
19
20
       14-May-89  05:04 PM     HAL
```

Changing the Case for Label Entries

HAL easily converts your data to uppercase, lowercase, or propercase.
Unlike with 1–2–3, you can convert the data with one simple request.
There is no need to enter a formula, copy it, freeze the values, and
move it over the original data.

To convert a column of labels to uppercase, use the verb **upper, uppercase**, or **capitalize**. If you enter the verb without a location, the current cell will be affected. To capitalize the entries in B4..B40, request
capitalize B4..B40.

HAL also supports lowercase and propercase changes. To convert entries
to lowercase, use the verb **lower** or **lowercase**. To convert entries
to propercase, use **proper** or **propercase**. The rest of the syntax for
these requests follows the pattern established for uppercase.

Abbreviating Entries

In 1–2–3, the @LEFT function extracts a specified number of characters
from the left side of a string. You can use this function to abbreviate
string entries in worksheet cells. For example, you might have a list
of part numbers in Column A and wish to display only the first three
characters representing the vendor code. Entering @LEFT(A4,3)

extracts the first three characters from an entry in this column. If you copy the function down the column, you will have the vendor codes for all the part numbers. After converting the entries with /Range Value, you can move the converted entries over the original entries.

HAL lets you accomplish the same task with the abbreviate request. You can use the verbs **abbreviate**, **shorten**, or **truncate** to express your request. Without a location, only the current cell is affected. You can enter the conversion request for the data in Figure 10.15 as **abbreviate column A**. To tell HAL how many characters you want in your abbreviated entry, add the qualifier **at n characters** where n is replaced by the number of characters you want. If you don't tell HAL how many characters you want in your abbreviated entry, it will have three. HAL does not provide an equivalent request for the @RIGHT or @MID function.

Figure 10.15 Data for abbreviate request

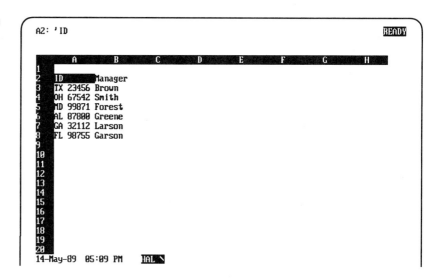

Replacing Text

1-2-3 provides the @REPLACE function to replace all or part of a character string. You specify the original string, the beginning location, the number of characters you want to replace, and the replacement text.

HAL can imitate @REPLACE in many cases. For example, to replace all occurrences of Paper in Figure 10.16 with Computer Paper, type

replace all "Paper" with "Computer Paper" in column A

Figure 10.16
Database set up in
a worksheet

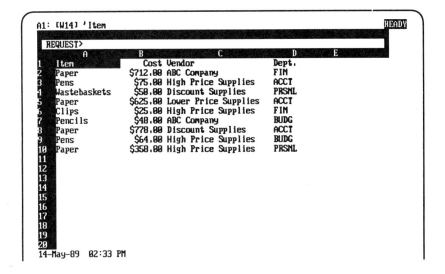

This request takes every occurrence of Paper in column A and replaces it with Computer Paper. While the quotes around Paper are optional, the quotes around Computer Paper are necessary since quotes are required with phrases. The results are shown in Figure 10.17. Capitalization in the text you are searching for is ignored. Capitalization in the replacement text controls the appearance of the completed entry. The word **all** in the request acts as a qualifier; without it, only the first occurrence is replaced.

Figure 10.17
Worksheet after
HAL replaces text

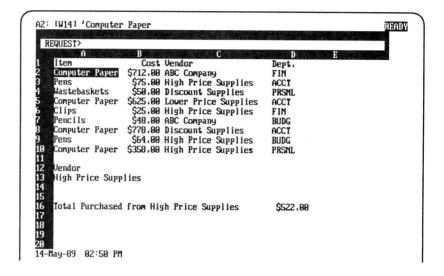

REPLACING AND ENHANCING 1–2–3'S DATABASE STATISTICAL FUNCTIONS

In 1–2–3, you can create databases and use the database statistical functions to extract summary statistics for records that meet criterion values which you enter on the worksheet. You can also create a Data Table to record the summary statistic values for a range of criterion entries.

HAL offers options that are a little different. There is no direct counterpart to the database statistical functions for a single criterion value. Instead, HAL automatically creates a table that tabulates the statistics for each value in the field representing criterion. HAL also provides a report feature that organizes database records and provides summary statistics for each group of records.

Although HAL's options offer greater sophistication, they are simpler to use. Depending on the type of report you need, you can use either the report or the tabulate features.

Using HAL's Report Feature

HAL's report feature combines a number of 1–2–3 features as well as some capabilities that 1–2–3 does not support. When you ask HAL to create a report, it automatically sequences the data by the field that you specify. This is equivalent to the effect of 1–2–3's /Data Sort command. HAL adds a blank line when a change occurs in the value in the field you are sequencing. This extra space allows room for a statistical computation on the values in a field that you specify. Unlike 1–2–3, which has no related feature to automatically add these subtotal type breaks, HAL can compute a total, average, or other statistical computation on the field for you automatically.

The verb for the HAL report feature is **report**. Simply tell HAL the sequence for your report with the word **on** followed by a field name as in **report on item**. HAL then sequences the records by item.

There is another part of the request that must be completed since HAL needs a field on which to perform its computations. For all statistical features except **count**, this field must contain value entries. To tell HAL which field you want to work with, append the word **and** to the request and follow it by a field name. Your request for the database in Figure 10.16 might be **report on item and cost**.

Since the request does not specify the type of statistical computation or the location for the results, HAL makes assumptions about both things. When the statistical computation is not specified, HAL assumes that you want to sum for each break in the controlling field. It also assumes that you want these results stored beneath the database. HAL provides a warning box before writing over this area. If you have other data stored there, you must reexecute the request, specifying a location for the report output.

HAL separates the different items into smaller groups below the current table. The original database records are left intact. This ensures that your original data is unharmed and allows HAL to perform another statistical function.

Figure 10.18 shows the results of HAL's actions. For each group, HAL adds the Cost column and puts the @SUM function below the group. To use a statistical function other than @SUM, insert the word representing the statistical function in place of the AND in the request. To perform the different statistical functions on the database in Figure 10.16, type the following requests:

To count: REPORT ON ITEM COUNTING COST
To average: REPORT ON ITEM AVERAGING COST

To find the lowest value: REPORT ON ITEM MINIMIZE COST
To find the highest value: REPORT ON ITEM MAXIMIZE COST
To compute the variance: REPORT ON ITEM VARIANCE COST
To compute the standard deviation: REPORT ON ITEM STANDARD COST

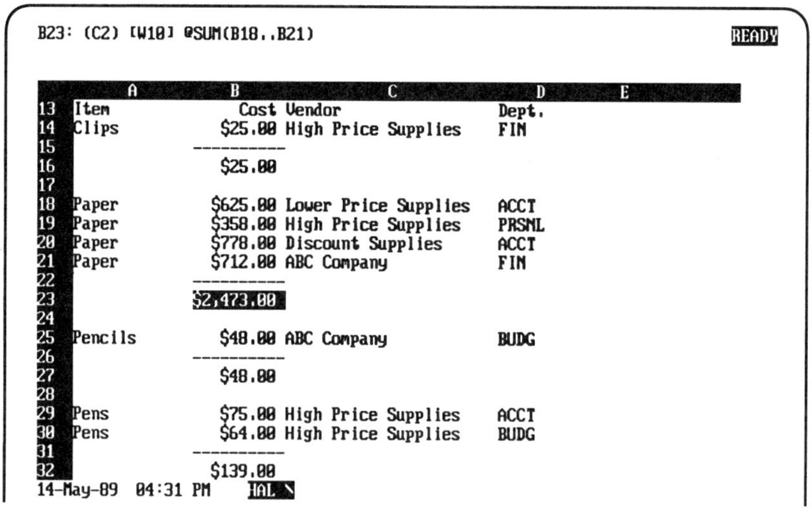

Figure 10.18
Database separated
into sections based
on item

Tabulating Statistics

Chapter 8 discussed 1–2–3's Data Table features for use with the database statistical functions. You found that you could create a table shell and have HAL fill in statistical computations for the database entries that you requested. HAL makes it easy for you since it can automatically create a one-way table. HAL sets up the table shell and the criterion area needed to produce statistics for each value in the table. When it creates the table shell, it uses every value it finds in the field that you specify. For example, if you specify the location field, HAL places each unique location down the left edge of the table before completing its computations.

To create your table request, you must position the cell pointer within the database. You can use the words **xtab**, **crosstab**, **crosstabulate**, **make a table**, or **create a table** to start your request. Next, specify the field that HAL will use to create the entries in the table column. HAL searches this field for unique entries. The next entry should be a statistical function like **averaging**, **totaling**, **counting**, **maximizing**, or **minimizing**. The next entry is a field or a group of adjacent fields like **salary** or **col s thru col z**. If you do not specify the location for the output, HAL warns you before overwriting the area beneath the database. To specify an output location, use **in** followed by the address of the upper-left cell in the output area. Some valid requests for tabulations might be

tab location counting employees
tab item summing costs
make a table of location averaging salary

Figure 10.19 displays a tabulation on the database shown in Figure 10.16. The request used to create this table was **xtab item totaling cost**.

Figure 10.19
Results from HAL's
tabulate feature

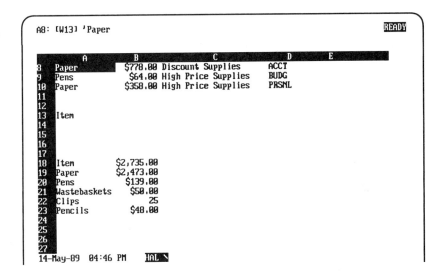

```
A8: [W13] 'Paper                                              READY

           A          B              C             D        E
 8    Paper        $778.00 Discount Supplies    ACCT
 9    Pens          $64.00 High Price Supplies  BUDG
10    Paper        $358.00 High Price Supplies  PRSNL
11
12
13    Item
14
15
16
17
18    Item       $2,735.00
19    Paper      $2,473.00
20    Pens         $139.00
21    Wastebaskets  $50.00
22    Clips             25
23    Pencils       $48.00
24
25
26
27
14-May-89  04:46 PM    HAL
```

ENTERING OTHER FUNCTIONS THROUGH HAL'S REQUEST BOX

The previous paragraph explained how HAL cannot always count worksheet columns properly. HAL lets you compensate by typing formulas into the request box directly. For example, if you move the cell to B19 and type **@COUNT(B3..B17)**, HAL places the formula in B19. You can then either have HAL copy the formula across the row or use 1–2–3's /Copy command. When you type a / in HAL's request box, HAL immediately transfers control to 1–2–3. Typing the entry is an option that provides access to all of the @functions that HAL does not directly support.

11

Using @Functions in Macros

1-2-3 lets you record menu selections and play them back later to perform a task without having to enter the keystrokes again. 1-2-3 also has an entire macro language that is similar to a programming language. With 1-2-3's macro command language, you can built sophisticated applications with menus, error and validity checking, and messages for the user. In addition to using the macro commands in the command language macros, you can use @functions, which add significant power.

Since macros themselves are already an advanced technique, you will want to use this chapter only after developing a set of macro creation skills. This book is not intended to provide the necessary training in macro techniques. You can refer to the 1-2-3 manual or books like *The Lotus Guide To Learning 1-2-3 Macros* or *The Lotus Guide To Advanced Macro Commands* for such instruction. Only a few macro basics will be reviewed in this chapter before looking at specific applications for using @functions in macros. The examples offer a creative approach to business solutions that incorporate one or more @functions in solving macro problems and will help to broaden your perspective when designing macros to meet your needs.

BASIC MACRO BUILDING BLOCKS

Macros are composed of two basic building blocks: recorded 1-2-3 menu selections and macro commands. In addition to these two components, you can use representations of special keyboard keys, keystroke entries that will be duplicated when the macro runs, @functions, and formulas.

To record 1-2-3 menu selections in a macro, you record the keystrokes that you would type to invoke the command. You must enter these keystrokes as a label, which means you must start your entry with a single quotation mark in some instances. For example, to enter the command to format an entry as currency, your entry is '/rfc0. The apostrophe causes 1-2-3 to store the entry in the current worksheet cell rather than executing the keystrokes immediately.

Note that each menu selection is made with the letter that begins the selection rather than using the arrow keys to move to the selection and pressing Enter. Although 1-2-3 will not reject the latter approach, avoid it because it might be incompatible with later releases.

Macro command language commands are keywords enclosed in curly braces { }. In most instances, one or more arguments are required to tell 1-2-3 how to use the command. For example, {BRANCH Print} tells 1-2-3 to change the execution flow of the macro instructions and to begin executing the instructions stored at Print.

Special keyboard representations include options for all of the cell pointer movement keys. Most of these keys are represented by keywords encased in curly braces { }. The Down Arrow is represented by {DOWN}. A shortcut for repeating it several times allows you to enter the number of repetitions after the keyword. You can use a number, formula, or function to convey the number of repetitions to 1-2-3. For example, {DOWN 7}, {DOWN 5*4}, and {DOWN @ROWS(DATABASE)} are all valid ways of telling 1-2-3 how many times you want the Down Arrow key pressed during the macro's execution.

The representation for the Enter key does not require braces. It is represented by the tilde (~). This key representation is frequently forgotten by novices as they learn to create macros. If you type /RFC0, 1-2-3 waits for you to finalize the selection of the number of decimal places and to specify a range for the instruction. Typing /RFC0 ~ ~ tells 1-2-3 to format the current cell as currency with 0 decimal places. The two tilde indicators make the important difference in the two entries.

@Functions and formulas can be used for many of the arguments in command language instructions. If the command expects a string, the function selected should be one that returns an appropriate label. If the macro command expects a value, the @function must return a value.

With the earlier releases of 1–2–3, @functions can be used as the main entry in a macro cell producing a string that is a macro command. This option allows you to create macros that dynamically alter the macro instructions as the macro is executed although it is an option that should be reserved for the power user since it is difficult to document, debug, and maintain.

Releases 2.2 and 3.0 have new options that allow you to avoid this approach. You can now include @functions that are arguments within macro commands, thereby eliminating the need to compute the function result and store it in a separate cell.

ENTERING, NAMING, AND EXECUTING MACROS

Entering macros requires that you choose an area of the worksheet that will not interfere with other worksheet entries. You will want to choose a column in this area for the macros since they are recorded in a continuous group of cells down a column of the worksheet. You can use 1–2–3's recorder for menu command entries, like /RFCI, but you will have to type the entries when you want to use the command language for entries like {GETNUMBER}. Since @functions are used primarily with more complicated macros that require the command language, use of the recorder feature is not included.

When you record a macro command, only the curly braces can be used; neither the square braces nor the parentheses can be used as a substitute. The keyword follows immediately after the open brace. It must be spelled exactly as shown in the examples and your 1–2–3 manual. Abbreviations for these words are accepted in limited circumstances, such as the use of {L}, {R}, {U}, and {D} for the direction arrow keys and several other keyname options. Although you have the choice of either uppercase or lowercase, all keywords are shown in uppercase in this book. Do not add extra spaces anywhere in the keyword.

For macro commands that require arguments, a space is expected after the keyword and before the start of the first argument. For a command with multiple arguments, a comma (,) is used as a separator after each argument as in {FOR counter,1,15,1,Start}. When one of the arguments is a function, it is recorded with the same method used in recording functions alone. For example, the same function for the preceding example can be modified to include a function for one of the arguments, as in {FOR counter,1,@ROWS(Database),1,Start}. For a keyword that does not have arguments, the closing brace follows immediately after the keyword as in {WINDOWSOFF}.

You must name the top cell in the macro with a special name that allows you to invoke it from the keyboard when using Releases 1A, 2.0, and 2.01. Releases 2.2 and 3 allow you to use a lengthy name although a different method is required to execute this type of macro, since only the letter name macros can be invoked with 1-2-3's shortcut method. The name that you must use begins with a backslash (\ ) and is immediately followed by any single alphabetic character. 1-2-3 does not distinguish between upper- and lowercase for these entries. To apply the name, move to the top cell and use the /Range Name Create command, enter the special name, and press Enter twice to end the name and establish the current cell as the one to which it applies.

Another approach for naming macro cells serves a dual purpose, since it documents the name on the worksheet and uses the entry for the name without reentering it. To use this approach, move one cell to the left of the top macro cell, then enter an apostrophe followed by a backslash and the letter for the macro name. The apostrophe is needed to prevent the backslash from being interpreted as a repeating label indicator. You can position your cell pointer on the name entry and use /Range Name Labels Right to assign it to the macro cell.

You do not need the special name to name other sections of macro code. You can use any name acceptable for a 1-2-3 range name.

To execute a macro, press the Alt key in combination with the letter used in the macro name if you use the backslash (\ ) and a letter for the macro name (Alt+m, for example). For a Release 2.2 or 3 macro with a longer name, use the Alt-F3 (RUN) key to execute the macro.

A LOOK AT SOME SPECIFIC @FUNCTION EXAMPLES

In this section you will have an opportunity to look at a variety of macro examples. Each macro presented uses at least one of the @functions to perform its tasks. After a general explanation of the macro's task, you will be able to look at an explanation of each step within the macro. Steps that do not contain functions are explained fully since it is important to understand the entire macro to utilize the function steps.

Although capitalization is not important in macro names or instructions, the following standards are observed for all of the function examples

- @Functions are shown in capital letters as in @ROWS.

- Range names are shown in proper case as in Print, Code, and Database.

- Macro keywords are shown in all capitals as in {BRANCH} and {GETNUMBER}.

- Cell addresses and range addresses are shown in lower case. The entries f11 and a1..a10 are examples.

Date Stamping a Worksheet

You can use @TODAY or @NOW to date stamp a worksheet. @TODAY is available in all releases of 1–2–3 and @NOW was introduced with Release 2. The @NOW function provides a time stamp in addition to the date stamp. The decimal fraction of the resulting number represents the time. When you enter @TODAY in Release 2, 2.01, or 2.2, your entry is converted to @INT(@NOW), which is equivalent to @TODAY since it drops the decimal fraction from the result. Release 3.0 reverts to the direct support of @TODAY without conversion, just as Release 1A did.

Figure 11.1 shows two different date stamp macros. The first macro, \d, provides a fixed date stamp equal to the current date. If you save a worksheet after using this date stamp macro and retrieve it several days later, the cell containing the date stamp will show the original date of entry.

Figure 11.1 Date
stamp macros

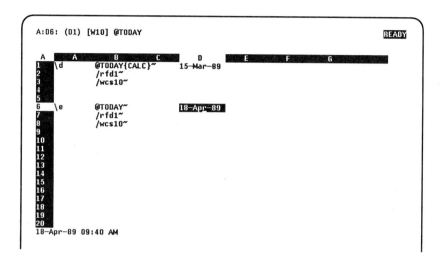

The second macro, \e, provides a date stamp that is automatically up-dated. When you first use this macro, the current system date displays in the cell containing the date stamp. If you save the worksheet and retrieve it several days later, the current system date displays.

Since only the top cell in each macro differs, we can examine them together. Cells D1 and D6 in Figure 11.1 contain the results after positioning on these cells and executing macros \d and \e respectively.

- **@TODAY{CALC}** ~—This command from the \d macro enters @TODAY to access the current system date. Before finalizing the entry, the entry is calculated with the F9 {CALC} representation. This records the serial date number in the cell rather than the function.

- **@TODAY** ~—This entry records the function @TODAY directly in the worksheet cell. 1-2-3 obtains a new value for the cell containing this entry anytime you retrieve the worksheet. When used in Release 3 or 1A, the cell entry is @TODAY. In other releases, the same entry results in a cell containing @INT(@NOW).

- **/rfd1** ~—This command formats the cell containing the date stamp entry as date format 1.

- **/wcs10** ~—This macro instruction sets the width of the column containing the date stamp to 10 since date format 1 requires 10 positions.

Using @IF Within a Macro to Record the Payment Type for a Loan

You can use @PMT to calculate loan payments anywhere in a worksheet. When you want to add a little sophistication to your application, you can design an entry screen for the required data that responds to one loan at a time. Figure 11.2 displays the entry screen with the first set of entries and results. Label entries were placed in D1..D11. Several spaces were added to the beginning of the label in D1 to achieve a centered effect above the data. C15 contains a label entry instructing users how to use the application.

Figure 11.2
Entry screen

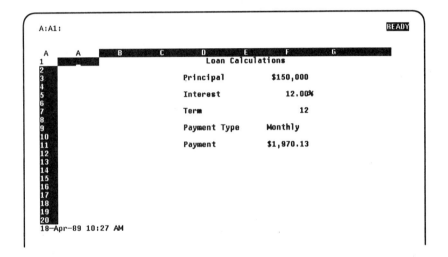

The @IF function plays an important role in this macro because it lets you use one of two entries for a variable. Note that @IF is different than the {IF} macro command; they both evaluate an expression as true or false, the similarity ends at that point. The {IF} command executes the macro instruction on the same line if the condition is true and executes the command on the next line if the command is false. @IF, however, contains two values within the expression. The first is the result for the if statement if the condition test is true, and the second is the result of the if statement if the condition is false. In many cases, the {BRANCH} command is used for the true value to prevent 1-2-3 from executing the false option on the next line. In essence, {IF} chooses a macro command and @IF selects a return value.

In the sample macro, cells F3, F5, and F11 are formatted to display the entries in the best form. Currency with zero places is used for F3, percent with two places is used for F5, and currency with two places is used for the computed payment amount. A 10.5% is entered in F5 as a constant with no user option for changing this entry, but you can modify the macro to allow the entry of an interest rate if you wish.

The macro that requests entries for the required fields is shown in Figure 11.3. It requests a principal, the payment schedule, and the term. Rather than asking the user to make the term and schedule consistent, the macro handles any data conversion that may be needed to ensure that the interest rate, term, and payment frequency are the same time period.

Figure 11.3 Data entry macro

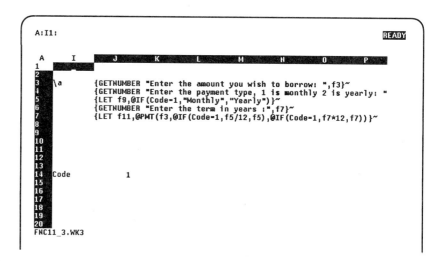

{GETNUMBER ''Enter the amount you wish to borrow :'',f3} ~

When this macro instruction executes, the message within the quotation marks displays. 1-2-3 waits for the user to type something and press Enter. Although a loan amount is expected, there are no controls to ensure that the proper type of entry was made. A space and a colon follow the message. These additions improve the appearance of the display when the user types a response.

The entry is stored in F3. The tilde (~) which follows the instruction causes 1-2-3 to update the entry in F3 immediately.

{GETNUMBER "Enter the payment type, 1 is monthly, 2 is yearly :",Code} ~

> This macro instruction provides a message stating the valid responses. No check is made to ensure that these are the only responses entered. The current macro code assumes that any entry other than 1 is yearly. You can add additional instructions to check the validity of the entry. The entry is stored in a range named Code. In this example /Range Name Labels Right was used to name J14, Code. This instruction assumes that Code was entered in I14 prior to executing the command. The tilde (~) is needed to effect immediate updating.

{LET f9,@IF(Code = 1,"Monthly","Yearly")} ~

> The schedule for the payments is displayed on the screen as a word rather than a numeric code. If Code contains a 1, the @IF statement places Monthly in F9. Any other entry places Yearly in that position. The tilde causes the update to be immediate.

{GETNUMBER "Enter the term in years :",f7} ~

> This statement displays a message and stores the value entered in F7.

{LET f11,@PMT(f3,@IF(Code = 1,f5/12,f5),@IF(Code = 1,f7*12,f7))} ~

> This statement sets F11 equal to the result of the @PMT function. Two of the function arguments, interest and term, are represented by @IF statements. These statements handle the necessary conversion of both quantities when you calculate a monthly payment.

> You could create this macro as a \0 macro to have 1–2–3 automatically begin executing this macro when you retrieve the worksheet file. You might also want to add an instruction to erase the entries from the previous calculation when you retrieve the file although another approach is not to save the file to disk each time.

Using @CHOOSE and @VALUE to Direct the Flow of a Macro

> 1–2–3's menu commands allow you to create menus that are identical to the type of menus that 1–2–3 uses. You can also create a full screen menu that allows you to design the appearance of the display. Figure 11.4 shows a menu that allows the user to enter the number representing their selection. With a full screen menu you will need a different method for processing the user's selections.

Figure 11.4 Full
screen menu

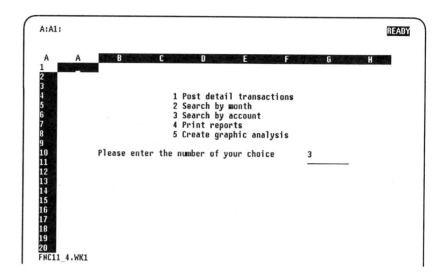

The macro can display the menu and wait for the user to enter a key-stroke. Based on the entry, processing can be completed by different routines. Figure 11.5 shows the short macro that processes the entry. The various routines currently function as place holders since the code has not as yet been entered for each of the options.

Figure 11.5
Processing the
menu selection

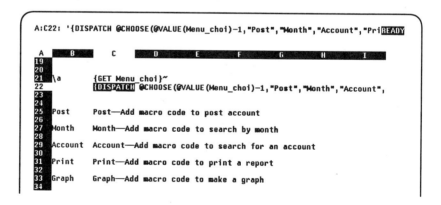

{GET Menu__choi} ~

This command accepts a single keystroke and places it in a variable that you named Menu__choi. Despite the fact that the user enters a number, this command stores the entry as a label.

{DISPATCH @CHOOSE(@VALUE(Menu__choi)-1,"Post","Month","Account",
"Print","Graph")}

> The DISPATCH command allows you to specify a cell that contains an address to which you want to branch. You can select a range name with @CHOOSE. 1–2–3 would look at that location for a routine name or a cell address. The important part of this instruction is selecting a range name based on @CHOOSE. Menu__choi is used to tell 1–2–3 which routine from the list you want. Because @CHOOSE expects a value and @GET returns a label, @VALUE is used to handle the conversion.

Post—Add Macro Code to Post Account

> This is the first of the routine names that can be selected. Instead of showing a cell address or range name to which the DISPATCH instruction can branch, this instruction contains text that will be entered in the current cell. This technique is effective in testing the main logic of a macro. You will want to be certain to press the Escape key when the macro ends to clear this entry from the control panel.

Using Time Functions When Displaying Messages

> In some instances, you will want to display a message to the user and leave it on the screen until they acknowledge it. Other less critical messages can be displayed for a brief time and removed or replaced. 1–2–3's macro command {WAIT} can be used in combination with time functions to achieve these results.

> The macro code is shown in Figure 11.6. The macro can continue with application instructions after the last message was displayed. The only preliminary task required is naming a cell Entry. Although you would probably choose an out-of-the-way location, the sample macro uses cell J13.

Figure 11.6
Displaying
messages

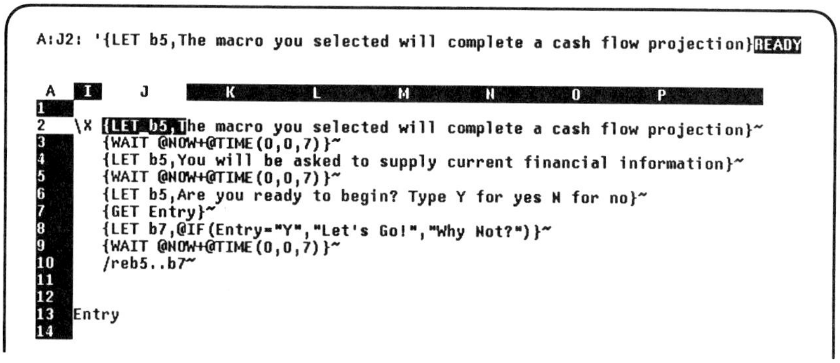

```
A:J2:  '{LET b5,The macro you selected will complete a cash flow projection}READY

   A  I    J        K        L        M        N        O        P
  1
  2  \X {LET b5,The macro you selected will complete a cash flow projection}~
  3     {WAIT @NOW+@TIME(0,0,7)}~
  4     {LET b5,You will be asked to supply current financial information}~
  5     {WAIT @NOW+@TIME(0,0,7)}~
  6     {LET b5,Are you ready to begin? Type Y for yes N for no}~
  7     {GET Entry}~
  8     {LET b7,@IF(Entry="Y","Let's Go!","Why Not?")}~
  9     {WAIT @NOW+@TIME(0,0,7)}~
 10     /reb5..b7~
 11
 12
 13  Entry
 14
```

{LET b5, "The macro you selected will compute a cash flow projection"} ~

> This instruction produces the first message display. The character string
> shown in the instruction is placed in B5. You may want to add another
> instruction at the beginning of the macro to position the cursor so the
> messages are in view. Entering {HOME} handles this task.

{WAIT @NOW + @TIME(0,0,7) } ~

> This statement is used three different places in the macro. Each use
> generates a seven-second wait before the macro proceeds to the next
> instruction. The length of the wait is dictated by the @NOW time plus
> an increment created by the @TIME function.

{LET b5, "You will be asked to supply current financial information"} ~

> This instruction replaces the message in B5 with a new entry.

{LET b5,"Are you ready to begin? Type Y for yes N for no"} ~

> After executing another wait instruction, the macro displays this new
> message in B5.

{GET Entry} ~

> Rather than using a wait instruction, you can use a get instruction to
> force the user to acknowledge the message with an entry.

{LET b7,@IF(Entry=''y'',''Let's Go!'',''Why Not?'')}~

> This instruction looks at the user response stored in Entry and deter-
> mines which of two messages to display with the @IF statement. A
> wait instruction follows this message to insure that the information is
> on the screen for a sufficient period of time. Figure 11.7 shows the screen
> with the last two messages displayed.

Figure 11.7
Message display

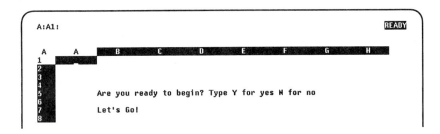

/reb5..b7~

> This instruction erases the entries in B5..B7. You would place the re-
> maining application instructions at this location in the macro.

Using String Functions to Verify Data Entry

> String functions can perform a variety of validity checking tasks. You
> can examine database entries with these functions by checking the entire
> entry or a small portion of the entry.

> The @LENGTH function determines the length of a character string.
> @MID, @RIGHT, and @LEFT allow you to look at part of an entry.

> The macro that you will examine uses @MID and @LENGTH to check
> aspects of a social security number entry. The macro is shown in Figure
> 11.8. The macro starts with four subroutine calls. (A subroutine call
> is nothing more than a macro name enclosed in curly braces.) Since
> the macro code does not need to be invoked with a keyboard command,
> you can use any valid range name when you name the macro. Each
> of these subroutine calls are designed to handle the entry of a specific
> type of data although only the Ss—no routine is shown. The subroutine
> begins in row 6 and executes this routine repeatedly until there is no
> error in the entry.

Figure 11.8 Validity
checking macro

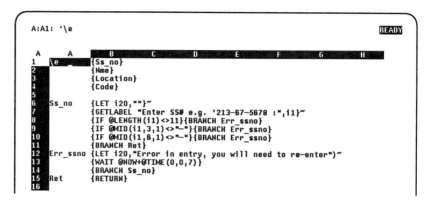

{LET I20,'' ''} ~

> This instruction initializes I20, the cell containing an error message when
> a problem occurs. You may want to add an instruction to the macro to
> ensure that this cell will be visible to display an error message. An entry
> of {GOTO i1} would handle the task. The double quotes in this instruc-
> tion are referred to as a null string. They set the cell equal to nothing.

{GETLABEL "Enter SS# e.g. '213-67-5678 :",I1 } ~

> This instruction requests the user to enter a social security number.
> It displays a proper format for the entry on the screen. This is impor-
> tant since the user must enter the label indicator as the first character
> or the dashes will be interpreted as minus signs. The entry is stored
> in I1.

{IF @LENGTH(I1) < >11 }{BRANCH Err__ssno}

> This is the first validity checking instruction, and it determines whether
> the length of the entry in I1 is not exactly equal to 11. When the length
> is any value other than 11, 1-2-3 branches to Err__ssno.

{IF @MID(I1,3,1) < >''-''}{BRANCH Err__ssno}

> This command checks for a dash (-) in the third position of I1. Since
> 1-2-3 begins counting string positions from 0 rather than 1, the instruc-
> tion must specify the third position. If position 3 is anything other than
> a dash, 1-2-3 branches to Err__ssno.

{IF @MID(I1,6,1)<>"-"}{BRANCH Err__ssno}

> This command checks for a dash (-) in the sixth position of the string. If 1-2-3 does not find the dash, it branches to Err__ssno.

{BRANCH Ret}

> If none of the branches to Err__ssno are taken, the macro executes this command. This command causes 1-2-3 to branch to a routine named Ret. This routine returns control to the instruction following the subroutine call.

{LET I20,"Error in entry, you will need to retry"} ~

> This is the first instruction in Err__ssno. It places an error message in I20. The cell pointer must be positioned to let the user read this message from their screen. The tilde at the end of the instruction causes 1-2-3 to display the message on the screen immediately.

{WAIT @NOW+@TIME(0,0,7)}

> This instruction generates a seven second wait. Two time functions are used with WAIT to control the length of the wait.

{BRANCH Ss__no}

> This instruction branches to the top of the subroutine and begins the process again.

{RETURN}

> This instruction causes the macro to return from the subroutine call. 1-2-3 executes the instruction immediately following the subroutine call.

Using @ROWS and @CELLPOINTER to Control Database Entries

> Many 1-2-3 users do not make use of the data management features because they do not like to enter data into the rows and columns to create a new record. After using the dedicated data base management packages, they prefer a full-screen entry method. Release 3 provides macro instructions that allow a data entry form. Another option is to control the placement of data for the user with macro control.

The example you will review uses the row and column entry system but moves the cellpointer from record to record for the user. The database shown in Figure 11.9 has four fields. Cells B1..E7 contain the database. As a preliminary step, use /Range Name Create to apply Database to these cells. Figure 11.10 contains the macro entries to add a new field.

Figure 11.9
Database

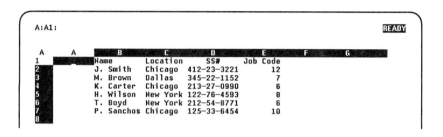

Figure 11.10 Macro
to add a field

{GOTO Database} ~

This instruction positions the cell pointer on the first cell in the range name Database. This allows you to proceed from a known position regardless of the number of database records.

{END}{RIGHT}{RIGHT}Salary ~ {DOWN}{CALC}

The first task this instruction handles is positioning the cursor on the last field name in the database. Next, it moves the cell pointer one position to the right. The macro contains the keystrokes to enter Salary at this location. It moves down one cell and recalculates the worksheet to update the position of the cell pointer.

/rfc0 ~

> This instruction starts the format command. It selects a format of currency with zero decimal places. You must enter a single quotation mark before entering this command to have 1–2–3 store the instruction in a worksheet cell.

{DOWN @ROWS(Database)-1 } ~

> This instruction completes the range format command. It specifies a range sufficient to allow a salary entry for each database record.

{FOR Rows,1,@ROWS(Database)-1,1,Add__sal }

> This instruction determines the number of times the macro instructions in Add__sal are executed. The instruction uses the range name Rows. You must create this range name before running the macro the first time. 1–2–3 uses this range name to control the loop. It is set a+1, based on the second argument value. @ROWS(Database)–1 determines the maximum value allowed for this variable. Once it exceeds the established value, 1–2–3 stops executing the loop. Since @ROWS(Database) includes a row for the field names, the –1 is added. The fourth argument, 1, determines the increment for the variable name Rows for each iteration of the loop. Add__sal is the location containing the first macro instruction in the loop.

+''{GETNUMBER Enter Salary,''&@CELLPOINTER(''address'')&''} ~ ''

> This macro instruction is a string formula. The string formula creates a macro command language instruction from string constants that do not change and a string function. The string function @CELLPOINTER (''address'') returns the current address of the cell pointer and incorporates it in the macro instruction. After the string function, a second constant completes the instruction. Note that a tilde (~) is part of the string to finalize the entry of the salary into the current cell. Without the tilde, the instruction does not update the screen display immediately. In Releases 2.2 and 3, you have a much better alternative than a string formula. Since these releases support the entry of @functions as arguments for macro keywords, simple enter **{GETNUMBER ''Enter salary:,'' @CELLPOINTER (''address'')} ~ .**

{DOWN}{CALC}

This instruction moves the cell pointer down one cell. It recalculates the worksheet to make the repositioning occur immediately.

In the example shown, the macro is designed to add a record to each field in the database although this concept is adaptable to entering complete records.

The macro code in Figure 11.11 is a continuation of the macro shown in Figure 11.8 and is designed to process a job code number. Although it is more efficient for an operator to enter a code rather than a job description, the entry of codes can raise the error rate in fields. To eliminate this problem, a check program located in B23 compares the operator's entry against the valid codes in a table. It looks up the value in the table's zero offset and compares the return value against the column with an offset of zero from the beginning of the table. An error routine is executed if the code is not in the table. If the code exists, it displays the description associated with the job code for verification. This is obtained by a second @VLOOKUP instruction that uses an offset of one instead of zero and looks at the column of the table that contains the job descriptions.

Figure 11.11
Checking a job code

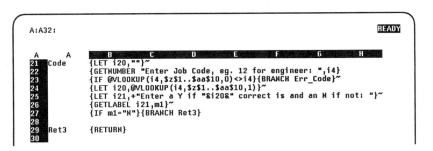

In this way, assurance is provided that the job code in a new employee record is valid. The macro can be modified to let the operator re-enter a code that is not valid. Additional code can be added to this macro to move the correct data to the next record in the database.

This macro can be adapted to use the multi-sheet features of Release 3. For example, the lookup table can be stored on a different sheet out of the way of macro code and other entries. The placement flexibility of multiple sheets in one file allows you to better organize the model design. Another option with Release 3 is storing the table in an external file that can be accessed with formulas when needed.

DEBUGGING TECHNIQUES

Correcting errors in macros can be trying, even for experienced users. Mistakes are not always obvious and 1-2-3 does not tell you exactly what is wrong. The process of eliminating the errors in your macros is referred to as *debugging*. In this process, you want to eliminate the obvious errors that prevent the macro from running as well as the errors that cause the macro to produce incorrect results.

Using STEP Mode

There are a number of techniques that you can use to manage the process and debug your macros with a minimal investment of time. One of the first techniques that you should try is activating STEP mode when the macro is not operating correctly. STEP mode slows the execution of the macro so that you can follow its actions.

After pressing Alt+F2 to invoke STEP mode, you will need to press the Spacebar for each instruction executed or each character entered. Slowing the macro makes it easier to pinpoint the instruction where problems start to occur. You can focus your attention on this one area of the macro rather than looking at every macro instruction.

Turning off STEP mode is as easy as invoking it; simply press Alt+F2 a second time to resume normal execution mode.

Test in Pieces

A lengthy macro might contain one hundred lines of code or more. If you execute all the macro lines at one time and realize that they contain errors, it is difficult to pinpoint the problem. Since a blank cell stops a macro, you can temporarily insert blank cells to stop the macro periodically so that you can assess its progress. You will want to assign a name to the beginning of each new section so that you can test all the pieces. These names can be deleted once the macro works correctly.

You can add {INDICATE} instructions to change the indicator in the control panel. These changes in the mode indicator are another way to monitor progress through the macro.

The use of small segments of code that perform a particular task can streamline macro code. These code sections are called *subroutines*. Whenever you need to perform the specific task, you can call the subroutine rather than incorporating all the lines of code into the main macro routine. This procedure helps you to develop code that is packaged in manageable size pieces. You can even test the main routine code without coding the subroutines. A simple placeholder instruction like {INDICATE} can tell you when you reach the subroutine code. When the main routine functions correctly, you can begin entering the subroutine code.

Dissect Instructions

If 1–2–3 encounters a keyword or a range name error in a lengthy macro instruction, all you will know is the cell address of the faulty instruction. You can spend a considerable amount of time deciphering the faulty instruction.

One solution is to make several copies of a long instruction and edit them so that each contains only one instruction. This technique is especially useful when you are using @functions as part of macro instructions. You can determine the result produced by the @function alone and can plug that entry into a copy of the formula to see the effect. The following macro command could be replaced with a more streamlined instruction but serves as a good example of this type of evaluation

+''{GETNUMBER Enter Salary,''&@CELLPOINTER (''address'')&''}˜''

When you evaluate @CELLPOINTER(''address''), you might find that it returns $F$3. Substituting this address into the command provides {GETNUMBER Enter Salary,@CELLPOINTER(f3)}˜ or {GETNUMBER Enter Salary,$F$3}. The components of the macro instruction work correctly so the combination should produce correct results.

Appendix A:
Complete List of @Functions

@Function	Type	Chapter	Available in 2.0 and Above	Available Only in 3.0
@@(cell address)	Special	8	●	
@ABS(number)	Math	4		
@ACOS(ratio)	Math	4		
@ASIN(ratio)	Math	4		
@ATAN(ratio)	Math	4		
@ATAN2(x,y)	Math	4		
@AVG(list)	Statistical	2		
@CELL(attribute,range)	Special	8	●	
@CELLPOINTER(attribute)	Special	8	●	
@CHAR(x)	String	7	●	
@CHOOSE(x,v0,v1, ...,vn)	Special	8		
@CLEAN(string)	String	7	●	
@CODE(string)	String	7	●	
@COLS(range)	Special	8	●	
@COS(angle)	Math	4		
@COORD(worksheet,column,row,absolute)	Special	8		●
@COUNT(list)	Statistical	2		
@CTERM(int,fv,pv)	Financial	6	●	
@DATE(year,month,day)	Date & Time	5		
@DATEVALUE(date string)	Date & Time	5	●	
@DAVG(input,field,criteria)	Database	9		
@DAY(date serial number)	Date & Time	5		
@DCOUNT(input,field,criteria)	Database	9		
@DDB(cost,salvage,life,period)	Financial	6	●	
@DGET(input,field,criteria)	Database	9		●
@DMAX(input,field,criteria)	Database	9		
@DMIN(input,field,criteria)	Database	9		
@DQUERY(function,ext-arguments)	Database	9		●

@Function	Type	Chapter	Available in 2.0 and Above	Available Only in 3.0
@DSTD(input,field,criteria)	Database	9		
@DSTDS(input,field,criteria)	Database	9		•
@DSUM(input,field,criteria)	Database	9		•
@DVAR(input,field,criteria)	Database	9		
@DVARS(input,field,criteria)	Database	9		•
@D360(start date,end date)	Date & Time	5		•
@ERR	Special	8		
@EXACT(string1,string2)	String	7	•	
@EXP(number)	Math	4		
@FALSE	Logical	3		
@FIND(search string,string,start number)	String	7	•	
@FV(pmt,int,term)	Financial	6		
@HLOOKUP(x,range,column number)	Special	8		
@HOUR(time serial number)	Date & Time	5		
@IF(condition,value if condition is true, value condition if false)	Logical	3		
@IFAFF(name)	Logical	3		
@IFAPP(name)	Logical	3		
@INDEX(range,column,row[,worksheet])	Special	8		
@INT(number)	Math	4		
@INFO(attribute)	Special	8		•
@IRR(guess,range)	Financial	6		
@ISERR(argument)	Logical	3		
@ISNA(argument)	Logical	3		
@ISNUMBER(argument)	Logical	3		
@ISRANGE(string)	Logical	3		•
@ISSTRING(argument)	Logical	3	•	
@LEFT(string,n)	String	7	•	
@LENGTH(string)	String	7	•	
@LN(number)	Math	4		
@LOG(number)	Math	4		
@LOWER(string)	String	7	•	
@MAX(list)	Statistical	2		
@MID(string,start number,n)	String	7	•	
@MIN(list)	Statistical	2		
@MINUTE(time serial number)	Date & Time	5	•	
@MOD(number,divisor)	Math	4		
@MONTH(date serial number)	Date & Time	5		
@N(range)	String	7	•	
@NA	Special	8		
@NOW	Date & Time	5	•	
@NPV(int,range)	Financial	6		

@Function	Type	Chapter	Available in 2.0 and Above	Available Only in 3.0
@PI	Math	4		
@PMT(prin,int,term)	Financial	6		
@PROPER(string)	String	7	•	
@PV(pmt,int,term)	Financial	6		
@RAND	Math	4		
@RATE(fv,pv,term)	Financial	6	•	
@REPEAT(string,n)	String	7	•	
@REPLACE(original string,start number,n, new string)	String	7	•	
@RIGHT(string,n)	String	7	•	
@ROUND(number,place)	Math	4		
@ROWS(range)	Special	8	•	
@S(range)	String	7	•	
@SECOND(time serial number)	Date & Time	5	•	
@SHEETS(range)	Special	8		•
@SIN(angle)	Math	4		
@SLN(cost,salvage,life)	Financial	6	•	
@SQRT(number)	Math	4		
@STD(list)	Statistical	2		
@STDS(list)	Statistical	2		•
@STRING(x,n)	String	7	•	
@SUM(list)	Statistical	2		
@SUMPRODUCT(list)	Statistical	2		•
@SYD(cost,salvage,life,period)	Financial	6	•	
@TAN(angle)	Math	4		
@TERM(pmt,int,fv)	Financial	6	•	
@TIME(hour,minute,second)	Date & Time	5	•	
@TIMEVALUE(time string)	Date & Time	5	•	
@TODAY	Date & Time	5		•
@TRIM(string)	String	7	•	
@TRUE	Logical	3		
@UPPER(string)	String	7	•	
@VALUE(string)	String	7	•	
@VAR(list)	Statistical	2		
@VARS(list)	Statistical	2		•
@VDB(cost,salvage,life,start-period,end-period,[depreciation factor],[switch])	Financial	6		•
@VLOOKUP(x,range,column number)	Special	8		
@YEAR(date serial number)	Date & Time	5	•	

Appendix B: Lotus International Character Set (LICS) and Lotus Multibyte Character Set (LMBCS) Codes

1-2-3 offers additional characters other than the keys you can select on your keyboard. You can include these characters by using one from a Lotus character set. The character set that you use is dependent upon the release of 1-2-3 you have.

Release 1A uses the ASCII character set, which includes the keys on your keyboard. Releases 2.0, 2.01, and 2.2 use the Lotus International Character Set (LICS). This set includes all of the keys on your keyboard as well as other characters that you can use by pressing the Alt-F1 (Compose) key and entering the compose sequence as described below. Release 3 uses the Lotus Multibyte Character Set (LMBCS), which includes more characters than the LICS. You can access these characters by typing the character on the keyboard, using the Alt-F1 (Compose) key once and entering a compose sequence, or using the Alt-F1 (Compose) key twice and entering the group number and the code within the group.

Most of the compose sequence characters are the same for both the LICS and the LMBCS. Although the compose sequences are the same between releases, the code numbers each character set uses for the characters vary. When you use a .WK1 file in Release 3 or save a Release 3 worksheet in an earlier format, 1-2-3 makes an automatic translation. If you are planning to use a worksheet in Releases 2.0, 2.01, or 2.2 and in Release 3.0, you do not have to convert character sets.

When you include a character other than a straightforward keyboard character, it may not appear or print as intended. Some monitors and printers cannot display and print all of the characters 1–2–3 makes available. When this happens, 1–2–3 substitutes a different character to represent the one that cannot display or print. Since your monitor and printer are separate, you may be able to display a character but be unable to print it, or your monitor may not be able to display a character but the character appears correctly in the printed output. The way the printer or monitor displays the character varies from monitor to monitor.

Most of the characters you will use in your worksheets are entered from your keyboard. When you want a character that your keyboard does not have a key for, use one of the following three methods to have 1–2–3 create the character.

Using the Compose Key

To create a LICS or LMBCS character, press the Alt-F1 (Compose) key and enter a two-character compose sequence. The compose sequence characters tell 1–2–3 which character you want. Most of the compose sequences use characters that resemble the character you want. For example, to create the ™ character, you would press Alt-F1 (Compose) and type a T and an M. When you type the M, 1–2–3 displays the ™ character.

Using the Compose Key Twice (Release 3 only)

To create a LMBCS character, press the Alt-F1 (Compose) key twice, enter the group number, and then enter the key code. All of the characters are divided into different groups. Each character in a group has a unique three-digit key code. For key codes such as 27, you must precede the code with a 0 so the resulting code is three digits. For example, to create the Œ character, press Alt-F1 (Compose) twice, type 1 for the group number, and 064 for the keycode.

Using the @CHAR Function

To create a LICS or LMBCS character, use the @CHAR function by entering @CHAR() with the LICS or LMBCS code. For example, to create ™ the character, you would type @CHAR("184") in Release 2.0,

2.01, or 2.2. In Release 3, you would type @CHAR("374"). The LICS and LMBCS use the same characters for codes 31 through 127. For other characters, the two character sets use different numbers.

The following characters are the same in both LICS and LMBCS. For LMBCS, these characters belong to Group 1 and the key code is the same as the LICS/LMBCS code.

Character	LICS/ LMBCS Code	Compose Sequence	Key Code	Description
	32		032	Space
!	33		033	Exclamation point
"	34		034	Double quotes
#	35	+ +	035	Pound sign
$	36		036	Dollar sign
%	37		037	Percent
&	38		038	Ampersand
'	39		039	Close quote
(	40		040	Open parenthesis
)	41		041	Close parenthesis
*	42		042	Asterisk
+	43		043	Plus sign
,	44		044	Comma
–	45		045	Minus sign
.	46		046	Period
/	47		047	Slash
0	48		048	Zero
1	49		049	One
2	50		050	Two
3	51		051	Three
4	52		052	Four
5	53		053	Five
6	54		054	Six
7	55		055	Seven
8	56		056	Eight
9	57		057	Nine
:	58		058	Colon
;	59		059	Semicolon
<	60		060	Less than
=	61		061	Equal sign

Character	LICS/ LMBCS Code	Compose Sequence	Key Code	Description
>	62		062	Greater than
?	63		063	Question mark
@	64	aa or AA	064	At sign
A	65		065	A, uppercase
B	66		066	B, uppercase
C	67		067	C, uppercase
D	68		068	D, uppercase
E	69		069	E, uppercase
F	70		070	F, uppercase
G	71		071	G, uppercase
H	72		072	H, uppercase
I	73		073	I, uppercase
J	74		074	J, uppercase
K	75		075	K, uppercase
L	76		076	L, uppercase
M	77		077	M, uppercase
N	78		078	N, uppercase
O	79		079	O, uppercase
P	80		080	P, uppercase
Q	81		081	Q, uppercase
R	82		082	R, uppercase
S	83		083	S, uppercase
T	84		084	T, uppercase
U	85		085	U, uppercase
V	86		086	V, uppercase
W	87		087	W, uppercase
X	88		088	X, uppercase
Y	89		089	Y, uppercase
Z	90		090	Z, uppercase
[	91	((	091	Open bracket
\	92	//	092	Backslash
]	93	))	093	Close bracket
^	94	vv	094	Caret
_	95		095	Underscore
`	96		096	Open single quote
a	97		097	a, lowercase
b	98		098	b, lowercase
c	99		099	c, lowercase

Character	LICS/ LMBCS Code	Compose Sequence	Key Code	Description
d	100		100	d, lowercase
e	101		101	e, lowercase
f	102		102	f, lowercase
g	103		103	g, lowercase
h	104		104	h, lowercase
i	105		105	i, lowercase
j	106		106	j, lowercase
k	107		107	k, lowercase
l	108		108	l, lowercase
m	109		109	m, lowercase
n	110		110	n, lowercase
o	111		111	o, lowercase
p	112		112	p, lowercase
q	113		113	q, lowercase
r	114		114	r, lowercase
s	115		115	s, lowercase
t	116		116	t, lowercase
u	117		117	u, lowercase
v	118		118	v, lowercase
w	119		119	w, lowercase
x	120		120	x, lowercase
y	121		121	y, lowercase
z	122		122	z, lowercase
{	123	(-	123	Open brace
|	124	^/	124	Bar
}	125	-)	125	Close brace
~	126	--	126	Tilde
⌂	127		127	Delete

The following list contains the characters with the LICS codes that create them. This information is specific to Releases 2.0, 2.01, and 2.2.

Character	LICS Code	Compose Sequence	Description
`	128	` (space)	Grave accent, uppercase
´	129	' (space)	Acute accent, uppercase
^	130	^ (space)	Circumflex accent, uppercase
¨	131	'' (space)	Umlaut accent, uppercase
~	132	~ (space)	Tilde accent, uppercase
	133		
	134		
	135		
	136		
	137		
	138		
	139		
	140		
	141		
	142		
	143		
`	144	(space) `	Grave accent, lowercase
´	145	(space) '	Acute accent, lowercase
^	146	(space) ^	Circumflex accent, lowercase
¨	147	(space) ''	Umlaut accent, lowercase
~	148	(space) ~	Tilde accent, lowercase
ı	149	i (space)	i without dot, lowercase
__	150	__ (space)	Ordinal indicator
▲	151	ba	Solid triangle
▼	152	ea	Solid triangle inverted
■	153	Square bullet	
•	154	{space}{space}	Hard space
←	155	mg	Left arrow
	156		
	157		
	158		
	159		
ƒ	160	ff	Guilder
¡	161	!!	Exclamation point, inverted
¢	162	c| c/ C| or C/	Cent sign

Character	LICS Code	Compose Sequence	Description
£	163	L= l= L- or l-	British pound sterling symbol
ˮ	164	ˮ ^	Low opening double quotes
¥	165	Y= y= Y- or y-	Yen sign
Pt	166	PT Pt or pt	Peseta sign
§	167	SO S0 so or s0	Section symbol
¤	168	XO or xo	International currency sign
©	169	CO C0 co or c0	Copyright symbol
ª	170	a__ or A__	Feminine ordinal indicator
«	171	<<	Left angle quotes
Δ	172	dd or DD	Delta
π	173	PI pi or Pi	Pi
≥	174	> =	Greater than or equals sign
÷	175	:-	Division sign
°	176	^0	Degree symbol
±	177	+ −	Plus or minus sign
²	178	^2	Two superscript
³	179	^3	Three superscript
,,	180	''v	Low closing quotes
μ	181	/u	Greek mu, lowercase
¶	182	!p or !P	Paragraph symbol
·	183	^.	Center dot
™	184	TM tm or Tm	Trademark sign
¹	185	^1	One superscript
º	186	o__ or O__	Masculine ordinal indicator
»	187	>>	Right angle quotes
¼	188	14	One quarter
½	189	12	One half
≤	190	< =	Less than or equals sign
¿	191	??	Question mark inverted
À	192	A`	A grave, uppercase
Á	193	A'	A acute, uppercase
Â	194	A^	A circumflex, uppercase
Ã	195	A ~	A tilde, uppercase
Ä	196	A''	A umlaut, uppercase
Å	197	A*	A ring, uppercase
Æ	198	AE	AE diphthong, uppercase
Ç	199	C,	C cedilla, uppercase
È	200	E`	E grave, uppercase
É	201	E'	E acute, uppercase

Character	LICS Code	Compose Sequence	Description
Ê	202	E^	E circumflex, uppercase
Ë	203	E''	E umlaut, uppercase
Ì	204	I`	I grave, uppercase
Í	205	I'	I acute, uppercase
Î	206	I^	I circumflex, uppercase
Ï	207	I''	I umlaut, uppercase
Đ	208	D-	Icelandic eth, uppercase
Ñ	209	N ~	N tilde, uppercase
Ò	210	O`	O grave, uppercase
Ó	211	O'	O acute, uppercase
Ô	212	O^	O circumflex, uppercase
Õ	213	O ~	O tilde, uppercase
Ö	214	O''	O umlaut, uppercase
Œ	215	OE	OE ligature, uppercase
Ø	216	O/	O slash, uppercase
Ù	217	U`	U grave, uppercase
Ú	218	U'	U acute, uppercase
Û	219	U^	U circumflex, uppercase
Ü	220	U''	U umlaut, uppercase
Ÿ	221	Y''	Y umlaut, uppercase
Þ	222	P-	Icelandic thorn, uppercase
ß	223	ss	German sharp, lowercase
à	224	a`	a grave, lowercase
á	225	a'	a acute, lowercase
â	226	a^	a circumflex, lowercase
ã	227	a ~	a tilde, lowercase
ä	228	a''	a umlaut, lowercase
å	229	a*	a ring, lowercase
æ	230	ae	ae diphthong, lowercase
ç	231	c,	c cedilla, lowercase
è	232	e`	e grave, lowercase
é	233	e'	e acute, lowercase
ê	234	e^	e circumflex, lowercase
ë	235	e''	e umlaut, lowercase
ì	236	i`	i grave, lowercase
í	237	i'	i acute, lowercase
î	238	i^	i circumflex, lowercase
ï	239	i''	i umlaut, lowercase
ð	240	d-	Icelandic eth, lowercase

Character	LICS Code	Compose Sequence	Description
ñ	241	n ~	n tilde, lowercase
ò	242	o`	o grave, lowercase
ó	243	o'	o acute, lowercase
ô	244	o^	o circumflex, lowercase
õ	245	o ~	o tilde, lowercase
ö	246	o''	o umlaut, lowercase
œ	247	oe	oe ligature, lowercase
ø	248	o/	o slash, lowercase
ù	249	u`	u grave, lowercase
ú	250	u'	u acute, lowercase
û	251	u^	u circumflex, lowercase
ü	252	u''	u umlaut, lowercase
ÿ	253	y''	y umlaut, lowercase
þ	254	p-	Icelandic thorn, lowercase
	255	Null	

The following list contains the characters of the first half of the second group with the LMBCS codes that create them. The key codes are the same as the LMBCS codes. This information is specific to Release 3.

Character	LMBCS Code	Compose Sequence	Description
Ç	128	C,	C cedilla, uppercase
ü	129	u''	u umlaut, lowercase
é	130	e'	e acute, lowercase
â	131	a^	a circumflex, lowercase
ä	132	a''	a umlaut, lowercase
à	133	a`	a grave, lowercase
å	134	a*	a ring, lowercase
ç	135	c,	c cedilla, lowercase
ê	136	e^	e circumflex, lowercase
ë	137	e''	e umlaut, lowercase
è	138	e`	e grave, lowercase
ï	139	i''	i umlaut, lowercase
î	140	i^	i circumflex, lowercase
ì	141	i`	i grave, lowercase
Ä	142	A''	A umlaut, uppercase

Character	LICS Code	Compose Sequence	Description
Å	143	A*	A ring, uppercase
É	144	E'	E acute, uppercase
æ	145	ae	ae diphthong, lowercase
Æ	146	AE	AE diphthong, uppercase
ô	147	o^	o circumflex, lowercase
ö	148	o''	o umlaut, lowercase
ò	149	o`	o grave, lowercase
û	150	u^	u circumflex, lowercase
ù	151	u`	u grave, lowercase
ÿ	152	y''	y umlaut, lowercase
Ö	153	O''	O umlaut, uppercase
Ü	154	U''	U umlaut, uppercase
ø	155	o/	o slash, lowercase
£	156	L= l= L- or l-	British pound sterling symbol
Ø	157	O/	O slash, uppercase
×	158	xx or XX	Multiplication sign
f	159	ff	Guilder
á	160	a'	a acute, lowercase
í	161	i'	i acute, lowercase
ó	162	o'	o acute, lowercase
ú	163	u'	u acute, lowercase
ñ	164	n ~	n tilde, lowercase
Ñ	165	N ~	N tilde, uppercase
ª	166	a__ or A__	Feminine ordinal indicator
º	167	o__ or O__	Masculine ordinal indicator
¿	168	??	Question mark inverted
®	169	RO or ro	Registered trademark symbol
¬	170	-]	End of line symbol/Logical NOT
½	171	12	One half
¼	172	14	One quarter
¡	173	!!	Exclamation point, inverted
«	174	<<	Left angle quotes
»	175	>>	Right angle quotes
░	176		Solid fill character, light
▒	177		Solid fill character, medium
▓	178		Solid fill character, heavy
│	179		Center vertical box bar
┤	180		Right box side

Character	LICS Code	Compose Sequence	Description
Á	181	A'	A acute, uppercase
Â	182	A^	A circumflex, uppercase
À	183	A`	A grave, uppercase
©	184	CO C0 co or c0	Copyright symbol
⊣	185		Right box side, double
‖	186		Center vertical box bar, double
⌐	187		Upper right box corner, double
⌐	188		Lower right box corner, double
¢	189	c| c/ C| or C/	Cent sign
¥	190	Y= y= Y- or y-	Yen sign
¬	191		Upper right box corner
└	192		Lower right box corner
⊥	193		Lower box side
⊤	194		Upper box side
├	195		Left box side
—	196		Center horizontal box bar
+	197		Center box intersection
ã	198	a ~	a tilde, lowercase
Ã	199	A ~	A tilde, uppercase
╚	200		Lower left box corner, double
╔	201		Upper left box corner, double
╩	202		Lower box side, double
╦	203		Upper box side, double
╠	204		Left box side, double
=	205		Center horizontal box bar, double
╬	206		Center box intersection, double
¤	207	XO or xo	International currency sign
ð	208	d-	Icelandic eth, lowercase
Ð	209	D-	Icelandic eth, uppercase
Ê	210	E^	E circumflex, uppercase
Ë	211	E''	E umlaut, uppercase
È	212	E`	E grave, uppercase
ı	213	i (space)	i without dot (lowercase)
Í	214	I'	I acute, uppercase
Î	215	I^	I circumflex, uppercase
Ï	216	I''	I umlaut, uppercase
┘	217		Lower right box corner

Character	LICS Code	Compose Sequence	Description
⌐	218		Upper left box corner
▉	219		Solid fill character
▄	220		Solid fill character, lower half
¦	221	/ (space)	Vertical line, broken
Ì	222	Iˋ	I grave, uppercase
▀	223		Solid fill character, upper half
Ó	224	O'	O acute, uppercase
ß	225	ss	German sharp, lowercase
Ô	226	O^	O circumflex, uppercase
Ò	227	Oˋ	O grave, uppercase
õ	228	o ~	o tilde, lowercase
Õ	229	O ~	O tilde, uppercase
µ	230	/u	Greek mu, lowercase
þ	231	p-	Icelandic thorn, lowercase
Þ	232	P-	Icelandic thorn, uppercase
Ú	233	U'	U acute, uppercase
Û	234	U^	U circumflex, uppercase
Ù	235	Uˋ	U grave, uppercase
ý	236	y'	y acute, lowercase
Ý	237	Y'	Y acute, uppercase
	238	^-	Overline character
´	239		Acute accent
-	240	-+	Hyphenation symbol
±	241	+-	Plus or minus sign
=	242	-- or = =	Double underscore
¾	243	34	Three quarters sign
¶	244	!p or !P	Paragraph symbol
§	245	SO S0 so or s0	Section symbol
÷	246	:-	Division sign
¸	247	''	Cedilla accent
°	248	^0	Degree symbol
¨	249		Umlaut accent
•	250	^.	Center dot
¹	251	^1	One superscript
³	252	^3	Three superscript
²	253	^2	Two superscript
■	254		Square bullet
!	255		Null

The following list contains the characters of the second half of the second group with the LMBCS codes that create them. The key codes are the same as the LMBCS codes. This information is specific to Release 3.

Character	LMBCS Code	Compose Sequence	Description
	256		000 Not Used
☺	257		001 Smiling face
☻	258		002 Smiling face, reversed
♥	259		003 Heart suit symbol
♦	260		004 Diamond suit symbol
♣	261		005 Club suit symbol
♠	262		006 Spade suit symbol
•	263		007 Bullet
▣	264		008 Bullet, reversed
○	265		009 Open circle
◉	266		010 Open circle, reversed
♂	267		011 Male symbol
♀	268		012 Female symbol
♪	269		013 Musical note
♫	270		014 Double musical note
☼	271		015 Sun symbol
►	272		016 Forward arrow indicator
◄	273		017 Back arrow indicator
↕	274		018 Up-down arrow
‼	275		019 Double exclamation points
¶	276		020 Paragraph symbol
§	277		021 Section symbol
▬	278		022 Solid horizontal rectangle
↨	279		023 Up-down arrow, perpendicular
↑	280		024 Up arrow
↓	281		025 Down arrow
→	282		026 Right arrow
←	283	mg	027 Left arrow
∟	284		028 Right angle symbol
↔	285		029 Left-right symbol
▲	286	ba	030 Solid triangle
▼	287	ea	031 Solid triangle inverted
¨	288	'' (space)	032 Umlaut accent, uppercase
~	289	~ (space)	033 Tilde accent, uppercase

Character	LMBCS Code	Compose Sequence	Description
°	290		034 Ring accent, uppercase
^	291	^ (space)	035 Circumflex accent, uppercase
`	292	` (space)	036 Grave accent, uppercase
´	293	' (space)	037 Acute accent, uppercase
''	294	''^	038 High double quotes, opening
'	295		039 High single quote, straight
. . .	296		040 Ellipsis
–	297		041 En mark
—	298		042 Em mark
	299		043 Null
	300		044 Null
	301		045 Null
〈	302		046 Left angle parenthesis
〉	303		047 Right angle parenthesis
¨	304	(space) ''	048 Umlaut accent, lowercase
~	305	(space) ~	049 Tilde accent, lowercase
°	306		050 Ring accent, lowercase
^	307	(space) ^	051 Circumflex accent, lowercase
`	308	(space) `	052 Grave accent, lowercase
´	309	(space) '	053 Acute accent, lowercase
''	310	''v	054 Low double quotes, closing
'	311		055 Low single quotes, closing
''	312		056 High double quotes, closing
__	313		057 Underscore, heavy
	314		058 Null
	315		059 Null
	316		060 Null
	317		061 Null
	318		062 Null
	319		063 Null
Œ	320	OE	064 OE ligature, uppercase
œ	321	oe	065 oe ligature, lowercase
Ÿ	322	Y''	066 Y umlaut, uppercase
	323		067 Null
	324		068 Null
	325		069 Null
╞	326		070 Left box side, double joins single
╟	327		071 Left box side, single joins double

Character	LMBCS Code	Compose Sequence	Description
▮	328		072 Solid fill character, left half
▮	329		073 Solid fill character, right half
	330		074 Null
	331		075 Null
	332		076 Null
	333		077 Null
	334		078 Null
	335		079 Null
⊥	336		080 Lower box side, double joins single
╤	337		081 Upper box side, single joins double
╥	338		082 Upper box side, double joins single
╙	339		083 Lower single left double box corner
╘	340		084 Lower double left single box corner
╒	341		085 Upper double left single box corner
╓	342		086 Upper single left double box corner
╫	343		087 Center box intersection, vertical double
╪	344		088 Center box intersection, horizontal double
╡	345		089 Right box side, double joins single
╢	346		090 Right box side, single joins double
╖	347		091 Upper single right double box corner
╕	348		092 Upper double right single box corner
╜	349		093 Lower single right double box corner
╛	350		094 Lower double right single box corner

Character	LMBCS Code	Compose Sequence		Description
⊥	351		095	Lower box side, single joins double
ij	352	ij	096	ij ligature, lowercase
IJ	353	IJ	097	IJ liguature, uppercase
fi	354	fi	098	fi ligature, lowercase
fl	355	fl	099	fl ligature, lowercase
'n	356	n	100	n comma, lowercase
ŀ	357	l.	101	l bullet, lowercase
Ŀ	358	L.	102	L bullet, uppercase
	359		103	Null
	360		104	Null
	361		105	Null
	362		106	Null
	363		107	Null
	364		108	Null
	365		109	Null
	366		110	Null
	367		111	Null
†	368		112	Single dagger symbol
‡	369		113	Double dagger symbol
	370		114	Null
	371		115	Null
	372		116	Null
	373		117	Null
™	374	TM Tm or t	118	Trademark symbol
ℓ	375	l r	119	Liter symbol
	376		120	Null
	377		121	Null
	378		122	Null
	379		123	Null
Kr	380	KR Kr or k	124	Krone sign
⌐	381	- [	125	Start of line symbol
£	382	Li Li or l	126	Lira sign
Pt	383	PT pt or p	127	Peseta

Codes 384 through 511 repeat the characters (and key codes) that the LMBCS characters use for codes 128 through 255.

Index

You're invited to preview – *free* – the most useful, practical, and reliable computing magazine for managers and professionals.

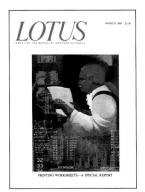

LOTUS enhances your ability to use spreadsheets and related products, and helps you get the most out of your computing system. Each month, **LOTUS** provides ready-to-use applications and time-saving tips and macros, tells you what your peers in other businesses are doing, and keeps you abreast of new products and developments that could make you even more productive.

Select the introductory offer that's right for you!

You can get six issues of **LOTUS** *absolutely free* just by returning the postage-paid card below.

Or you can order a one-year subscription now, and receive a free copy of the **LOTUS** **Guide to @Functions**. This sturdy flipchart, developed exclusively for **LOTUS** subscribers, is the fastest way to find information about the structure and operation of the Lotus @functions.

Introducing *LOTUS* with Two Special Offers!

☐ 6 Issues *Free*

Please enroll me as a trial subscriber for six issues. If I like the magazine, I will be able to extend my subscription later at the basic rate. To qualify for this free offer, I have signed and dated this request, and indicated which software program(s) I use.   TL19

☐ 12 Issues and a *Free* Guide

Yes, please send my free **LOTUS** **Guide to @Functions** and bill me just $18 for a one-year (12 issues) subscription, a savings of 50% off the annual newsstand rate. If I'm not satisfied with **LOTUS**, I understand that I'll receive a prompt refund on all undelivered issues, and the free guide is mine to keep.   5L199

Which software program(s) do you use?

☐ 1-2-3   ☐ Symphony

SIGNATURE (required for free offer)

NAME

COMPANY

ADDRESS

CITY   STATE   ZIP

Please allow 4-6 weeks for delivery of your first issue. Send foreign orders prepaid in U.S. funds: $24 Canada, $80 (airmail) all others.

NO POSTAGE
NECESSARY
IF MAILED
IN THE
UNITED STATES

BUSINESS REPLY MAIL
FIRST CLASS   PERMIT NO. 1264   BOULDER, CO

POSTAGE WILL BE PAID BY ADDRESSEE

LOTUS

Subscription Department
P.O. Box 52349
Boulder, CO 80321-2349